MINNESOTA FARMERS' DIARIES

William R. Brown, 1845-46
Mitchell Y. Jackson, 1852-63

With an Introduction and Notes
by
Rodney C. Loehr

SAINT PAUL
THE MINNESOTA HISTORICAL SOCIETY
1939

Copyright, 1939, by the
MINNESOTA HISTORICAL SOCIETY
St. Paul

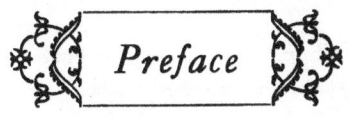

Preface

Though much has been said and written about the farmer and his contributions to American life, comparatively little has been done toward making available to the public the farmer's own records—his letters, diaries, account books, and reminiscences—which present the homely, authentic detail of his everyday life. In fact, no volume containing the texts of actual diaries kept by American farmers, published because of their value as farmers' diaries, has hitherto appeared in print. This book, therefore, should have an almost unique interest, for it contains two such diaries, each recording in faithful detail the everyday life of an American farmer.

These diaries were kept by Minnesota farmers in the frontier era of the Middle West, and they have, therefore, a special value for the history of Minnesota and the Middle West. Their general interest, however, transcends locality and region. William R. Brown and Mitchell Y. Jackson, who wrote the diaries, were American farmers. Their way of life was like that of millions of Americans. The problems and difficulties which they met were like those that have faced pioneer farmers on a hundred American frontiers. Their joys and disappointments echo those of countless others who have broken sod, tilled the field, and built frontier homes. They serve, therefore, as spokesmen for the unknown farmer, whose contribution to the epic of America has not yet been told with the wealth of detail and authenticity of flavor that alone can lend the story the eloquence of truth.

Both the detail and the flavor are in these diaries. Here, in entries marked by simplicity and honesty, is the concrete tale of pioneering, of community life on the frontier, of persons and places. Here are chronicled the farmers' "work and days," in the same immemorial cycle that Hesiod sang of in ancient times. Here is the story of the crops, in concrete terms of potatoes, corn, wheat, oats, barley, and other products. Here, too, are contemporary reports on tools and implements, on plowing and threshing, on markets and prices, on oxen, pigs, poultry, and sheep. And here is the record of the farmer's goings and comings, of his interests and diversions—comments on visits to such near-by centers as pioneer St. Paul, Fort Snelling, and Stillwater; information about roads and transportation, weather, people, politics, economic conditions, and special happenings; and glimpses of his home, his social activity and recreation, and occasionally, if not often enough, of his wife, whose humble role was that of a wilderness Martha.

The diaries should be read in the setting of the scholarly introduction contributed by Dr. Loehr, whose services as the editor of the volume are deeply appreciated by the society.

THEODORE C. BLEGEN

MINNESOTA HISTORICAL SOCIETY
ST. PAUL

Contents

INTRODUCTION	1
THE DIARY OF WILLIAM R. BROWN, 1845-46	37
THE DIARY OF MITCHELL Y. JACKSON, 1852-63 . . .	85
APPENDIX	223
INDEX	233

Illustrations

WILLIAM R. BROWN	38
A PAGE FROM BROWN'S DIARY	39
MAP OF WASHINGTON COUNTY	62
MITCHELL Y. JACKSON	86
A PAGE FROM JACKSON'S DIARY	87
JACKSON'S SKETCH OF PRAIRIE DU CHIEN	106
JACKSON'S HOME AT LAKELAND	107

MINNESOTA FARMERS' DIARIES

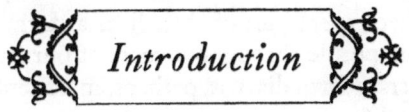

Introduction

Diaries are frequently of value and always of interest to the historian. Giving, as they do, a chronological record of events witnessed or impressions felt by an individual, they are often useful in helping to re-create past times. Diaries of the great or near-great, or of those who have lived in stirring times, provide intimate pictures of memorable lives or events which the historian strives to retell and the novelist or poet sometimes succeeds in portraying. Not all diaries are of such a spectacular nature. Sometimes those whose fortunes have kept them from the halls of the mighty, or have not permitted even a gallery view of a stage where great dramatic actions were being unfolded, have nevertheless recorded the occurrences of their smaller worlds in diaries kept for personal pleasure, as the record of a useful life, or for the instruction of children and grandchildren. Some of these personal records have found their way into the archives of historical societies, where they preserve for following generations the story of the common man; probably many others now lie tucked away in some half-forgotten dusty niche.

Here are the diaries of two farmers—not ordinary farmers, perhaps, for the ordinary farmer did not keep a diary. But they are the records of men who, like many of our fathers, spent part of their lives as farmers. Since most of our people throughout most of our history have been farmers, a farm diary is, perhaps, more representative of the past life of our people than one recording a different occupation.

In addition to being farm diaries these records have other virtues. The Brown Diary is one of the few sources for the history of Minnesota in the 1840's. The Jackson Diary was kept by a man who came to Minnesota in the first great wave of immigration and whose acute perception and wide range of observation place him above the ordinary farm diarist. Few other Minnesota farm diarists showed an equal facility with the pen or exhibited an interest in so wide a range of subjects. This is not censure of those whose records yield little information; the wonder is that any farm diaries were kept at all. But a determined and faithful few, who sat down night after night to record by the flickering light of a candle or kerosene lamp the events of their daily existence, have made it possible for us to follow the daily life of the farmer from the plowing and seeding in the spring, through the cultivation and haying in the summer, to the harvest in the late summer or early autumn.

William Reynolds Brown, who kept the first diary printed below, was born in 1816 near Urbana, Ohio. His parents were well-to-do farmers and he spent his boyhood on the farm. After receiving a common schooling, in 1833 he was apprenticed as a carpenter in Mount Carmel, Illinois. As a young man he was of a religious turn of mind, and he remained so throughout his life. He read a good deal, and in the lyceums, which were held every winter at Mount Carmel, he was considered a good debater.[1]

After the crash of 1837 Brown, as a young journeyman carpenter, found it difficult to earn more than a bare subsistence. Hoping to better his position, he bought a boat in the autumn of 1840 in partnership with a relative, Charles T. Cavileer, a saddler, and the two planned to float down the Wabash, Ohio, and Mississippi rivers, with Texas as their ultimate destination. A few days before their journey was to begin they met Benjamin T. Kavanaugh, superintendent of the Methodist missions to the Sioux and Chippewa Indians in Minnesota. His glowing descriptions of the territory which he had just left, of Minnehaha and St. Anthony falls and the scenery of the upper Mississippi, of prairies with an abundance of game, and of lakes swarming with fish, at once captured the enthusiasm of the young men and led them to change their destination. Kavanaugh promised Brown a year's work at good wages; Cavileer was to be on his own.[2]

Brown and Cavileer left Mount Carmel in April, 1841, and went down the Wabash and the Ohio to Cairo and thence to St. Louis, where they joined Kavanaugh, his

[1] Biographical material concerning Brown is given in two short biographical sketches of him, in manuscript form, in the possession of the Minnesota Historical Society. One, written by Charles T. Cavileer, is in the Cavileer Papers; the other is contained in a letter from John A. Ford to J. Fletcher Williams, dated December 10, 1874. Another sketch of Brown, written by Williams and based on Cavileer's account, is in the *Saint Paul Daily Pioneer*, January·7, 1875.

[2] Cavileer's sketch of Brown, 1. In a letter dated June 18, 1841, Kavanaugh wrote to the Reverend E. R. Ames, western corresponding secretary of the Missionary Society of the Methodist Episcopal Church: "From Mt. Carmel, Ill., we obtained a carpenter William Brown, and Charles Cavalier, as a kind of trader, to relieve the mission from any traffic with the Indians or settlers." The letter was published in the *Western Christian Advocate*, 8:70 (August 20, 1841).

brother William Barbour, and others of the mission party. On May 8 the party took passage on a steamer bound for Fort Snelling and ten days later landed at Red Rock, Minnesota, on the east side of the Mississippi River across from the Sioux village of Kaposia. At Red Rock Brown erected buildings for the accommodation of the mission party. In the autumn of 1841 he married Martha A. Boardman, a widow who taught in the Methodist mission school at Kaposia. The Browns and Cavileer lived in the mission buildings at Red Rock for a time, and then both men took up claims of about a mile square near Red Rock. Claim jumping came into vogue and the two men, who were farming as partners, were forced to cut down their claims to 160 acres. It is evident from the diary that, in addition to their farming activities, Brown acted as local justice of the peace and did carpenter work for settlers in the neighborhood, and that Cavileer pursued his trade as a saddler.

In 1846, or soon thereafter, Brown and Cavileer dissolved their partnership and Cavileer removed to St. Paul. In 1851 he went to the Red River Valley. Brown sold his Red Rock farm in 1851 and moved across the river to West St. Paul, where he engaged in land speculation. In the summer of 1857, according to his own statement, he was worth $50,000; but his fortune disappeared in the panic of 1857, and, a bankrupt, he was forced to fall back upon farming. For three years during the Civil War he served with the Sixth Minnesota Volunteer Regiment. His wife died during the war and on his return he remarried in Newport, where he built a house and a shop. He bought forty acres of land adjoining Newport, laid out an addition, and sold several lots. Soon after he settled in Newport he was appointed justice of the peace, an office he held until his death in 1874.[3]

The second diarist, Mitchell Young Jackson, was of old American stock. He was born near Mt. Vernon, Ohio, in 1816, the sixth generation in descent from Robert Jackson, who came from England in 1643 and settled in Hempstead on Long Island. His boyhood days were spent on a farm in Fayette County, Indiana, where his father, Daniel Jackson, settled in 1821. Nostalgic glimpses of his boyhood are given in the diary, when he recalls maple-sugar making on a frosty spring night, or remembers eating bread made from wheat of his family's raising during his youth. He went to a little country school and for a time attended a private school, but for the most part his education came from reading.[4]

[3] J. Fletcher Williams, *A History of the City of Saint Paul*, 115 (*Minnesota Historical Collections*, vol. 4—St. Paul, 1876); Cavileer's sketch of Brown, 2–5; Ford to Williams, December 10, 1874; *Minnesota in the Civil and Indian Wars, 1861–1865*, 1:340 (St. Paul, 1890). Red Rock was just north of the present village of Newport in Washington County. See Warren Upham, *Minnesota Geographic Names*, 570 (*Minnesota Historical Collections*, vol. 17—St. Paul, 1920). For accounts of the Methodist missions at Kaposia and Red Rock, see William W. Folwell, *A History of Minnesota*, 1:204–207 (St. Paul, 1921), and Chauncey Hobart, *History of Methodism in Minnesota*, 23 (Red Wing, 1887).

In the *Minnesota Pioneer* for August 30, 1849, the editor, James M. Goodhue, gives the following description of Cavileer's and Brown's claims: "Farther along [*below the mission buildings*], the prairie becomes wider between the timber upon the river and the bluffs which majestically sweep up on the left to a height of at least 100 feet. The prairie is here from one to two miles in width. Here is the improvement of Mr. Charles Cavileer, of St. Paul. . . . Farther along is the field of Mr. W. R. Brown, comprising some fifty acres, in an excellent state of cultivation. Upon the left, high up the ascent, amid a colonnade of large oaks, is his home; a cheerful scene."

[4] Biographical material concerning Jackson was obtained through an interview with Preston T. Jackson, a son of the diarist, in June, 1937, and from a letter from Preston Jackson to Dr. Grace Lee Nute, dated March 28, 1930, in the Jackson Papers in the possession of the Minnesota Historical Society.

In 1833, when Mitchell was seventeen, the family removed to a farm near the present city of Wabash. When Wabash County was organized two years later, Daniel Jackson was elected one of the two associate justices of the circuit court, and he held the office for several years. He was a leader in school affairs, one of the first and most active members of the Wabash County Agricultural Society, and an elder in the Christian Church, which he helped to organize.[5]

In 1841 Judge Jackson established at Wabash a warehouse, forwarding, and commission business under the name "D. Jackson and Sons." At the end of the first year the capital of the business had increased from $3,000 to $3,800—a situation with which Mitchell Jackson was "well satisfied considering the hardness of the times." A side line in dry goods was soon added, and Mitchell made a number of trips to the East to buy goods, which were then offered for sale at a storeroom in Wabash. Buying goods in New York City raised some difficulties. The goods were slow to arrive, and, since they were bought on credit, there was the further difficulty of arranging for long distance payment. This payment was made in a roundabout way. Jackson gave his notes to the New York creditor, who then turned them over to an individual in Indiana. The new creditor then received a stock of goods and some new notes in exchange for the old ones. The Jacksons erected their own warehouse in 1844, and four years later Mitchell and his brother Alexander bought out their father's interest in the business.[6]

[5] *Post*, p. 119; T. B. Helm, *History of Wabash County, Indiana*, 96, 101, 122, 124, 125, 131, 222 (Chicago, 1884).
[6] Jackson Diary, September 1, 1842; June 12–16, 1843; March 4, July 10, September 29, December 15, 20, 1844; April 14, 1849. The

Mitchell Jackson was appointed school commissioner at Wabash in 1847, and in 1850 he was elected treasurer of the board of trustees of the town of Wabash. In 1844 he married Martha Ann Caldwell, whose sister Prudence married Alexander Jackson a few years later. Shortly after the first anniversary of his marriage, Jackson computed the cost of his first year of housekeeping. His provision bill, including wood and light, came to $147.58. From this sum he deducted $114, the amount received from three boarders. The cost of boarding himself and his wife for a year, then, came to $33.58. This did not include the cost of clothing and furniture, which Jackson estimated would bring the total up to $200 for the year.[7]

As early as 1846 Jackson considered leaving Wabash. He recorded in the single entry of his diary for September of that year that he and his wife had "had chills nearly half the time." "We are getting pretty well tired of Wabash," he continued, "but dont know how to mend the matter without leaving the Mississippi valley entirely and crossing the mountains, which we will certainly undertake if we are spared till we can sell out." But it was not until the railroads threatened to destroy their means of livelihood, which was dependent on the Wabash Canal, that the Jacksons made their final decision to leave Indiana.[8]

Together with a number of other Wabash citizens, Judge Jackson, Mitchell, and Alexander joined the

diary for these years, which is not included in the present volume, is in the possession of a grandson of Mitchell Jackson, Mr. Raymond A. Jackson of Minneapolis, who has also an account book containing records of the warehouse business at Wabash.

[7] Jackson Diary, March 26, 1844; April 6, 1845; November 22, 1846; June 11, 1847; Helm, *Wabash County*, 219.

[8] *Post*, p. 90, 91.

Western Farm and Village Association, an Eastern organization which proposed to form a colony to settle on government lands to be selected by the association. When the Wabash members set out in the spring of 1852 for the location that was finally selected—Rollingstone, near the site of Winona, in Minnesota—Mitchell and Alexander Jackson were not ready to leave. Judge Jackson meantime had sold his membership in the association. By the time their business affairs in Wabash were settled, the brothers had apparently lost interest in the Rollingstone settlement, for in the winter of 1853-54 they sold their household goods with the intention of emigrating to Oregon. But again they changed their minds, and the late winter of 1854 found Mitchell journeying to Minnesota to find a suitable location for himself and his brother. The lands that he finally selected were in Washington County, between Afton and Lakeland, and about half a mile west of Lake St. Croix. There the two brothers brought their families in the spring of that year.[9]

Mitchell Jackson lived on his Lakeland farm for seventeen years. He was active in Republican party affairs and held several county offices—assessor from 1855 to 1858, county commissioner in 1859 and 1860, and register of deeds from 1866 to 1870. From the spring of 1863 until he became register of deeds in 1866 he spent most of his time traveling about Minnesota selling books, maps, pic-

[9] *Post*, p. 96, 97; manuscript reminiscences of Preston Jackson, dated June 9, 1937, in the Jackson Papers. Much information about the Rollingstone colony and the Wabash people who were interested in it is given by Edward B. Drew in his manuscript reminiscences in the possession of Mr. James M. Drew of St. Paul. The Minnesota Historical Society has a typewritten copy of these reminiscences. Drew, who was originally from Wabash, settled at Rollingstone in 1852, and Jackson on his first trip to Minnesota in 1854 visited him there. See *post*, p. 107.

tures, and a patent money drawer. In December, 1870, he sold his Lakeland farm for $2,400, and in the spring of 1871 he removed to a farm near Otisville, Iowa. In the autumn of the same year he traded his new farm for the Vermont House, a hotel in Mason City, Iowa, worth about $5,400. After a few weeks in the hotel business he leased the hotel, and the next summer he removed to Shakopee, Minnesota, where he went into the lumber business. Two years later he sold the lumber yard and again removed to Mason City, where he sold insurance. He remained there until his death in 1900.[10]

To place the Brown and Jackson diaries in their proper settings it is necessary to give a picture of agricultural conditions in Minnesota during the earlier years covered by them. Lack of a comprehensive agricultural history of the state and the scarcity of special studies in this field make it difficult to tell the complete story; but a few of the threads of the agricultural tapestry can be followed in these diaries, and from other diaries, newspapers and farm magazines of the period, and the recollections of pioneers part of the story can be pieced together.

The years covered by the Brown and Jackson diaries are those during which the first wave of pioneer farmers opened the Minnesota prairies to settlement. Washington County, in the southeastern part of the triangle of land formed by the Mississippi and St. Croix rivers, is one of the oldest, if not the oldest, settled regions of the state.

[10] Preston Jackson to Dr. Nute, March 28, 1930, Jackson Papers; diary of Preston Jackson, April 17, May 15, November 5, 28, 1871; June 30, 1872; May 30, 1874. Preston Jackson's diary is in the possession of his son, Mr. Myron B. Jackson of St. Paul. There is a brief mention of the Jacksons in George E. Warner and Charles M. Foote, eds., *History of Washington County and the St. Croix Valley*, 323, 324 (Minneapolis, 1881).

It was probably first seen by white men when Du Luth entered the St. Croix Valley in 1680. Few Frenchmen, however, found their way down the river valley, which was occupied by the Indians. Not until the late 1830's was there any permanent white settlement in the St. Croix Valley; and then it was timber, and not land, which attracted settlers.[11]

In those early days Minnesota's prairie lands were covered with timber, hazel brush, or long coarse grass. Wild plum and crab-apple trees were scattered through the forests, and wild roses dotted the prairies in the spring. Washington County had a diversified surface. Its southern portion was rich, rolling prairie; the central part had many small prairies and oak openings; and the northern portion was rough, being cut up by deep ravines whose depths were covered with timber.[12] Except for the disappearance of timber through lumbering, the general clearing of the land, the erection of houses and farm buildings, and some erosion in the northern and central portions, the county probably has not changed much in general appearance since the early days.

Agriculture as an independent occupation did not exist in Minnesota until 1840. Before that time some incidental agriculture had been carried on about the fur posts, forts, missionary stations, Indian agencies, and lumber camps, but, except for the refugees from the Selkirk settlements who were permitted to squat on government land near Fort Snelling from 1821 to 1840, no persons were solely dependent upon agriculture for a livelihood. Among the earliest farmers in Minnesota,

[11] Folwell, *Minnesota*, 1:24.
[12] Warner and Foote, *Washington County*, 337.

and probably the earliest in Washington County, were Joseph Haskell and James S. Norris. Haskell, who had worked for a lumber company at St. Croix Falls, and Norris commenced farming as partners near Afton in 1840. Using four yoke of oxen and a cast-iron plow, these men turned three acres of sod in six days at a cost of fifteen dollars an acre. They planted corn and potatoes, and the following winter baked bread on a barn shovel, an indication of the poverty of kitchen utensils in a pioneer bachelors' establishment. In 1841 Norris took up a claim in what is now Cottage Grove Township, built a cabin, broke forty acres of prairie sod, and seeded wheat. This is said to have been the first wheat of any quantity sown north of Prairie du Chien. The next year he sowed ninety acres of wheat, but since no flour mills were available, much of his harvest could not be disposed of.[13]

The early settlers in Washington County did not have long to wait for mills in which to grind their wheat and other grain. Few of them were reduced to the expedient of grinding wheat in coffee mills in order to secure flour for their bread. About 1845 Lemuel Bolles, on the creek bearing his name near Afton, erected the first privately owned mill in Minnesota for grinding corn and wheat. After salvaging slabs from the shore of Lake St. Croix, Bolles carried them on his back a mile and a half to the site of his mill. Lacking nails, he used wooden pins in the construction of the small mill, which had only eighteen-

[13] Warner and Foote, *Washington County*, 194, 365, 408; Robert Watson, *Notes on the Early Settlement of Cottage Grove and Vicinity, Washington Co., Minn.* (Northfield, 1924); *Minnesota Farmer and Gardener*, 1: 9, 59 (November, December, 1860). William A. Benitt, in his "Introduction to History of Agriculture in Southern Washington County," in the *Hastings Herald*, May 15, 22, 1936, gives an account of the farming activities of Haskell and Norris.

inch stones. For a few years it had no bolting cloth, and farmers who had their grain crushed at the mill sifted it at home. The mill, which was later rebuilt, was in operation as late as 1875. This was the mill to which Jackson carried his wheat and which, as he says, permitted him to eat bread from wheat of his own cultivation.[14]

Gradually settlers came into Minnesota. Because of its geographical location and the existence of the lumber industry, Washington County was one of the first regions in Minnesota to be settled. In 1850 it had a population of 1,056. Of these, 621 lived in Stillwater, which derived its importance from the fact that it was a center of the lumber industry. At the same time there were 157 farms in Minnesota, of which 48 were in Washington County. By 1850 market gardening in the county had begun in a small way to supply the needs of the lumber camps. Two men, Samuel and William Middleton, reported raising nearly a thousand bushels of potatoes in the census year; another crop was beans, which were popular in the lumber camps.[15]

Treaties with the Indians in the early fifties opened Minnesota to settlement on a wide scale, and in the next few years the trickle of immigration became a flood, which poured into the river valleys, where transportation was assured, and, with the coming of the railroads, spread

---

[14] Warner and Foote, *Washington County*, 404; William H. C. Folsom, "History of Lumbering in the St. Croix Valley," in *Minnesota Historical Collections*, 9:305; Edward V. Robinson, *Early Economic Conditions and the Development of Agriculture in Minnesota*, 43 (University of Minnesota, *Studies in the Social Sciences*, no. 3 — Minneapolis, 1915).

[15] Robinson, *Early Economic Conditions*, 41, 43; *United States Census, 1850, Statistics*, 994; *Compendium*, 334; manuscript schedules of the census of 1850 for Minnesota, in the possession of the Minnesota Historical Society.

over the rolling prairies. Transportation to a new region such as Minnesota was difficult and expensive, money was scarce, and household utensils and furnishings were not easily come by, so that settlers tended to economize what they brought with them. Household goods brought from the East were usually packed in large boxes made of inch-thick pine boards. These boxes, or their boards and nails, found many uses in the houses of the new settlements. Temporary cupboards, tables, chairs, and many other articles of furniture were made from these materials.[16]

In many parts of Minnesota the early settlers lived in log cabins or even in sod dugouts, but in Washington County the proximity of the lumber industry made it possible for some of the pioneers to build frame houses. The frame house into which Jackson moved, which still stands near Lakeland, was an unusually large one. It had two bedrooms, two parlors, a sitting room, a kitchen, four fireplaces, and a brick oven downstairs, and two bedrooms, a storeroom, and a closet upstairs. Underneath the house was a cellar in which vegetables such as potatoes, turnips, carrots, cabbages, and rutabagas were stored in the winter.[17]

Sod houses and sod dugouts were the most primitive types of dwelling used by the early settlers in Minnesota, and these shelters were used only where lack of timber prevented the construction of anything more elaborate. For building the walls of a sod house, pieces of sod a foot wide, a foot and a half long, and four inches thick were dug on the prairie, and, after being placed in position,

---

[16] H. V. Arnold, *Old Times on Portland Prairie, Houston County, Minn.*, 13 (Larimore, North Dakota, 1911).

[17] Preston Jackson in June, 1937, gave the editor a description of his father's home.

were secured with a mortar composed of white clay mixed with buffalo grass. The roof was formed of poles closely fastened together with willow withes, and was covered with sod. Windows and door frames were cut into the walls with an ax, and the floors were sometimes fashioned from loose boards. Dugouts were made in much the same way, except that the dugout was built into the side of a hill. Heat was furnished by a round, sheet-iron stove, and in the winter, when drifts of snow sometimes completely hid these dwellings, ventilation was obtained through the stovepipe, which protruded high above the roof. Wisps of dry prairie hay twisted into a hard coil were used as fuel, and lasted longer than might be supposed.[18]

In the eastern counties of Minnesota most of the settlers' cabins, however, were log buildings whose chinks were filled with a mixture of mud and hay or straw. Frequently the roof leaked, especially if it was made of shakes, and sometimes it was necessary to raise an umbrella to protect part of the interior. The Jackson home, then, represented quite an advance over the usual pioneer dwelling. But Jackson's stable, if it was made in the usual way, consisted of logs with a roof of wild hay or straw. Sometimes, however, barns were built of straw. Corner posts were set in the ground, and over a latticework of rails and poles wheat straw was piled in threshing time. The frames of these straw barns lasted a long time, but the straw had to be renewed each year. Only a few farmers had granaries; the rest used bins made of rails and lined

[18] The construction of sod houses and dugouts in Blue Earth County is described by James H. Quinn on page 18 of his manuscript autobiography written in 1928, in the possession of the Minnesota Historical Society.

with hay or straw to keep the grain from running out. Frame houses, barns, granaries, and drilled wells were not available in many parts of Minnesota until the seventies.[19]

In the early days all cultivated land was fenced, since livestock was allowed to run at large. Fences were usually made of rails, or, in some cases, of strips of sod piled four feet high; but in Washington County they were made of rough boards obtained from the lumber mills in exchange for corn and grain. Here again is an example of the benefits of cheap lumber to the inhabitants of the St. Croix Valley.[20]

Little is known concerning the agricultural implements used by Brown or the other pioneers of the 1840's, but probably most of their implements were made of wood. The settlers who came in the next decade were better equipped. Jackson had a steel plow, but, like other early steel plows, it was difficult to get it to scour properly, especially in clay. Fortunately he had little sod-breaking to do, since his was an improved claim. The tough prairie sod was not easily broken, and sometimes the settlers united to plow the land. Occasionally as many as ten yoke of oxen were hitched to the breaking plows. Some men made a business of breaking land, for which they charged from eight to twelve dollars an acre. Land was usually broken in June and was allowed to lie fallow until the next year. But before the prairie land was

[19] H. V. Arnold, *Forty Years in North Dakota*, 6, 8 (Larimore, North Dakota, 1921). An excellent description of the methods used in building log houses in pioneer Minnesota is given by Evadene A. Burris, in "Building the Frontier Home," in *Minnesota History*, 15:43–49 (March, 1934).
[20] Watson, *Early Settlement of Cottage Grove;* Drew Reminiscences, 49; Benitt, in the *Hastings Herald*, May 29, 1936.

broken, the wild meadow hay, or turkeyfoot grass, was gathered. This hay, which yielded as much as three or four tons an acre, was cut with a scythe, and it was carried in cocks on peeled poles to the stacks.[21]

Grain was sown broadcast by hand, and with a little practice it could be scattered quite evenly. In the early days grain was harvested and threshed without the aid of mechanical contrivances. It was cut with a cradle, which was a scythe with five long, tapering wooden fingers fastened to the blade and parallel to it, in such a manner as to cause the grain to fall upon the fingers. The advantage of the cradle was that grain could be deposited upon the ground in a gavel, that is, in a small pile with the heads all one way. The binder then raked the grain into bundles and bound it with a band of grain. An expert cradleman could cut four acres of an average stand of grain in one day, and occasionally a binder could keep up with him; but ordinarily from two to three acres of grain was considered a good day's work for either cradleman or binder. Bound grain was stacked and left until late autumn or early winter to be threshed.[22]

The first reaper to invade Minnesota—in 1854 or earlier—was hardly more than a mowing machine. It

[21] See *post*, p. 74, 81; George Smith, "Austin's Barefoot Boys of 70 Years Ago Recall Fun," in the *Austin Daily Herald*, August 31, 1935, p. 7; Quinn Autobiography, 5; Marshall T. Comstock Reminiscences, 9, a manuscript in the possession of the Minnesota Historical Society. These reminiscences were published in the *Mankato Daily Free Press* for August 9, 15, and 31, 1916.

[22] Watson, *Early Settlement of Cottage Grove;* manuscript reminiscences of Thomas R. Stewart, 1:177, in the possession of Mrs. Edith Stewart Hall of Pengilly. The Minnesota Historical Society has a photostatic copy of volume 1 and a typewritten copy of volume 2 of Stewart's reminiscences. Volume 1 was published in installments in the *Caledonia Journal* from May 1 to October 2, 1929.

was equipped with a platform on which a man stood and raked off the grain as it was cut. The grain was then bound by hand. The next important improvement, which appeared in the 1860's, replaced the man on the platform with a series of revolving rakes. These reapers cost three hundred dollars, and, since few settlers could afford them, the fortunate few cut grain by the acre for their neighbors. Another reaper had a platform on which two men stood and bound the grain as it was elevated to them on a table. Improvements followed quickly. The wire binder, which appeared about 1873, cut the grain and bound it into bundles fastened with pieces of wire, but it earned a bad reputation because bits of the wire got into threshing machines, causing damage, and, according to rumor, cows occasionally died from eating pieces of the wire which had found their way into the straw. This difficulty disappeared with the invention of the Appleby twine binder in the late 1870's. Jackson apparently did not have a reaper until 1856. The reaper that he purchased in that year, according to later entries in his diary, was probably a Manny reaper. In 1861 he bought a Brockport self-raking reaper.[23]

Until the threshing machine came to Minnesota, grain was threshed with the flail or by the hoofs of horses and oxen, which trod out the grain spread over an earthen threshing floor, made by smoothing off a bit of ground

[23] Leo Rogin, *The Introduction of Farm Machinery in Its Relation to the Productivity of Labor in the Agriculture of the United States during the Nineteenth Century*, 110–112, 114, 115 (University of California, Publications in Economics, vol. 9 — Berkeley, 1931); Smith, in the *Austin Daily Herald*, August 31, 1935, p. 7; Quinn Autobiography, 5; Stewart Reminiscences, 1:178; *post*, p. 151, 195, 204. An advertisement for "Manny's Adjustable Reaper and Mower Combined!" in issues of the *Hastings Independent* for 1860 includes an illustration of the reaper.

and pounding it down hard. The use of the flail entailed
a large amount of hard labor. It was made of two pieces
of hard wood, one about four feet long and the other
two and a half feet, fastened together at one end with a
piece of cord or rawhide. The thresher held the free end
of the longer piece in his hand, and, whirling the shorter
over his head, brought it down flat upon the grain. A
flail had to be used skillfully or it might strike the thresher
on the head.[24]

The first mechanical thresher to come to Minnesota
was the old horsepower treadmill thresher, which threshed
out the grain with a cylinder, but threw the grain and
straw out together. The straw was removed with a pitch-
fork or rake, and the chaff was blown off by a fanning
mill. This thresher was improved by attaching a shaker
to the cylinder, which shook out the wheat from the straw,
but left the grain and the chaff together. When the
fanning mill was added to the threshing machine, grain
and chaff were separated, the last going into the straw
pile. Jackson had a threshing machine as early as 1854,
and, since he had sold threshing machines in Indiana
before coming to Minnesota, he was familiar with the
frailties of the early machines. Threshing crews were
small, and the farmers whose grain was being threshed
did most of the work themselves. The bands on the
bundles were cut by hand and fed into the machine by
the "feeder," who wore snow goggles to protect his eyes
from kernels of grain flying from the cylinder. The
feeder's job was considered the most laborious in the
threshing operations and he received the highest wages

[24] Rogin, *Introduction of Farm Machinery*, 178; Watson, *Early Settle-ment of Cottage Grove;* Stewart Reminiscences, 1:175.

of the threshing crews. In 1869 a feeder was paid a dollar and a half a day.[25]

Steel or iron implements had to be brought from the East or fashioned by the local blacksmith, although even in metal work some farmers became proficient. Many of the farmer's tools were of necessity made by himself. Using an ax, he shaped sleds, ox yokes, and harrows from timber of his own cutting. Large sleds, fashioned entirely of wood by the farmers, were used for winter hauling.[26]

Cattle which the pioneer farmers brought with them were of no particular breed, but Jackson's cattle resembled Shorthorns somewhat, according to his son Preston, and his best cows had graded Shorthorn sires. Thoroughbred Shorthorns were reported coming into the state in 1860, and Freeborn County, where six thousand dollars' worth of beef cattle were sold in the same year, had both Shorthorn and Devon cattle. When twenty cattle raised at Cannon Falls were driven to St. Paul and sold it was evidently an unusual occurrence, for it won this comment from the *Stillwater Messenger:* "Stock raising will yet become a source of great wealth to our State."[27]

Little or no attention was paid to the improvement of the breeds of livestock on the prairie frontier, and animals such as hogs were allowed to run wild in the woods. Hogs which thus ranged the woods and fed upon acorns

[25] Rogin, *Introduction of Farm Machinery,* 163; Stewart Reminiscences, 1:176; Win V. Working, "Old Time Blakeley Township Thresher Is Still on the Job," in the *Belle Plaine Herald,* August 1, 1929; *post,* p. 131.

[26] Stewart Reminiscences, 1: 67–70, 85–88; Drew Reminiscences, 115; Arnold, *Forty Years in North Dakota,* 7.

[27] Interview of the editor with Preston Jackson in June, 1937; *Minnesota Farmer and Gardener,* 1:63, 72 (December, 1860, January, 1861); *Stillwater Messenger,* June 5, October 2, 1860.

acquired a fine flavor and a lean bacon. By 1861 pork-packing was an industry of some importance in the young state. During the season of 1860–61 about 282,000 pounds of pork were packed at St. Peter and were sold at an average price of 3¾ cents a pound. Chickens were scarce on the frontier, and one man recorded that in 1855 he had paid five dollars in gold for a hen. He raised sixteen chickens and in the autumn of the same year sold them for twenty dollars. The same man paid five dollars for a cat, a great necessity where mice were prevalent.[28]

In Washington County vegetables were grown mainly for table use, although potatoes were sold in St. Paul and beans were marketed in the lumber camps. Stillwater was the chief market for Washington County farmers, who brought there flour, oats, beans, potatoes, corn, hides, furs, hams, shoulders, butter, and eggs. Heavy shipments of produce were made from Stillwater. One boat in 1859 carried 2,370 sacks of grain and potatoes, while another loaded 3,500 sacks of the same produce. Cranberries and blueberries were abundant, and picking the latter was a favorite recreation of the Jacksons. Broom corn was grown by the farmers and manufactured by them into brooms during stormy days and long winter evenings, or, as in the case of Jackson, taken to a broom factory. The finished product was then sold by the farmers in St. Paul or Stillwater. Another side line was the production of sorghum sirup. In 1860 a man at Lakeland produced nearly five hundred gallons of this sirup.[29]

[28] *Minnesota Farmer and Gardener,* 1:73 (January, 1861); *Stillwater Messenger,* June 15, 1858; Comstock Reminiscences, 16.
[29] *Stillwater Messenger,* August 24, 1858; March 22, May 24, 1859; February 28, August 7, 1860; *Minnesota Farmer and Gardener,* 1:69 (January, 1861); *post,* p. 201; Jackson Diary, July 7-9, 1864.

In the fifties such a flood of immigration came to the newly opened territory that its infant agriculture was unable to supply sufficient food to meet the increased demand. Food was brought up the Mississippi from the older settled regions, and as late as 1857 flour was imported into Minnesota. At first the prices of farm commodities in Minnesota were fairly high, but during the depression of 1857 they fell rapidly and they remained at low levels until the demands and inflation of the Civil War years forced prices up. On January 31, 1863, Jackson noted in his diary the effect on prices of the issuance of paper money by the federal government, but pointed out that farm prices lagged behind industrial prices. Of the purely agricultural exports from Minnesota before the Civil War, oats, potatoes, and wheat alone were of any importance. Oats were shipped to Illinois for seeding purposes, potatoes to St. Louis and even to New Orleans, and in 1859 one hundred barrels of Minnesota flour were shipped to Boston, but at the prohibitive transportation cost of $2.25 a barrel. The first wheat to be shipped from Washington County, some two thousand bushels, was sent from Hastings in 1852 and probably went to St. Paul.[30]

Before the coming of the railroad, transportation costs were high and not only added to the cost of what the farmer bought, but also reduced the price of his exports; in the case of wheat the reduction ranged from thirty-five to fifty per cent of the price at the terminal market. St. Louis and Milwaukee were the principal markets for Minnesota wheat. In 1860 wheat prices at Stillwater were from twenty to twenty-three cents per bushel below the

[30] *Saint Croix Union* (Stillwater), November 3, 1854; May 12, 1855; *Stillwater Messenger*, June 12, 1860; Robinson, *Early Economic Conditions*, 44, 45; Benitt, in the *Hastings Herald*, May 29, 1936.

Milwaukee price, the best Eastern market. The following table shows why there was such a large spread in prices between Stillwater and Milwaukee:

	Cents per Bushel
Commission for buying, sacking, and shipping	4
Insurance and wastage	½
Wear and tear on sacks	1
Expense of sale at Milwaukee	1½
Freight from Stillwater to Milwaukee	15
Total	22

In spite of the difficulties and expense involved in marketing Minnesota produce to an outside market, however, the settlers in the new country, suffering from a shortage of cash, welcomed their growing exports as a method of rectifying their adverse balance of trade. This feeling was expressed in 1860 by the editor of the *Minnesota Farmer and Gardener,* who wrote: "Three years ago the St. Paul landing was covered with sacks and barrels of flour from the States below, for which we had to pay a good price, and then we did not get anything to compare with Minnesota flour. In 1860, the flour trade of this State goes down stream and the gold comes up."[81]

Minnesota experienced a land boom in the years preceding 1857. Many persons came to the territory with the expectation of making their fortunes through land speculation. Some of these speculators were stranded by the panic of 1857 and were forced to turn to farming to make a living. During the land boom, prices rose as much as two hundred or three hundred per cent. In 1857

---

[81] Henrietta M. Larson, *The Wheat Market and the Farmer in Minnesota, 1858–1900,* 36, 46, 53 (New York, 1926); *Stillwater Messenger,* September 4, 1860; *Minnesota Farmer and Gardener,* 1:56 (December, 1860).

Jackson sold for fifteen dollars an acre lake shore land which had cost him only five dollars an acre in 1854. At the same time, he reported, his prospects for selling the rest of his land for forty dollars an acre, or about double what he had paid for it, were good. He relates in his diary how his personal wealth had increased since he came to Minnesota, and how he felt that this increase was due, not to farming, but to the rise in land values.[32]

The panic of 1857 brought to an end the bubble of land speculation in Minnesota. Hard times settled down in the autumn and winter of that year and the pall did not lift until the Civil War years. As Jackson noted in December, 1857: "Since 1836 there has been no such Revulsion in money affairs." Minnesota farmers suffered greatly from the almost total lack of a trustworthy circulating medium. Money and banking facilities always seem to be scarce in a frontier community; normally currency is drained from the frontier to the older communities in payment for the supplies and capital necessary to keep the new community going during the years of settlement and clearing, while banking and credit services are both rudimentary and expensive. The lack of actual currency was a hardship, since it made trading difficult, and farmers in many instances were reduced to barter. As early as 1855 Jackson noted the growing scarcity of money, and in the early days of 1858 he declared that it was difficult to sell even farm produce for money. Although the issuance of greenbacks by the federal government during the Civil War helped somewhat to supply

[32] *Stillwater Messenger,* September 7, 1858; John H. Stevens, "Annual Address before the Crow River Agricultural Society, October 2, 1861," in *Minnesota Farmer and Gardener,* 1:327 (November, 1861); *post,* p. 156, 157.

the need for a trustworthy circulating medium, from the panic of 1857 on Minnesota experienced a need for currency which was felt as late as the 1870's. The situation was at its worst in the years from 1857 to 1859, when Illinois and Wisconsin "stump-tail," or scrip, currency drove out of circulation almost all other money. In Stillwater "stump-tail" currency was refused circulation, and the city authorities and the school board combined to issue school bonds in five and ten dollar denominations to the amount of several thousands. For a time these bonds were the only circulating medium in the county.[33]

In other parts of Minnesota at a later date this monetary stringency seems to have been almost as great. A settler in Stearns County wrote in 1879: "I haven't seen but about ten $ in cash during the whole of the winter thus far." He added: "Still I am fully convinced even during this tight pinch, that a young man can make more money in a year, & live upon less than half, than he could in the East."[34]

Agricultural fairs made their appearance in Minnesota in the early 1850's. At the agricultural and horticultural fair of the Hennepin County Agricultural Society, held in Minneapolis in 1854, cash premiums of several hundred dollars were distributed, and there were more than fifty exhibitors. The first fair in Minnesota which was fully representative of the products of the territory was held in Minneapolis in 1855. It was sponsored jointly by the Hennepin County association and the Minnesota Territorial Agricultural Society. There were two thousand

---

[33] *Post,* p. 141, 166, 167; *Saint Croix Union,* November 18, 1854; Warner and Foote, *Washington County,* 334.

[34] Bertha L. Heilbron, ed., "Pioneering in Stearns County," in *Minnesota History,* 19:323 (September, 1938).

admissions. Among the exhibits were a Durham bull, Leicester sheep, a few hogs, Shanghai, Chittagong, and Brahmaputra chickens, yellow dent corn, wheat, rye, buckwheat, cabbages, squash, pumpkins, potatoes, turnips, onions, house plants and flowers, butter and cheese, needlework, homemade rugs and carpets, and three apples. These last were exhibited by Gideon Pond, who gathered them from a tree which he had planted at Oak Grove in 1844. Jackson attended the Ramsey County fair in 1863, but he was not impressed by it. It was, he wrote, "a meagre collection of Cattle & horses brought in by their owners & offered for sale at auction."[35]

Most of the farmers' diaries consulted by the editor have few entries concerning politics, and those entries are confined to short comments such as: "Voted today." The Jackson Diary has more than most in this respect, because of Jackson's political activities. Likewise his comments on the coming conflict and on the Civil War itself are fuller than those in most farmers' diaries. There are no entries concerning the Grange, and, in the recollection of Jackson's son Preston, no Grange meetings were held in the neighborhood. Farmers' clubs, such as the one which Jackson helped to organize, met sometimes to discuss local affairs, but apparently no organizations existed in the neighborhood, apart from the regular political parties, which took part in national affairs. A number of persons in the neighborhood of Lakeland belonged to the Good Templars, which Jackson and his wife joined in 1866, and

[35] See *post*, p. 217; Earle R. Buell, "When Uncle Sam's Army Gave up Raising Wheat in Minnesota," in the *Daily News* (Minneapolis), September 9, 1922, section 3, p. 6; *Saint Croix Union*, November 3, 1855; *Stillwater Messenger*, September 7, 1858; *Minnesota Farmer and Gardener*, 1:35 (December, 1860).

others were members of other fraternal organizations. Jackson was a Mason, having joined the order at Wabash.[36]

The center of the farmer's social life was the schoolhouse. Many of his amusements were of an educational nature. Lyceums were held at the schoolhouse in the winter evenings and questions of local or national interest were debated. Jackson records temperance and the Kansas question among the subjects debated at lyceums that he attended. Singing schools, spelling bees, Christmas celebrations, panorama shows, and dramatic entertainments were all held in the schoolhouse. In one community a "Thespian Society" gave plays written by a member who used Scott's and Campbell's poems as sources of inspiration. That such amateur plays and acting were not always of the highest quality is indicated by an entry in the diary of Allen W. Dawley of Smithfield: "Attended a Dramatic Entertainment in the Evening given by a Kellogg company for a free Reading Room. Performance poor."[37]

Library associations, books, magazines, and newspapers were far from unknown on the farm; and the Lakeland neighborhood, as well as other districts, prized reading matter. Jackson noted a meeting of the library association in Lakeland, and the formation of a club of subscribers to the *Northwestern Farmer and Horticultural Journal*. In the Jackson home, according to the recollection of Preston

[36] *Post*, p. 123, n., 154; Jackson Diary, June 13, September 28, 1848; Helm, *Wabash County*, 230. Jackson was secretary of his Masonic lodge at Wabash in 1848.

[37] *Post*, p. 146, 168; Rodney C. Loehr, "Minnesota Fairmers' Diaries," in *Minnesota History*, 18:293 (September, 1937); Eugene W. Randall, *Reminiscences and Reflections*, 1 (n.p., n.d.); Comstock Reminiscences, 12; Dawley Diary, February 24, 1879. The Dawley Diary is in the possession of the Minnesota Historical Society.

Jackson, there could be found the New York *Weekly Tribune,* the Stillwater newspapers, and *Harpers Magazine.* Out of a dozen or more books in the Jackson library the family still has B. F. Tefft's *Speeches of Daniel Webster* from the *Young American's Library* series and James Fenimore Cooper's *Stories of the Sea.*[38]

Not all the farmer's recreation was connected with the schoolhouse or library. In some communities dancing and card-playing were not frowned upon. Farmers played euchre, "pea Nuckle," backgammon, parchesi, and checkers. Dancing clubs were formed, and at some of the dances each couple was expected to pay the fiddler fifty cents. Oyster suppers, candy pulls with sorghum molasses candy, parties, sewing and quilting bees, housewarmings, ice-cream festivals, and sleigh rides provided entertainment. Individual recreation was sought in skating, berrypicking, hunting, fishing, and swimming.[39]

Hunting and fishing provided food as well as sport for the farmers. Large fish were easily caught in the rivers and lakes, and trout could be found in some creeks. Game birds were plentiful; quail and prairie chickens were flushed in the long grass of the prairies and in the brush, while ducks and geese rested on the many lakes during their spring and autumn flights. In the winter rabbits and sometimes deer could be tracked over freshly fallen snow, and they provided welcome additions to the farmer's larder. Using steel traps, the boys in the farmer's family caught muskrats, minks, raccoons, and skunks, whose skins had a ready sale. Weasel skins were sold in

[38] *Post,* p. 154, 180; interview of the editor with Preston Jackson in June, 1937.
[39] Quinn Autobiography, 5, 9; Loehr, in *Minnesota History,* 18:294 (September, 1937).

the neighborhood to women who used them as powder puffs on babies.[40]

Following the American custom, the farmer's wife was ordinarily kept out of the fields. Brown mentions his wife, Martha, helping him in the field, but that was an unusual occurrence. Even so, the farmer's wife had a busy life. Besides the care of the children, no small task in a day of large families, she had three meals a day to prepare, washing and ironing to do, fruit to put up or dry, and a large amount of sewing and patching of clothes and darning and knitting of stockings and mittens as spare-time tasks, besides such chores as taking care of the fowl yard, churning, and sometimes milking. She also made hard and soft soap, put up preserves and pickles, and for threshing day, Thanksgiving, and Christmas prepared great amounts of food.[41]

The piano was not unknown on Minnesota farms in 1854, as Jackson notes, and the sewing machine was also available in the fifties. Screen doors were possible by 1881, and papered walls and washing machines were on the farm by 1885, but in earlier days conveniences and comforts were few and household utensils primitive. Our first farmers had crude, homemade lanterns or none at all. When manufactured lanterns were available, they were poor affairs until the tubular lanterns appeared about 1870. Interior illumination came from fireplaces or, if the home had a stove, from a dish of lard with a strip of rag hanging over the edge for a wick. This "lamp" was kept on the stove to keep the lard melted. Candles were of three

[40] Heilbron, in *Minnesota History*, 19:322 (September, 1938); Arnold, *Old Times in Portland Prairie*, 16; Stewart Reminiscences, 1:88; Quinn Autobiography, 5.
[41] Randall, *Reminiscences and Reflections*, 4; *post*, p. 80.

kinds—sperm, tallow, and wax. Before the Civil War tallow candles sold six for fifteen cents, and sperm or "Star" candles, six for twenty-five cents. Many persons molded their own candles, and honeycomb from bee trees found in the summer was saved for this purpose. In making tallow candles, hot tallow was poured into the molds, each of which had a cotton wick in the center. After the tallow had hardened the molds were often placed in hot water to loosen the candles. Illumination remained poor and unsatisfactory until the introduction of the kerosene lamp, which became available during the Civil War. The first kerosene on the market was dangerously explosive and the lamps had to be handled with care. To remedy this condition agents peddled liquids and powders which, if placed in the lamps, were supposed to reduce the danger of explosion, but some people found common salt just as useful for that purpose.[42]

Early frontier homes frequently lacked spring beds. In the place of springs a latticework of half-inch ropes was stretched across the bedstead. A tick filled with straw was placed upon this, and over the tick, a feather bed made from the feathers of wild geese and ducks. A few farmers had sheep of their own and, like Jackson, used the wool from their sheep to provide clothing. But unlike Jackson, who took his wool to a mill to be spun and woven into cloth, other farmers allowed their wives to card the wool, spin it into yarn, and knit stockings and mittens. Using black and white threads—sumac gave a black dye—the

[42] Drew Reminiscences, 122; Stewart Reminiscences, 1:114; Quinn Autobiography, 22; Evadene A. Burris, "Keeping House on the Minnesota Frontier," in *Minnesota History*, 14:264 (September, 1933); J. E. Townsend, "Commodity Prices of 75 Years Ago," in the *Belle Plaine Herald*, February 21, 1935; *post*, p. 112.

wife knit the mittens double, which added to warmth and wearing qualities. Occasionally a farmer had a cobbler's outfit and was able to sew bootstraps, patch holes, and even put half soles on the cowhide boots worn by men and boys. These boots were greased every night with tallow, and even then, shrunken and hard, they were difficult to get on in the morning.[43]

Soapmaking was a task which was sometimes left to the women, but more often, as Brown records, it received the labors of the whole family. Two logs were rolled close together and an empty barrel was placed upon them. The barrel was packed with hardwood ashes and water was allowed to seep through them. The seepage constituted lye, which when boiled with grease gave soft soap. To get hard soap, salt was added. When cold, the soap was cut into cakes, and although it was hard on hands, it was efficient in removing grease and dirt.[44]

Doctors were not plentiful on the frontier, and women acted as midwives for each other at the frequent childbirths. Child life was harsher than it is today; there was always plenty of work to do, and children took their place in the fields at an early age. Yet they were not without amusements. At school recess they played "ante ante over," two old cat with yarn balls made from old stocking ravelings wrapped around cotton, and such games as crack-the-whip, fox and geese, and pom-pom-pullaway. Picnics were held in the summer, and in the winter sleigh rides or spelling contests with neighboring schools provided excitement.[45]

[43] Quinn Autobiography, 15, 21; Jackson Diary, September 6, 7, 1865.
[44] Quinn Autobiography, 32; Burris, in *Minnesota History*, 14:273 (September, 1933); *post*, p. 38, 80.
[45] Interview of the editor with Preston Jackson in June, 1937; Randall, *Reminiscences and Reflections,* 8; Quinn Autobiography, 22.

One writer has described the school building where he went to school in the 1850's as a little log building about fourteen by eighteen feet, with desks consisting of a board about sixteen inches wide running around three sides of the building and fastened to the logs. The room was heated by an old box stove. School terms ran from three to four months in the winter, and sometimes three in the summer. Children were drilled in reading, writing, spelling, grammar, history, geography, and arithmetic. On Friday afternoons they spoke pieces and held spelldowns. The last day of school was a day of open house to parents; the scholars spoke pieces, and in the evening a spelling bee was held in which all could participate.[46]

Then, as now, children hung up their stockings on Christmas Eve. Gifts, however, were apt to be limited in variety, and sometimes, as Jackson records, the difficulties which Santa Claus faced in coming to Minnesota prevented his arrival. The usual gifts were of the homemade variety, and stockings bulged with popcorn, a pair of knitted mittens or something else which was useful, and, down in the toe, a big, red apple.[47]

Preachers, like doctors, were scarce on the frontier, and, according to Jackson, the frontier had a leveling effect upon sectarianism. Missionaries and circuit riders held services in schoolhouses and private homes, but even their absence did not prevent the holding of services. An elder might preach a sermon, or the services might be limited to the singing of hymns. In spite of the difficulties facing the pioneer farmers, they maintained a tenacious hold upon certain common religious tenets, such as refraining

[46] Stewart Reminiscences, 1:115.
[47] Interview of the editor with Preston Jackson in June, 1937; Randall, *Reminiscences and Reflections*, 13; *post*, p. 132.

from work on Sunday and assembling for common worship. Jackson felt rather strongly on the matter of keeping Sunday as a day of rest; this is demonstrated by his refusal to move cattle across the St. Croix River on Sunday, in spite of the fact that his family desired to get their stock to their new home as quickly as possible.[48]

Farming on the frontier, as these diaries show, was not without its hardships and perplexities. Opening a new country to settlement, converting virgin soil to cultivated land, and establishing the social conveniences common to older settled regions were not easy tasks. To the story of this pioneer period these diaries contribute a vivid, first-hand account. They are useful first, simply as farmers' diaries, and second, as Minnesota frontier diaries. As farmers' diaries they give something of the flavor of the life of many of our people in past times, and as frontier diaries they relate part of the life of pioneer farmers, figures well known to American history.

The Brown Diary covers the period from October 25, 1845, to June 14, 1846, and is written in a small leather-bound notebook. The Jackson Diary, which begins on September 8, 1841, and ends on December 20, 1873, comprises ten small volumes—the first three unbound and cut and sewed by hand, and the remaining seven bound, some in leather and some in cloth. The editor has selected for publication in the present volume the part of the Jackson Diary covering the dates from August 8, 1852, to June 5, 1863, which gives enough of Jackson's life in Wabash to serve as a background, and describes his journeys to Minnesota and his life on the farm at Lake-

[48] Randall, *Reminiscences and Reflections*, 2; Loehr, in *Minnesota History*, 18:294 (September, 1937); *post*, p. 127, 139.

land until the time when activities other than farming engaged the greater part of his time and attention.[49]

Except for their division into chapters according to years and some changes in paragraphing, the diaries are reproduced below as they were written, with the spelling, capitalization, and punctuation unchanged. In a few instances omitted words, letters, and punctuation have been supplied in brackets as an aid to readability. Paragraphing has been omitted in short entries for the sake of the appearance of the printed page; and unusually long entries have been paragraphed in the interest of readability. Wherever possible, the editor has indicated the full names of persons mentioned in the diaries, except in cases of names generally familiar, using brackets to indicate the portions supplied. Accounts, planting and harvesting dates, descriptions of land, and other memoranda which Jackson wrote in the front and back of his diaries have been gathered together and printed as an appendix to the volume.

The editor wishes to thank the present owners of the diaries—Mrs. Clarence H. Johnson of St. Paul, a great niece of William R. Brown, and Mr. Raymond A. Jackson of Minneapolis, a grandson of Mitchell Y. Jackson—for permission to print the diaries, as well as for their cooperation during the preparation of the volume. He also wishes to thank Dr. Theodore C. Blegen, superintendent of the Minnesota Historical Society, and Mrs. Mary W. Berthel and Mrs. Selma P. Larsen of the society's staff for their aid and encouragement.

RODNEY C. LOEHR

UNIVERSITY OF MINNESOTA
MINNEAPOLIS

[49] Extracts from Jackson's diaries, selected by Solon J. Buck, are printed in *Agricultural History*, 4:92–120 (July, 1930).

THE DIARY OF
WILLIAM R. BROWN, 1845-46

1845

The Prope[r]ty of Wm R. Brown of Kaposia Red Stone Prairie St Croix Co. and Territory of Wiskonsan   Oct. 25th 1845

Oct. 25   Finished Harvesting & burying our Rutabagas and flat Turnips   Weather Remarkably warm and pleasant, smokey & dry.

26th Sunday   smokey, dry, warm and pleasant   [James S.] Davis[1] went home this morning   assisted us two days last week.

27   Warm & pleasant   gathered up the pieces of rails & Bark around the fences today   put up 2 barrels of ashes to leach   Sold our yoke of Steers 2 years old to young Lavicinia for $36 also our pair of yearlings for $16. Hauled up sand and lime for Daubing purposes.   Settled with & paid Hopkins and Fords Store Act.[2]   Firm also settle[d] with and paid Hopkins & Ford.   Bot. 10 yds of Marriners Shirting of H. & F   paid 16⅔ cents per yd.

28   Martha made pot of soap[3]   used 22 lbs Tallow in makeing it.   Charles [Cavileer] & I. Daubed the Hen

---

[1] Davis settled in what is now Cottage Grove Township about 1844. Warner and Foote, *Washington County*, 365.

[2] Daniel Hopkins and John A. Ford kept a supply store at Red Rock. Ford had been the blacksmith for the Indians at Kaposia, and he continued to do blacksmith work for settlers in the neighborhood. William H. C. Folsom, *Fifty Years in the Northwest*, 385, 386 (St. Paul, 1888); Watson, *Cottage Grove and Vicinity*.

[3] Martha was Brown's wife.

House. [Edmund] Brissette [Brissett] took his Prairie Plow away. [Henry] Belland sent for his ox yoke.[4]

29th Very warm rather cloudy. Commenced daubing the old Kitchen. Went just at night to burn around our hay stacks but the grass would not burn. looks very much like rain.

30 Warm & cloudy in the morn. at 1 oclock commenced raining & continued untill night. Lavisinia came for his cattle & I rode all over Creation in search of them & found them just at night. L. stayed over night. Continued the daubing operation on the old Kitchen Martha made a pot of Hard soap excellent.

31 Went out after Breakfast to catch Lavisinias cattle Caught 3 of them [but] the 4th jumped the fence and cleared Sold him our yearling of the Doe [?][5] stock in Lieu of one he bought the other day he payed $11 for this one for the other he was to have paid $8 Sold him Star & Swans yoke for $4.50[6] Continued Daubing the old Kitchen & the House Martha made a pot of Hard soap.

Nov. 1st Finished daubing Kitchen and Stable. commenced on House. Castrated 4 Pigs Martha made 2 kettles soap 3rd she had trouble with, would not thicken think salt was the cause

[4] On Cavileer, see *ante,* p. 3, 4. Brissett lived on a farm near the mouth of the slough on Gray Cloud Island from 1842 to 1848. Belland, a trader in the employ of the American Fur Company, purchased a claim on the site of St. Paul in 1840 and lived there for seven years. Brissett Reminiscences, 6, 8, a manuscript in the possession of the Minnesota Historical Society; Thomas M. Newson, *Pen Pictures of St. Paul, and Biographical Sketches of Old Settlers,* 333 (St. Paul, 1886).

[5] The word is either "Dar" or "Doe." One Hilton Doe, who had been an Indian farmer at Red Wing from 1840 to 1844, lived at Prescott, Wisconsin, in 1845, and it is possible that Brown refers to cattle purchased from him. Folsom, *Fifty Years in the Northwest,* 215.

[6] Star and Swan were a pair of oxen.

just night the Hurlbut
Cow had a heifer calf

Tuesday 17th
Harrison hauled wood on
the sled untill noon, after
which he took the Waggon
& hauled 3 loads of Wood
for Ford, I finished the
Wood Saddlers,

Wednesday 18th
Sold Lacture 3 lbs of
Butter at 25 cent per lb
on credit, Mail arrived
received a letter from
the Department stating
we were to have the
Mail, Harrison hauled wood
for Ford, Haskell came over
to assist thresh our Oats

A Page from Brown's Diary

Sunday 2nd   Steamer Cecilia arrived.   I went up to Fort [Snelling] on foot

Monday 3rd   To day I arrived at home from Fort in the evening   found Harrison had arrived from Ohio[7]

Tuesday 4   Harrison and I talked a great deal about Home

Wednesday 5th   Continued daubing House & shop tryed at night to burn around hay stacks but the grass would not burn

Thursday 6th   Continued daubing Shop   Burned around hay Stacks.

Friday 7th   Continued daubing Shop and root House [B. L.] Rockwood came & Borrowed Waggon[8]   Weather very pleasant   We banked the dirt up around the Houses.

Saturday 8th   Daubed Root House   Weather rather cool but pleasant   Robert Cummings commenced suit against E[lijah] A. Bissell for Wages   Jacob Faulstram [*Falstrom*] Wanted me to Petifog for him on the [Edward] Worth case befor[e] H[enry] Jackson[9]   I agreed to do so on Monday next.   cattle got in the Garden &

---

[7] Harrison apparently was Brown's brother, and the "E. H. Brown" referred to *post*, p. 41.

[8] Rockwood, a bachelor familiarly known as "Rock," had a small farm in Denmark Township, near the St. Croix River.   Watson, *Cottage Grove and Vicinity*.

[9] Cummings settled at Cottage Grove in 1845, and Bissell made a claim in Afton Township in 1842. Falstrom, a one-time trader in the employ of the American Fur Company, settled near Lakeland in 1840. After his conversion to Christianity at the Methodist mission at Kaposia, he became a missionary and conducted services at various points in the St. Croix Valley.   Worth settled at St. Croix Falls, Wisconsin, in 1842. Soon afterward he obtained the contract for carrying the mail from Point Douglas to St. Croix Falls, and held it until 1848.   Jackson, a fur trader and pioneer storekeeper, was justice of the peace at St. Paul.   Warner and Foote, *Washington County*, 295, 296, 399, 407; Hobart, *Methodism in Minnesota*, 20; Folsom, *Fifty Years in the Northwest*, 109, 524; Warren Upham and Rose B. Dunlap, *Minnesota Biographies, 1655–1912* (*Minnesota Historical Collections*, vol. 14—St. Paul, 1912).

destroyed some Cabbage the balance we caried in in the evening

Sunday 9th Morning Frosty but clear & pleasant Harrison & I walked out on Prairie he was well pleased with the country Jacob Faulstram came over and stayed all night also Mr Grigrich [?] stayed over night.[10]

Monday 10 Started early for St Paul Charley [,] Harrison and myself to attend the trial between Worth Pla[i]ntiff and Faulstrom Def. Case of Forcible entry and detainer I acting as council for F. Jury could not agree trial again on 29th Worth commenced an action of Burglary against Faulstrom trial on 15th Sold 1 Barrel onions to L[ouis] Robert for $4.00 also 32 heads Cabb[a]ge @ 2.00[11] Started from St Paul at sunset Weather very moderate.

Kaposia W. T. Tuesday 11th Very moderate weather Charly & Harrison went Fishing brot home 9 Today the people begin to talk of openly resisting the administration of Justice by Henry Jackson of St. Paul he seems to pay no regard whatever to the sanctity of Oaths or the obligation of his Office. So much so that the people talk of declareing that we in St Croix have worse than *no Law*

Wednesday 12th Morning opens the day clear and pleasant Charles Cavileer[,] E. H. Brown & myself went out and measured off a half Claim or Steped off a half Claim for Cavileer & Brown the same on which we have

[10] This may be the Joseph Grigerige who is listed in the 1850 census schedules under the Stillwater precinct of Washington County. In the 1860 census schedules his name is spelled "Gregridge." These census schedules are in the possession of the Minnesota Historical Society.

[11] Robert, a fur trader on the upper Missouri River in his early life, settled in St. Paul in 1844, where he engaged in the Indian trade. He later became owner and captain of several steamboats.

been improving. Went to renew the lines around the Town Claim but Ford insisted on having 20 acres which we agreed to give him and Hopkins. John W. Brown called to witness the contract[12]

Tuesday 12th [*sic*] Rockwood brot. waggon home, & 3 bushels Corn   Harrison found a Claim which pleased him   I bot. 6 yards of flannel for Harrison at 37½ per yard $2.25

Thursday 13th   Steam Boat Otter arrived   did not stop   I walked up to Fort   intended bringing Flour sugar molases &c down but Capt. Mumford[13] charged me so much I could not afford to pay Freight   received the Mail. Walked down from Fort. E. A. Bissell paid note of $9.96   weather Very Warm.

Friday 14   E. H. Brown Marked off for himself a Claim   C. Cavileer & myself witnessed the corners & lines. I went over to Esq [James S.] Norrises   bot some corn   went from there over to see [Joseph] Haskell[14] was not at home   he came over to Red Rock   I came home in the night   found Haskell at my house.

Saturday 15   Haskell & myself went up to Esq Jacksons to council   Jacob Faulstrom[,] Worth[,] Edward[,] haveing Warranted him for Burglary   had not sufficient evidence to commit Faulstrom   We have pretty stron[g] proof that Worth perjured himself at the trial   Jackson seemed to show Worth great partiality by pleading his case & assi[s]ting him to give in his testimony

---

[12] Brown was a half-brother of Joseph R. Brown, the well-known Minnesota pioneer.   John H. Case, "Historical Notes of Grey Cloud Island and Its Vicinity," in *Minnesota Historical Collections*, 15:373.

[13] Brown may refer to A. C. Monfort, a steamboat captain in the upper Mississippi trade.   The editor has found no record of a "Captain Mumford."

[14] On Haskell and Norris see *ante*, p. 11.

Sunday 16   Haskell went home   borrowed 1 barrel of Flour.   Warm & pleasant

Monday 17   C. Cavileer & myself went to the Fort in a canoe. brot home our canoe loaded with Leather & sadlery, sugar, molasses, &c   got home late at Night.

Tuesday 18   Did not feel well   did not do much

Wednesday 19th   Went to drive home our cattle looked through the Bottom for them but found them not   went down below Brissettes House on the Slough then found them. heard that [John] Holtons cattle were destroying our hay.[15]   some fears that John Miller is drowned.[16]

Thursday 20   Charles Cavileer & Harrison went out to secure our hay   they found the cattle had destroyed considerable of it.   Windy & quite cool   has the appearance of Winter.

Friday 21   Harrison & I went to Fort   drove up 2 cows for [Franklin] Steel[e][17]   Started home Just at sunset. Commence[d] snowing about 9 oclock   snowed ½ an inch

Saturday 22   This morning looks wintry indeed   pretty cold   snowing quite fast   first snow this Fall   after Breakfast H. & I went down & piled the rails around W[illiam] B. K[avanaugh]'s place.[18]   Snowed all day   geting quite cold.

[15] Holton was a member of the missionary party, led by Alfred Brunson, which established a Methodist mission at Kaposia in 1837. He later settled on a farm near Red Rock.

[16] Miller, a stonemason, was drowned at Gray Cloud Island, where he lived at the time. He did the masonwork on the Sibley House in Mendota in 1835.   Brissett Reminiscences, 1; Williams, *Saint Paul*, 84.

[17] Steele was sutler at Fort Snelling from 1838 to 1858. He made a claim at St. Anthony in 1838, and took a prominent part in the development of the water power and the lumber industry at the falls.

[18] On Kavanaugh, see *ante*, p. 4.

Sunday 23rd   Clear & still, somwhat more moderate than yesterday. Ice runing quite thick.

Monday 24th   Quite cold   river full of ice. Harrison & I choped & hauled 5 loads of fire wood   wind from the south has the appearance of moderating. Wind changed about 10 oclock tonight

Tuesday 25th   Wind in North   quite cold   Harrison & I hauled a load of hay so windy it was bad work. River closed over about 1 oclock today. after dinner H. & I Butchered a hog. at sunset Martha[,] Harrison & Charley & myself went over to Mr Holtons & helped to eat a fine fat Roast goose. wind has fallen.

Wednesday 26th   Wind in the no[r]th & pretty cold. Harrison & I killed one hog, after which Charles[,] Harrison & I killed a young hiefer for Beef one of the Doe [?] Cattle that would not Breed.   After supper H & I Cut up the Beef.

Thursday 27th   Wind in the North & very cold   H & I ground up our axes   concidered it too cold to kill a Beef   I loaned H. my large choping axe during the Winter   At about one oclock today Harrison frosted the Tip of his nose going from the shop to Hopkins store.

Friday 28th   Very cold. Harrison Chopped some wood to haul.   I went over to Esquire Norris's then met Haskell & returned home with him   Then first heard of [James] Purintons intention to serve upon Norris a writ of Injunction.[19]   I think he means to distress Norris

Saturday 29th   Haskell & myself called up to St Pauls to Council [—] Jacob Faulstrom in suit of Forcible Entry

---

[19] Purinton settled in 1842 at St. Croix Falls, where for a time he leased the lumber mills.   He later became part owner of them.   Folsom, *Fifty Years in the Northwest*, 161.

& Detainer brot. against him by Edward Worth. This case was tryed by a Jury of 12 men as the Law directs, & I believe had Justice Jackson not so mystified the subject & showed the g[r]os[s]est partiality by missconstureing [*sic*] the Law & over ruling every motion made by the Defen[d]ant we should have got a Verdict in favor of Folstrom   In this case the Jury gave a Verdict for Worth stating at the same time that they did not deside the Question as to who the property belonged to—a stragen [*strange*] Verdict indeed as I think.   There appeared to be considerable excitement on the day of trial.   about half of the Jury was from Still Water   Haskell & I left immediately after the rendition of the Verdict

Sunday 30eth   Quite cold. I rode over to Norris with Haskell   found that Purinton had served a writ of Injunction on Norris   he (N) seemed quite concerned at his present situation   does not know what to do.   Saw Orange Walker of the Marine Mills at Esq Norris House[20]   he does not understand the power of the Writ   believes that the people should not suffer Norris to be crushed by so heartless a Villian as old Purinton is   so say I & so says Haskell.

Monday 1st of Dec   I went from Haskells to Mr E. A Bissells   Stayed & took dinner with him   bot. of him 8 bushels Barley at .75 per Bushel.   he payed the cost on the suit that Robert Cummings brot. against him on the 8th of Nov. for 35 days work   I returned to Bissell the Note that he gave me for Star and Swan because I did not consider the form a good one, that is I thought the security

[20] Walker was one of a company of settlers who went to Marine in 1839 to develop the lumber resources of the region. They erected a sawmill and began operations as the Marine Lumber Company. Walker was active in the lumber industry for many years.

was not holden I left with him the form I wanted filled he promised to have it filled Haskell & I went down to J. Faulstroms house with Depty Sheriff [David] Hone to see that he did not distress the Family in the absence of Mr. F.[21] Hone went there with the Intention of Leve[y]ing on any & all the property he could find, as he said, but after our showing him the Law exemp[t]ing property to a certain amount he left without executing any property I went home with Mr Haskell & spent a pleasant night as I had done the night before also. Settled with Haskell & took his note for $83.42 payable Dec. 1st 1846

Tuesday 2nd I Started from Haskells about 10 oclock came to Mr [James] Middletons[22] rested an hour. came on to McHatties[23] stayed and took Dinner. found they highly disapprove of the course that old Purinton is pursueing towards Norris I came on home found Blake at the House[24] he stayed over night

Wednesday 3rd Blake & Charles started to Fort Snelling. Harrison & I killed the small Cow called Sheep She was not as fat as I expected. Wind south Weather a little more moderate. Brissette came & took the steer that

---

[21] Hone, who was one of the founders of the Marine Lumber Company in 1839, removed to Gray Cloud Island in 1841 and, in 1843, to Point Douglas. He held the office of deputy sheriff until 1849. Folsom, *Fifty Years in the Northwest*, 365.

[22] James Middleton, with his large family of sons and daughters, settled in Woodbury Township in the spring of 1845 on claims which his son William had made the previous year. Warner and Foote, *Washington County*, 386, 396; Folsom, *Fifty Years in the Northwest*, 393.

[23] John and Alexander McHattie settled on claims in Woodbury Township in the spring of 1845. Warner and Foote, *Washington County*, 386, 396.

[24] Probably Edward Blake, who came to the St. Croix Valley in 1840 and engaged in lumbering. Folsom, *Fifty Years in the Northwest*, 57, 59.

we sold to Lavisinia   Mail did not stop.   Mr Middleton paid me the $1.75 for one Bushel onions that he bought of us some days since

Thursday 4th   Snowed ab[o]ut 2 inches last night. Fine day   Harrison & I hauled 1 load of hay & loaded on another very large load but corossing [sic] the Creek our sled upset & we left most of our hay.   Blake & Charley Returned from the Fort & brot. the mail   one letter from home to Harrison from Robert.   I pa[i]d over to Charly his part of the money I Received of Middleton for the Onions

Friday 5th   Harrison & I hauled in the balance of the hay we left yesterday & we hauled one load of Rails from Barber W. Kavanaugh's[25] place to build a pen around the old Leith House for our calves   We commence puting up the fence.   This evening J. A Ford came over for Harrison to go over & help him forge out some horse Shoes.   I borrowed one bushel of Corn of Holton   Weath[e]r very pleasant indeed

Saturday 6th   Since the trial between E. Worth & J. Falstrom some of the Jury have I understand come to the conc[l]usion that they erred in rendering the Verdict they did.   They see now that they should have decided the right of Possession.   There is some considerable excitement in [the] county in consequence of the course pursued by Purinton towards Ja^s S. Norris   the people talk of resisting it openly which I think would be right.

Saturday 6th [sic]   Harrison & I finished makeing the fence around the Leith stable & house   Old Lavisinia came & took his steers away   he engaged an ox yoke at $2 without Bows   Harrison & I about 2 oclock went down

[25] Brown probably refers to William Barbour Kavanaugh.

to Mr [Hazen] Mooers   Stayed and sung untill 10 oclock at night then came home. [Andrew] Robertson seemed quite cool towards me[26]   I wished to borrow a Train[27] for the purpose of going to the Fort but Mr Mooers has none of his own

Sunday 7th   More moderate than it has been for 8 or 10 days past   Cloudy all day

Monday 8th   Weather moderate, south wind. Harrison commenced cutting Rail Timber   I worked a little in the shop. Put up some shelves for Charley. Done some little Jobs about the house   opened a Barrel of Flour. Talked with Charley about buying him out[,] that is, his interest in the Firm   did not come to any definite conclusion   I made him an offer of an hundred dollars for him [sic] share   he took me up on condition that I would board him untill the 6th of March next   I think I will acceed to his Terms.[28]

Tuesday 9th   Quite moderate   wind in the southwest, then sprung up a very high Northwest wind this morning about 9 oclock.   Abated again at sunset & very cold

Wednesday 10th   Very cold untill about 12 oclock when it began to moderate. in the evening it was pleasant   Cloudy & has some the appearance of snow

[26] Mooers and Robertson had a trading post on Gray Cloud Island, which they had established in 1839. Thomas A. Robertson Reminiscences, 3, a manuscript in the possession of the Minnesota Historical Society.

[27] Undoubtedly short for *traineau de glace,* which was a long sleigh or toboggan, drawn sometimes by oxen but more often by dogs or ponies, and used by traders for conveying supplies and merchandise in winter.

[28] These plans apparently were not carried out until later, for Cavileer was still with Brown in June, 1846. See *post,* p. 81.   In his sketch of Brown, pages 4 and 5, Cavileer says that he sold out to Brown because he, Cavileer, was not "much of a farmist."   The two men disagreed on religious matters.   "He went for me on the old Brimstone order," wrote Cavileer, "while mine was a more liberal school for sinners."

Thursday 11th Pleasant. Cloudy snowed a little. John McHatties stayed with us last evening, says Haskell will be here today with his sisters. here is 10 oclock and no Haskell yet so we shall give him up

Friday 12th Wind from southeast not very cold. Toward evening very mild. I commence makeing Mrs. Davis a cinque [*sink?*].

Saturday 13th Weather very mild what little snow we had has nearly all dis[a]ppeared. Harrison & I went out in the morning & hauled a load of hay Broke our sled. When we arrived at home found a party of our Neighbors there [—] a Weding party consisting [of] James S. Norris & Sophia Haskell to be married attended by Joseph Haskell[,] Mrs Mary Davis [29] & Clara Haskell they arrived at 11 oclock took dinner tarried untill 8 in the evening took supper I married Norris & Sophia & they all went home Clara from the exposure to the cold & the warmth of the house after her arrival took the headache & did not enjoy the evening. we spent a pleasant evening

Sunday the 14th Very warm, cloudy Snow still melting. yesterday it snowed quite fast from 10 in the morning untill 2 in the afternoon but melted nearly as fast as it fell. Cleared away in the evening & the moon shone beautifully so that the weding party had a beautiful evening to go home. This morning I discovered that 2 of my Turnip holes have commenced Roting & caved in they had on them 3 inches of straw & 4 of Dirt and a small chimney fixed in the Top with a flue of 2 inches square[30]

---

[29] Mrs. Davis, a sister of the Haskells, later married William Oliver. Folsom, *Fifty Years in the Northwest*, 372.

[30] This was the usual way of keeping vegetables in winter. Barns gave little protection and had no storage room, and cellars were rare.

these had been stoped up when the weathe[r] set in very cold but still the Rutabagas were too warm. Last year I put on my Rutabagas ab[o]ut 8 or 10 inches of dirt & lost most of them in consequence of their being too warm this year I only put on 4 inches & still they are Roting this is astonishing to me for we have had very cold weather since winter set in

Monday 15th This morning I mended the sled we broke on Saturday. Harrison & I opened those Turnip holes that had commenced Roting we found them badly Roted, say the first hole was half gone. Mr Mooers was here this morning going to Fort Snelling I sent by him two letters to be mailed I also sent by him the Post Office Laws to Mr Steel he had borrowed them of me some time since

Tuesday 16 E. Brissette & I went out on the hills to look for his hogs which have been lost for several weeks. I found them on the hills Back of Harrison's Claim. Brissette & I followed them all day but could not get to them. In the evening Mr Mooers brot down the mail one letter for [Alexander] Maige [Mege] & [John R.] Irvine.[31]

Wednesday the 17th Brissette & I went out & built a pen over his hogs bed (we found where they slept) hopeing at night we could slip up & shut the door at night & thus fasten them in so we made a pen & at night went down but only 3 of them were in we fastened those in intending to shoot the others & haul them home, next day his old Black sow had pigs this evening

---

[31] Irvine in 1843 settled in St. Paul, where, with Mege, he ran a general store. Williams, *Saint Paul*, 126–130; Charles D. Elfelt, "Early Trade and Traders in St. Paul," in *Minnesota Historical Collections*, 9:164.

Thursday 18th   Wind in the Northwest   very cold indeed   could not go down to get the hogs. Concluded to wait & go next day but opened the pen & let out those we had shut up.

Friday 19th   Very cold   Brissette did not appear untill late   did not go for the hogs   are to go tomorrow   John McHattie stayed with us last evening   he wants the floor laid in his house next week   John McHattie says he intends to marry in a few days[32]   he took dinner with us today then started home   it was very cold & the wind blowing from the Northwest.

Saturday 20eth   Harrison & I went out this morning for a load of Hay intending to be Back in time to go down for Brissettes hogs so got home at twelve oclock but Brissette did not come untill late in the evening too late to go.

Sunday 21st   More mild than yesterday   wind was last evening in the South but today it is in the Northwest again though it does [not] Blow very hard.   Some little cloudy all day   snowed a very little

Monday 22nd   This morning Harrison & I went down accor[d]ing to appointment to haul Brissett's hogs from the woods but Brissette had not gone & shut them up in the pen as [he] was to have done, so we had to defer the job untill tomorrow Brissette promising to pay us for [the] trip. We came home   Harrison hauled some wood for Charley   I & Martha went down to Mr Mooers   he had gone to the Fort

Tuesday 23rd   Harrison & I went down to haul Brissettes hogs home   he had shut them all up but one little pig   it ran away.   we tied them & put them in the sled.

---

[32] McHattie married Jane Middleton on January 15, 1846. See *post,* p. 57, and Warner and Foote, *Washington County,* 396.

Put ours out [on] the train (one sow I traded with Brissette for) and brot her home killed & dressed her. Just at night Mr [Joseph W.] Furber came & stays all night with us³³ Brot. a deed to record for McKnight. Harrison went down to Mr Mooers for Martha She came up on the River with John Mooers his wife & Mary [Mooers]³⁴ they stayed only a few minutes in the House then went home. John Borrowed our Lantern it being quite Dark

Wednesday 24th I Started over to Stillwater went by the way of McHatty's left my match planes for davis to lay McHattys Floor Went on to Stillwater Stayed at [John] McKusick's Sold him 18 bushels Beans at $2.00 per bushel bot. an axe at $2.00 The Beans are to be delivered by the 1st of February McKusick is to sell me articles at cash prices or the cash as soon as he gets a Return from a Raft in the spring³⁵

Thursday the 25 Christmas day. I started home from Stillwater came to McHattie's found Davis had layed McHatties Floor Came home fround [sic] [Walter R.] Vail had been here³⁶ wants a copy of Purintons Bill of

---

[33] Furber settled at Cottage Grove in 1844, after engaging in lumbering for four years at St. Croix Falls. In 1846 he was a representative in the Wisconsin legislature from St. Croix County, and he served as speaker of the House in the first territorial legislature of Minnesota. Henry L. Moss, "Biographic Notes of Old Settlers," in *Minnesota Historical Collections*, 9:151.

[34] John Mooers was probably a son of Hazen Mooers. He is listed in the 1850 census schedules as an Indian farmer in Wabasha County. Mary Mooers, a daughter of Hazen Mooers, married John W. Brown in 1846. See *post*, p. 54, and Case, in *Minnesota Historical Collections*, 15:373.

[35] McKusick was a member of the Stillwater Lumber Company, which in 1844 began the operation of the first sawmill in Stillwater. The beans were probably for the lumber camps.

[36] Vail had a store in Stillwater. Folsom, *Fifty Years in the Northwest*, 59.

Sale Recorded in the Registers Book or Rather it is a Deed of Trust

Friday 26th   Haskell & I went to Fort Snelling   took my pork   Brot home my Flour 4 Barrels, 4 Barrels Beans   7 Bushels Corn   Bot. a Buffaloe Robe at $2.50   bot 40 lbs of Harness leather for Charley at [Henry H.] Sibleys.[37]   learned of Steel that the Black & White cow of the Doe [?] Cattle that I sold to F. Steel weighed lighter than 400 lbs.   Bot 7 Bushels Beans of Lieutenant [Robert S.] Granger[38]   paid $1.50 per Bushel   took a Receipt of him   arrived at home at about 7 oclock.   found John McHattie had been here with his sled & 2 horses   brot over 3 of the Middleton girls on a Visit

Saturday 27th   Haskell & Charley went to Fort Snelling   Haskell bot on account at Steels for me ½ bushel Cranberries.   Harrison & I hauled Haskell's freight up off of the Ice to Hopkins Store.

Sunday 28th   Haskell went home today.   Charley went over with him.   Harrison & I went down to see John Brown but he was not at home

Monday 29th   Harrison took over for Haskell to his house a load of Flour & Beef   I am assisting Ford to make a Train.   I went over at Haskells Request and Bot a Buckskin at 2.25 with the priviledge of Returning it provided it does not suit Haskell   John Brown was here &

---

[37] Sibley, a partner in the American Fur Company, was in charge of the affairs of the company in the Northwest, with headquarters at Mendota.

[38] Granger was a first lieutenant in the First Regiment of United States Infantry, which was then stationed at Fort Snelling. George W. Cullum, *Biographical Register of the Officers and Graduates of the U. S. Military Academy at West Point*, N. Y., 1:719 (Boston and New York, 1891).

invited us all down to his Weding on New year's day I bot a neck comforter at Hopkin's for .62½

Tuesday 30eth Harrison Returned today and took over a load consisting of 4 Barrels of Pork & 5 of Flour for Mr Haskell. I sent over the Buck Skin to Haskell, he kept it. Brissette sent an order by F[rancis] McCoy & Amab[le] for the steer I sold him but [as] we have had no settlement I declined sending him untill B. & I settled[39] I sent him the Ballance of 3 lbs of Candles I sold him some time since.

Wednesday 31st Charley came home today from the Lake. Says Harrison has gone to the head of the Lake with the team for Haskell Mr Pond came down today[40] preached at Mr Holtons [John] Bush & [Harley D.] White happened along just in time to hear[41] I this day settled with Brissette & took his Note for the Balance due me which was $14.50 I am still assisting Ford with his Train Mr Pond stays with us over night

[39] Francis McCoy, a carpenter, settled in St. Paul in 1844. See Williams, *Saint Paul*, 145. The 1850 census schedules list two Francis McKoys, both farmers and probably father and son, in the St. Croix precinct. Amable Brissett, a son of Edmund, is also listed in the 1850 census schedules.

[40] Samuel W. and Gideon H. Pond, early Presbyterian missionaries among the Sioux, were stationed on the Minnesota River near Bloomington in 1845.

[41] Bush came to Fort Snelling in 1825 and engaged in the fur trade. He removed to St. Paul in 1837 and later to Prescott, Wisconsin. He is listed in the 1850 census schedules as an Indian farmer in Wabasha County. White came to Red Rock in 1844 and acquired an interest in Ford and Hopkins' store. A. T. Andreas, *Illustrated Historical Atlas of the State of Minnesota*, 266 (Chicago, 1874); Folsom, *Fifty Years in the Northwest*, 367.

1846

January 1st 1846   This is the first day of the year 1846 how time flies.   We came here in 1841   Mr Pond left for Redwing Village[1]   I & Harrison went down to John W. Brown's weding   I married them.   Saw Lucy Prescott and Jane Lamott [*Lamont*].[2]   we stayed untill 10 in the evening & came home   White and Bush stayed over night with us   Bot. ½ Bus[he]l Beans & 7 lbs Butter paid for them. left early, before day   Weather very warm   all the snow gone

Jan. 2nd   Last evening the wind changed round in the North   grew some colder & snowed a little   This morning cloudy & has the appearance of snow.   10 oclock cleared away and became very warm & pleasant   thawed fast.   Harrison took the waggon and went down to the Island[3] for six bbls of lime   we measured up 18 Bushels

---

[1] This was an Indian village on the site of the present city of Red Wing.   In 1837 two Swiss missionaries, Daniel Gavin and Samuel Dentan, established a mission there.   Folwell, *Minnesota,* 1:203.

[2] Lucy Prescott was a daughter of Philander Prescott, who is mentioned *post,* p. 59.   She married Eli Pettijohn.   Jane Lamont, a half-breed daughter of Daniel Lamont, a fur trader, married Moses S. Titus. *Minneapolis Daily Chronicle,* April 2, 1867; copy of a letter from Charles A. Eastman to M. C. Bacheller, March 4, 1931, in the possession of the Minnesota Historical Society.

[3] Gray Cloud Island, in the Mississippi River at the southwestern tip of Washington County.   It is cut off from the mainland by a small channel of the river.

of Beans for McKusic[k] of Stillwater Harrison Reports the Ice weak across the slough

Saturday 3rd   Harrison & I hauled one load of hay on the waggon for John A Ford and one for ourselves   It was so warm that it was unpleasant to work. After we had started home with [the] last load I was taken with a pain across my bowels   a very severe pain indeed so much so that I could not walk home   A Mr Howe stays with us tonight.

Sunday 4th   Morning cloudy & more cool than we have had   Howe left for St Paul

Monday 5th   Finished Fords Train.   Started for Stillwater   went as far as Haskells   found the Road Icy & bad

Tuesday 6th   Left Haskells for Stillwater   Road very Icy.   arrived there at 3 oclock P.M.   delivered McKusick 6 bbls Lime & 13½ bushels Beans   these Beans I sold M^cK. for $2.00 per Bushel   the Lime I hauled up from Hazen Mooers for McKusick.   I got my waggon Repaire[d] at McK's shop   Started home on

Wednesday 7th   Got as far as Haskell   Stayed all night with Haskell.   Start home in the morning

Thursday 8th   Came home by the way of Rockwoods place   Got of Rockwood 6½ bushel[s] corn.   Came to Esq Norris   took Dinner there then saw Hone, [William C.] Renfro,[4] Jackson & Vail.   Came home   J. S. Davis came over & Received his Fees on the Bissell & Cummings suit.   found the mail had arrived.   While at Stillwater I bot. 1 pair coarse boots $3.00, 1 table cloth .60 cents[,] 1 pr pants for C. Cavileer $3.00[,] 2 lbs saleratus .37½[,] 1 small chisel .25

[4] Renfro was a cousin of Henry Jackson.   He died in St. Paul in 1848. Williams, *Saint Paul,* 166, 177.

Friday 9th   yesterday it snowed about 1½ inches, but this morn. is clear & pleasant.

Saturday 10   Harrison & I haul[e]d 1 load of hay in the waggon   our ladders Brok[e] & let our load fall off. We then took the Sled but found it hard on the cattle and hauled another load

Sunday had the appearance [of] Snow all day.

Monday 11th   Started early for Haskells   Arrived there at sunrise   stoped at McHatties   saw Robertson there   John invited me to his weding on Thursday next   Haskell & I started to Marine Mills in his old Jumper   had but little snow so we went up the Lake.   Stoped at Stillwater   took Dinner at [Elam] Greelys   Saw Miss Greely for the first time   also Mrs. [Albert] Harris.[5]   was well pleased with them on first sight   We went on to Marine Mills   arrived there after sunset   they are making great improvements there.   in the evening they had a dance. They appear to be prepareing for a party that is to come off there on Thursday next   There were 4 young Ladies there.

Tuesday 12th   I settled my & Cavileers Lumber Bills & took their Receipt.   Also I settled W. B. Kavanaughs account with the Marine Co.[6] and Received of them on Kavanaughs account in goods $6.00   at my Request Haskell bought too [sic] mill saws one at $6. the other at 3.50   I bought me a new Cap at 7.00, Marthat [Martha] a Clothes Basket at 1.25, 4 lbs alum 50[,] pint shoe pegs 12½, 4 prs small Butto[ns] .40, 2½ yds flannel 1.62[,]

---

[5] Greely settled at St. Croix Falls in 1840 and engaged in lumbering. In 1843 he removed to Stillwater and became one of the original owners of the Stillwater Lumber Company.   The Miss Greely referred to was probably one of his five sisters.   Albert Harris was a carpenter who lived in Stillwater.   Folsom, *Fifty Years in the Northwest*, 56–58, 61.

[6] The Marine Lumber Company.

Martha pair shoe[s] 1.25 and some other little articles
We started home stoped at Still Water took supper at
Greelys house There saw Mrs Vail for the first time.
She appears to be Very fond of gameing Was playing
at Back Gamon & Cards taking her *by & large* I was not
much please[d] with her. I [think] the Ladies at Still
Water are rather *straining* a point to appear *Refined*.

We came on down to Haskells & stayed all night next
morning started home [Henry W.] Crosby came along
& stayed over night with us.[7] Bot of me one Barrel Flour
at 8.00 to be paid early in the Spring Also one qu[a]rter
of Beef I went up to the store and bot a few sundries
amounting to 1.25. got Ford to make me a pitch Fork.
Charley & Harrison had gone Fishing Harrison droped
Charley['s] axe through the Ice. they came home with
8 fish

Thursday 15th Our Horse was among the missing
consequently Martha cannot go to the Weding[8] I promised Crosby I would take his Churn over to McHattie's
place in the Jumper, but as the horse was gone I can't
take it. Harrison & I went over to the Weding on Foot.
Had a very pleasant time. They had Liquor & drank of
which I disapproved. We indulged in the simple plays
usually played on such occasions I hope the day is not
far distant when such things will not be countenanced by
the better sort of people We started home at 2 oclock
at night. I saw Mrs Andy McCay [Mackey] for the first
time I think her a good Woman[9]

[7] Crosby, a machinist, settled at Lakeland in 1842. Folsom, *Fifty Years in the Northwest*, 373.
[8] The wedding was that of John McHattie and Jane Middleton.
[9] Andrew Mackey, who had been a lumberman on the St. Croix from 1838 to 1840, lived in Afton. He married a Miss Hamilton in 1845. Warner and Foote, *Washington County*, 409.

Friday 16th I went out to look for the Horse I expected he was with the Indian Horses so went up to the Lodges to find out where their horses were[10] found they were below our ho[u]se came on down home found a man by the Name of Pearce here waiting to see me he wanted a Warrant for a Frenchman by the name of Venoia for an assault with intent to kill, but it appears that they have had a general row so I declined having any thing to do with the affair at all So Pearce left. Before Pearce got [out] of sight Venoia appeared wanting a Warrant for Pearce Was as Ready as the other to Swear his life was in danger &c but I declined acting in the matter at all so he left.

Saturday 17th Weather continues p[l]easant no snow on the ground I have not seen such a Winter in this country, such fine weather and no snow I went up & tryed to get the axe out of the Lake the one Harrison droped for Charly I found the water 14 feet deep I could not feel the axe at all. I got an Indian to fish for it but he could not get it so gave it up and came home. Found Capt. [William] Holcombe at the House.[11] he recor[d]ed some papers. administered the Oath of Office to me as Deputy Register of Deeds and paid the 1.75 for Recording one Deed a conveyance from Purinton to Withnell of St Louis The Capt left about sunset for Esq Norris's place. I settled with J. A. Ford this evening he Receipted his account in full & I mine he was in my debt $3.32 he paid me the money.

[10] The Indian lodges were probably those of the Sioux at Kaposia.
[11] Holcombe settled at Stillwater in 1839 and engaged in lumbering and steamboating. He was register of deeds of St. Croix County, Wisconsin, from 1843 to 1846, a member of the Minnesota constitutional convention in 1857, and the first lieutenant governor of the state. Upham and Dunlap, *Minnesota Biographies*.

Sunday the 18th   Davis[,] J. S.[,] was here today   he left an account against Dr. [Christopher] Carli to be collected.[12]

Monday 19th   I worked in the shop today   Made 2 fork stakes. Harrison & I ground our axes & my planes   Brissette sent today for his Bed cord.

Tuesday 20eth   Harrison & I hauled hay   3 loads   2 of them the first & the last sliped off before we got home   The weather is remarkably warm & pleasant.

Wednesday 21st   Warm & pleasant. Cloudy   has the appearance of Snow   Harrison & I hauled hay   3 loads finished just at dark

Thursday 22nd   Harrison & I hauled hay for Ford. 3 loads at 1.25 = 3 75   Mr [Albert] Harris of Still Water stayed over night with us. was looking out a claim. I sent him down to see the prairie just below my claim

Friday 23   I rig[g]ed out a set of harness for Mink.[13] Harrison Choped wood

Saturday 24th   I borrowed J. A Fords train and went to Fort Snelling   bot. 1 Barrel Beans @ 3.50   Bot Cloth for 2 Vests one for myself & 1 for Harrison   Bot 2/3 of a Bushel fine salt   took up to Mr [Philander] Prescott a jar of Butter. found the Ice Very Bad. Stayed over night with Mr Prescott.[14]

Sunday 25th   Came home from the Fort   Ice Bad.

---

[12] Carli, a physician born and educated in Germany, settled at Stillwater in 1841. Upham and Dunlap, *Minnesota Biographies*.

[13] Mink apparently was Brown's horse.

[14] Prescott was an Indian trader who came to Fort Snelling in 1820. According to John H. Stevens, *Personal Recollections of Minnesota and Its People*, 44 (Minneapolis, 1890), Prescott's "hospitable house was always full of people. It was the only roof at Fort Snelling that afforded a stopping-place for travelers and strangers."   Prescott was killed during the Sioux Outbreak in 1862. His "Autobiography and Reminiscences" may be found in *Minnesota Historical Collections*, 6:475–491.

Rockwood came over & Brot 2 wedges. Martha & I went over to see Mrs Holton she being sick. Weather so warm that the water is runing in the Ravines along the Road.

Monday 26th Wind in Northwest Snowing quite fast has the appearance of a change in the weather

Tuesday 27 Clear & pleasant. cut some Wood & piled [it] over the Potatoe holes to Keep the Cattle from scrapeing the dirt off Esqr Norris came over brot over the county Books & left them here. paid me his Marriage Fee. I promised to make him some doors & window Frames for his New house sold him W. B. Kavanaughs sash, at 10½ per light. for the work that I do for him he is to let me have some grain & pork next fall

Wednesday 28th I started for Stillwater got as far as Haskells Stayed over night commenced Raining at 7 oclock in the evening. rained all night.

Thursday 29th Very foggy looked likely for Rain did Rain some through the day. I stayed at Haskells all day in hopes it would clear away so that I might go to Stillwater the next day.

Friday 30eth Wind in the north cold had the appearance of a great change Snowed some in the morning I cam[e] home. left my Beans for Haskell to take up to Stillwater. Stoped at John McHatties got some Boards to make him a cupboard came home & hauled 2 loads of wood one for Charles, & one for the House.

Saturday 31st Clear & has the appearance of fair weather again Harrison & I choped wood to haul to the House I & Martha over hauled our Pickles took them out of the Liquor they were in, washed them put them in Vinegar, since which they look well.

February Sunday 1st Windy all day. Harrison went

over to see Esqr Norris was well pleased with Visit. Russell presented an order from the Department for what Post Office Money I had on hand I paid him 35. dollars.

Monday 2nd Harrison Choped wood I worked in the shop.

Tuesday 3rd Harrison hauled wood I worked in the shop.

Wednesday 4th Hary. [*Harrison?*] & [I] went out with the waggon to look for some good oak timbers for gates Harrow &c we got some good white oak. H. found a Bee tree the first he ever found in his life he feels quite lifted up about it

Thursday 5th Harrison commenced threshing the oats, takes the job at 6¼ cents per bushel.[15] Packed down ab[o]ut 300 lbs Beef in Barrels & made a pickle to preserve it To every gallon of water I put 1½ lbs Rock salt 1 oz saltpeter & 1 gill of molasses Boiled & skimed & let stand to cool.

Friday 6th I finished salting down my beef found that 7½ or 8 gallons brine was sufficient for a Barrel. Harrison continued threshing

Saturday 7 Harrison went to Fort for the mail I Received a letter from Joseph my Brother also one from the P[ost] O[ffice] D[epartment] Stating I had been Reported by the contractor as haveing refused to pay over the Balance due the P. O. D. The contractor has Reported me falsely.

Sunday 8th Clear & pleasant. I answered Jo's letter also the one from the P. O. D. wrote to the Contractor [Hercules L.] Dousman[16] Wrote to H L. Stewart P[ost]

[15] This threshing was probably done by tramping with horses.

[16] Dousman, a partner in the American Fur Company, was in charge of the affairs of the company at Prairie du Chien. Mail intended for the

M[aster] Chicago Requesting him to use his influence in haveing the mail stop at this office

Monday 9th   Clear & pleasant   Harrison threshed oats.

Tuesday 10th   Harrison & I hauled 3 loads hay   found Holtons cattle had destroyed some considerable

Wednesday 11th   H threshed oats.   I prepared to go over to Haskells but some man came from Still Water with an order from Vail for a copy of a Deed of Trust from James Purinton to John H. Ferguson, which detained me untill it was too late to start over to Haskells

Thursday 12th   Haskell came over, brot over Fords sleigh & our Candlemoulds   I went over with him in the evening   got over there after dark   went by Bissells place and got haskells wind mill.

Friday 13th   Came home from Haskells   Brot over some Deers hair for Charles & I   Brot over the 8^d nails H. had Borrowed of me.   J. S. Davis was here   left a Deed to be Recorded.

Saturday 14th   Harrison & I winnowed 60 or 70 Bushels of oats   brot. home about 30 bushels & put them in my shop.   McLeod[,] A. K. [*Alexander R.*,] and E[dward] Faylan [*Phelan*] came down to have a Deed acknowledged & Recorded.[17]

Minnesota region was sent to Prairie du Chien and from there to Fort Snelling by boat in summer and by sledge in winter. Williams, *Saint Paul*, 44.

[17] McLeod came to St. Paul in 1843 and purchased land in what is now downtown St. Paul. In 1846 he removed to a claim on Phalen Creek in present-day northeastern St. Paul, and the deed of which Brown speaks was a quitclaim deed for this land. Phelan, whose name sometimes appears as "Phalen," was a soldier who was discharged at Fort Snelling in 1838. He made several claims in St. Paul, one of them being on the creek that bears his name. Williams, *Saint Paul*, 71, 104, 135; Folsom, *Fifty Years in the Northwest*, 535; Upham, *Geographic Names*, 440.

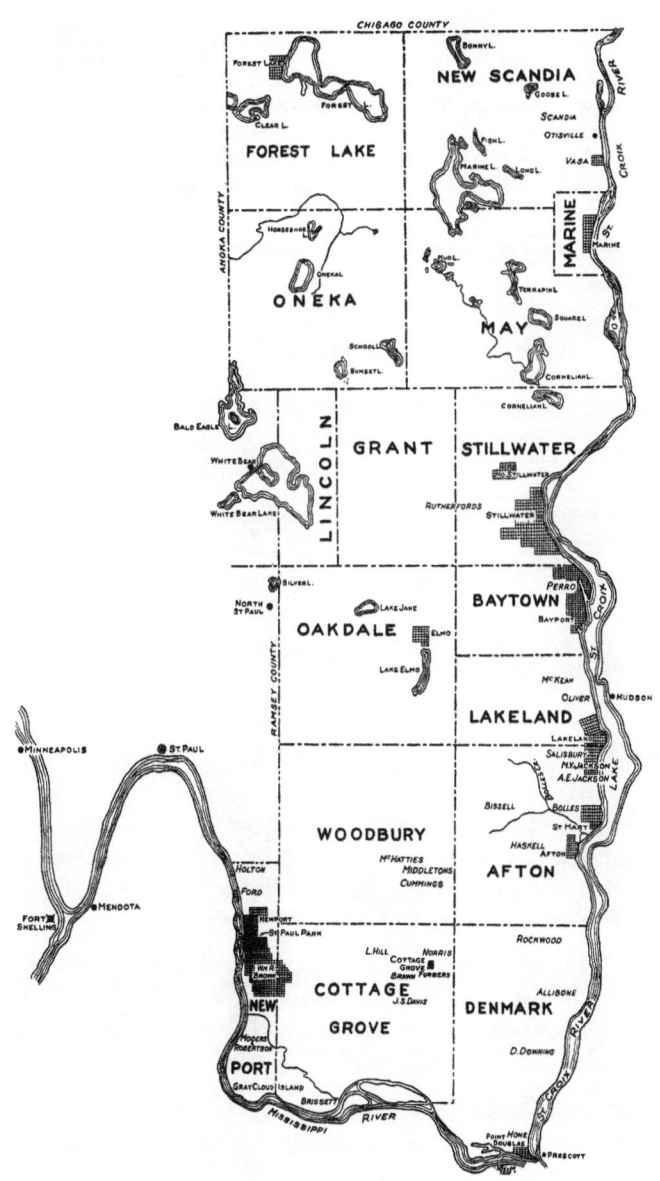

Sunday 15th Wind in the Northwest geting cold Snowed ½ an inch has the appearance of cold weather.

Monday 16th Harrison hauled wood half of the day. I commenced makeing a set of wood Ladders Morning quite cold. at noon more pleasant. just night the Hurlbut Cow had a heifer calf[18]

Tuesday 17th Harrison hauled wood on the sled untill noon, after which he took the waggon & hauled 3 loads of wood for Ford. I finished the wood Ladders.

Wednesday 18th Sold Laclare [*Le Claire*] 8 lbs. of Butter at 25 cent[s] per lb on credit.[19] Mail arrived received a letter from the Department stating we were to have the mail. Harrison hauled wood for Ford. Haskell came over to assist thresh our Oats

Thursday 19th Haskell & Harrison tramp Oats. I made a door for the Hen House & put up Pigion holes for the Hens nests. Holton got the waggon to go to Mill

Friday 20eth Borrowed Holtons mare to Tramp oats. Haskell, Harrison, & I all worked at the oats. Tramped out 1200 Sheaves with 4 horses. I returned Holtons mare

Saturday 21st Holton Returned the waggon Haskell[,] Harrison & I finished threshing the oats.

Sunday 22nd Haskell left for home bought 6 lights sash for James Parker & 6 for himself & ½ lb putty.[20]

Monday 23 Harrison & I winnowed oats it was very windy & cold for that kind of Work

---

[18] This may have been a cow of the Devon breed. Lemuel Hurlbut of Connecticut popularized the breed in this country in the years from 1815 to 1835, and sometimes the name Hurlbut was applied to Devon cattle.

[19] Brown refers to either Michel or Antoine Le Claire, both of whom settled at St. Paul in 1839. Williams, *Saint Paul*, 87.

[20] Parker was a member of the Marine Lumber Company. Warner and Foote, *Washington County*, 470.

Tuesday 24th Very cold so much so that Harrison & I concluded not to winnow oats. did not do much of any thing.

Wednesday 25 Very cold did not do any thing. John Mooers was here took Dinner with us

Thursday 26th Harrison & Charley took a bee tree got a good deal of Honey I walked up to the Fort to see Mr Steel, but he was gone over to St Croix sold [Samuel J.] Finly [*Findley*] one hundred Bushels of oats at .50 cents per Bushel[21] Bot. 1 paper of Ink powders 1 Bottle Indelible Ink ¼ lb white linen Thread

Friday 27th Took 46¼ Bushels oats up to Steel. bot. 10 lbs Chalk. Brot down 3 bbls damaged Beans at 1.25 per barrel. found my oats weighed 33 lbs to the Bushel Weather stormy. Durham Cow had a Calf.

Saturday 28th Weather moderate. Started to the Fort with 57½ bushels oats got to St Pauls & sold my load to [David] Ferribo [*Faribault*][22] took an order on H. H. Sibley for 28.75 dollars Bot. [of] Ferribo 3 yds sheep grey Cloth for pants @ 1.25 = 3.75 Sold him my whip @ $1.00 bot. of [James W.] Simpson 10 lights glass .50[,] 1 tin cup 18¾ = 68¾ Went with A. K. McLeod to Faylin [*Phalen*] falls to take the Acknowledgement to a Deed. Harrison went over to Haskells

Sunday March 1st Warm & pleasant

Monday March 2nd Harrison returned from Haskel's & Cleaned up & houve [*hove?*] one load of Oats he & Charley. I went up to the Fort & carried up 40⅓

[21] Findley was Steele's bookkeeper. Upham and Dunlap, *Minnesota Biographies*.

[22] Faribault, a son of the well-known fur trader, Jean Baptiste Faribault, had a trading post in St. Paul. Williams, *Saint Paul*, 159.

[23] Simpson opened a store in St. Paul in 1843. Elfelt, in *Minnesota Historical Collections*, 9:164.

BROWN'S DIARY, 1846 65

bushels of Oats Steel was well pleased with them they were Clean & the grain well filled I took to St Pauls 9 doz Eggs & sold 2 doz to [Leonard H.] LaRoch[e] @ 37½ per doz = .75 & 7 doz to L. Robert @ 37½ = 2 62½ [24] Bot. at the Fort 51½ lbs Pork at 8 cents per lb = 4.12½ and one bushel Peaches @ 1.50 got 2 Rings & staples at [Joseph] Robinet[te]s & paid him the Balance due on them[25] Presented a draft on H. H. Sibley from David Ferribo which was accepted als[o] delivered a Quit Claim Deed from Wm Douglass [*Dugas*][26] to A. McLeod of St Pauls to Mr Sibley he paid my fees. The mail arrived today no letters for any of us

Tuesday March 3rd Ford & I went up to St Pauls I took up some Butter sold 8 lbs to LaRoch @ 25 per lbs which together with the Eggs I sold him the day before paid the Balance I was owing them of $2.75. I let L. Robert have the Balance of the Butter & settled with him and found I still owed him .37½ cents I bot Martha a pair of Prunell shoes at Ferribos at 1.50 for which I still owe him. I bot of Jackson one Morticing Chisel .25 bot 10 lights glass & one Large Tin cup of J. Simpson all amounting to .75 cents which was a Balance due me.

Wednesday March 4 Harrison & I went down in the Bottom to haul out Rails hauled out about 2.20 at night the Prairie was on Fire Charles[,] Harrison & I went out to fight fire found it was comeing to B. W. Kav-

[24] La Roche, who came to St. Paul in 1845, was in partnership with David Faribault. Williams, *Saint Paul*, 150.
[25] Robinette was a blacksmith at Mendota. Census schedules, 1850.
[26] Dugas came to St. Paul in 1844, purchased 160 acres of land on Phalen Creek from Edward Phelan, and erected a saw and grist mill at the falls of the creek. In February, 1846, he sold the land and the improvements to McLeod. This is the transaction that Brown refers to in the diary. Williams, *Saint Paul*, 144.

anaughs house so we fired around his place & left found the fire had done no damage on my Claim.

Thursday March 5th We found that a Tree had Burned down & fallen across the place we had burned around B. W. K's place & set the grass on fire again and had Burned most of his Rails—had run around & under his house But had not Burned it Harrison & I hauled out Rails 2.20 The Ice in the River started down today Mr E. A. Bissell was here today but I did not see him

Friday March 6th H. & I hauled out the Balance of the Rails & got some yok[e] Timber 8 st[i]cks Broke in the Slough through the Ice had our Timber to unload. Esq Jackson was here today. I saw him not. Harrison & I mooved our Bees out doors today found the old swarm had been Kept too warm Most of them had died.

Saturday March 7th Harrison took up a hole of Turnips I done up some little Chores about the house Cleaned out the shop &c &c ground up our axes &c &c Ice run pretty smartly today H. Jackson was here today and had the county seal affixed by Esq Nórris order to paper for [*ms. illegible*] a pension [*ms. illegible*]

Sunday March 8th Very warm & pleasant This day completes my 30eth year. What 30 years old and no grace, wicked as ever yes Truly it is so.

Monday March 9th Harrison took Haskells Windmill Home. I fixed up the old Kitchen for Martha

Tuesday March 10th Harrison & I went down in the Bottom to look for Cabbin logs to buil[d] a shanty on the Claim. Cut 33 logs 15 feet long The Ice went out of the River today. Raining a little in the evening. Charley Killed 4 ducks & 2 Partridges.

Wednesday 11 March Rained all day the first Rain

this spring I worked in the shop Made a 9 light sash for the Old Kitchen also a Transom sash for Haskell 4 lights Filed up the old Crosscut saw mooved Marthas stove out in Kitchen

Thursday March 12th Still storming. Harrison went out & choped blocks for fence corners untill Dinner Mail went down about 12 oclock. I Primed & glazed one sash for the old Kitchen & one for the Hen House & made Martha a small Flour Box. got Ford to mend McHatties yoke staple.

Friday March 13th Harrison Choped Blocks for the fence. I Glazed Haskells Transom sash, hung the Kitchen Window, put a latch on the Kitchen door, &c, &c. Commenced makeing a yoke

Saturday March 14th Harrison choping Blocks. I spread out my seed onions found they were growing. Worked at yoke makeing. Warm & pleasant, though the wind is in the Northwest & blows very hard.

Sunday March 15 Wind in the Northwest froze some last night & quite cool today

Monday March 16th Morning Clear & pleasant Harrison hauling Rails. I prepared a Barrel to steam Potatoes for the Pigs.[27]

Tuesday March 17 Harrison Hauling Rails. I made 5 ox bows, hauled one load [of] wood to the house. heard of the Death of Paul Carli.[28] bot Harrison 7 yds of Marriners shirting at 16⅔ cents per yd = $1.16⅔

---

[27] It is unusual to find a frontier farmer steaming food for livestock. English farmers were accustomed to steam turnips and other vegetables for livestock, but the practice was not followed to any extent in this country. In this case it is probable that the potatoes were frozen and Brown was simply thawing them.

[28] Carli, who settled near Afton in 1844, was drowned in Lake St. Croix. His widow, Lydia Ann Carli, a half-sister of Joseph R.

Wednesday March 18th   Harrison assisted at the shop untill Dinner after which he went to hauling Rails. I made 2 whip stocks finis[h]ed 1 yoke put in the Bows &c seared & greased the Bows to prevent their swelling in wet weather. bot 1 lb Powder at Hopkins .37½   Wᵐ Middleton & Alec. MᶜHattie came & got each of them 3 oz of onion seed   Wᵐ Middleton bot 1½ lbs Rutabaga seed @ 1.00 lb   Alec. MᶜH. bot. 1 Peck. seed onions. I sent by MᶜHattie 3 oz of onion seed to James S. Davis Wᵐ Middleton paid me 75 for onion seed & 1 50 for Rutabaga seed & 50 for hauling 2 Barrels of Flour from Stillwater in all $2.75   What MᶜHattie got I charged to him. Young Cummings was here[29] brot a Note from Esq Norris.

Thursday March 19th   Wind sprung up in the night & blew very hard from the southwest & became quite cold & snowed at times through the Day.   So stormy Harrison & I did not work.   I sorted out my garden seeds & put up some seeds for Wᵐ Middleton[,] MᶜHattie & James S. Davis   Mail arrived today.

Friday March 20   Wind still in the southwest & very cold. Harrison & I hauled 2 Loads of Wood 1 to Charley & 1 to Hopkins, in the forenoon   in the after noon H. hauled Rails   bot 4 bushels of Corn of Hopkins at 50 cents per Bushel.   bot. for Harrison one wooden Bucket 37½

Saturday March 21st   Harrison hauled rails. I attempted to make some oak ox bows but they would not

Brown, married Carli's brother, Christopher, in 1847. Warner and Foote, *Washington County*, 498, 564.

[29] Probably Robert Cummings, the younger of the two Cummings brothers who were in Washington County at the time. Lindsey, the elder, was about Brown's age, according to the 1850 census schedules, and Robert was twenty-four in 1850.

bend they snaped like pipe stems. Made a long coeuppleing pole for the waggon in hauling hay. this morning was Clear & pleasant had the appearance of fair weather[.] in the evening it became cloudy snowed & was stormy

Sunday March 22 Stormy Snowed quite hard but melts as it falls.

Monday March 23. Wind in the North not very cold Harrison hauled 3 loads of hay killed seven Fish in the small Creek by Holtons with sticks

Tuesday March 24 Harrison hauled Rails. Crosby came over today & brot. Mink home he had been gone some 8 or 10 days over to Haskell he was tramping out Oats with him. C[r]osby brot over a Choping knife. I commenced 3 ox yokes. Crosby left with me $2.00 to [be] paid to Mr Robertson for Rockwood

Wednesday March 25 I went over to Norris' to get a Load of Lumber had to go to the Lake for it. Went by Rocks. Sold him 42 bushels of oats @ 37½ per bushel. he pays me for delivering them Made arrangements with him about Prairie Breaking to this affect. If he concludes to Break any for himself he will join his Team with mine & assist us to break ours & we his. But if he concludes not to Break any for himself, The[n] he is to let me have his Team any how to Break mine & I am to furnish him as much *Team next year* I went on to Haskells & stayed over night. had a pleasant time. Martha paid to Mr Robertson the $2.00 left for him by Crosby for Rockwood.

Thursday March 26 Went down to the Lake for a load of Boards put on a load. Came Back to Haskells took dinner Came on to McHatties found I had too much Load for my Team got a yoke of oxen of John

McHattie & came on home. Young Red River heifer[80] had her Calf but was so deformed about the head that it will have to be killed its under jaw does not work & on one side it has none

Friday March 27th Harrison went with the waggon for a Load of Boards to the Lake I attempted to Milk the young Red River Heiffer She was a Terrible thing. The weather windy & cold. I worked at yoke makeing. Stuck up the Boards I brot from the Lake.

Saturday March 28th Weather very wintry, snowing & blowing. I killed & skined the deformed Calf. At work on the yokes. Harrison Returned We took up a hole of Turnips & put them in the Stable.

Sunday the 29 March Cool but Clear & Beautiful Harrison went down to Mr Mooers, brot home some hard sugar. got it at Brissettes. I wrote a letter to Uncle J. W. Hitt of Ohio

Monday 30eth March Harrison hauled corner blocks for the Fence. I recorded a Deed for Edward Pierce Went over the River & cut enough Timber to make 10 Sets of Ox Bows. Steamed & Bent six of them. Our Brindle cow had Twin Calves one a Bull the other a heifer Calf.

Tuesday the 31st of March Harrison hauled Rails I made ox bows. We had a Steam Boat arrival today the Steamer Lynx. She brot the mail Harrison Received his Trunk by the Boat. Received a Letter from W. B. Kavanaugh.

Wednesday April 1st Harrison hauled Rails I finished 2 ox yokes. Mail did not stop

Thursday April 2 Harrison & I Measured our Land

---

[80] Probably a cow brought from the Red River settlements.

that is Broke made 23½ acres of it. I finished my yokes measured up 42 Bushels oats for Rockwood.

Friday April 3rd Rained all day very hard Harrison & I took up a hole of Rutabagas. I had Ford to paint Norris' plow[,] one that I used last year. I filed the wood saw. We today put a New yoke on Buck & Berry.

Saturday April 4th Harrison laid up Fence. I went over to Rockwoods delivered him 42 bushels of Oats. got of him, 12 bushels & ¾ of Corn. Returned to Esq Norrises got him 8 joists 16 feet long 2 inches thick 5 of them 7 inches wide & 3, 6 inches wide. Stayed over night with him

Sunday April 5th Returned home from Esq Norris. Very pleasant, today

Monday April 6th Harrison hauling Rails. I painted J. S. Norris sash. Ford dressed the Pick & dressed the Harrow teeth.[31]

Tuesday April 7th Wind Changed last Night & became very cold. Wind in the Northwest.

Wednesday April 8th Harrison hauled Rails. Mail went down. hauled Charley a load of dry wood.

Thursday April 9 Hauled hay all day. Holtons Cattle have been into our hay. [Jonathan] Brawne[32] Came over & wanted to commence an action of Forceable Entry & detainer against Lindsey & Robert Cummings. I persuaded him not to commence untill I could see the Cummings & endeavor to have the matter settled by Arbitration.

[31] This probably was done by placing iron on the wearing parts.
[32] Brawn settled at St. Croix Falls in 1842 and in 1844 removed to a farm in Cottage Grove. Folsom, *Fifty Years in the Northwest*, 361; St. Croix Valley Old Settlers Association, Obituary Record, 151, a manuscript volume in the possession of the Minnesota Historical Society.

Friday April 10th   Harrison took up a hole of Rutabagas   found them half Rotten   I went over to see the Cummings to endeavor to settle the difficulty between them & Brawne   it stormed most tremendously snowed & Blowed very cold   I called at Lewis Hills[33] left him some garden seeds. left some garden seeds at Brawnes some that he had Bot. of me   saw the Cummings   they are willing to defer their difficulty with Brawn, to Referees.   Stayed all night with Brawne   our little Black sow took the Boar   our Red River Cow had a Calf.

Saturday April 11th   Got Brawne & Cummings together   they Chose [Theodore] Furber[,][34] Haskell & myself as Referees to meet on Monday next.   Brawne & I went down to the Lake with Brawnes Team & hauled my lumber from there to Brawnes house.   I was at Haskells, came home by McHatties

Sunday April 12th   Clear & tolerably pleasant.

Monday April 13th   Harrison hauled Manure on the garden   Martha went over to Esq Norris on a Visit found Mrs Davis and Clara Haskell there. They all went down to see Mr [and] Mrs Furber.   Was much pleased with them   I sat on the Brawne & Cumming Trial as one of the Arbitrators (Joseph Haskell, & Th. Furber & myself were the Arbitrators)   After hearing the Testimony we came to the Conclusion that Brawne had a just title to the Land in dispute, and decided that each of the Parties should pay half of the Costs   At night it Clouded up & snowed tremendously   Martha & [I] Came home

[33] Hill settled at Cottage Grove in 1844. Folsom, *Fifty Years in the Northwest*, 363.

[34] Furber settled at St. Croix Falls in 1845 and in the spring of 1846 removed to a claim in Cottage Grove Township. Folsom, *Fifty Years in the Northwest*, 363; Warner and Foote, *Washington County*, 375.

in the night it [was] snowing very fast. I hired J. S. Davis for the summer & untill we get our Roots saved in the Fall Brawne has promised to let me [have] a yoke of Oxen to do my plowing this spring.

Tuesday April 14th Still snowing this morning very fast. 10 oclock cleared away. I weighed out for J. Brawn 140 lbs of Beef, & for Lewis Hill 238 lbs I boiled the Brine over again.

Wednesday April 15 I this day opened one of my Potatoe holes for the first time this spring I found them sound & good contrary to my expectation for I had on them only 2½ feet of dirt & we have had no snow so that I expected my potatoes were badly frozen. I oiled up my harness. Martha took a hen & Chickens from the Nest today. Harrison went over to Brawnes took him over 140 lbs beef [and] ½ Bushel pickles & took Lewis Hill 238 lbs Beef, all of which I am to charge them with. Harrison brot. home a load of Board[s]. (mail arrived) got 1 yoke of oxen of Brawne to help him home another yoke he got to bring him part of the way then turned them out & let them go home. in the evening it Rained

Thursday April 16th Harrison went for another load of Boards. this is a most delightful day clear & warm Steam Boat passed up. Lewis Hill paid me $6.00. I commenced makeing Norris Window Frames.

Friday April 17th Harrison hauled out Manure ½ the day. I fixed up a hen Coop Sawed out some window Frame stuff. After dinner H & I went down & run out a Timber Claim. In the evening I settled with Holton, every thing but the postage on his papers from the first of January last.

Saturday April 18th Morning Clear but Cool. Hulburt Cow took the Bull Harrison hauled Manure. I painted Holtons Waggon

Sunday pleasa[n]t

Monday April 20 Harrison & Davis planted onion seed & set out some small onions, also seed onions one Bushel. I painted Holtons waggon a second time. I bought one of Greelys plows price 13 dollars paid $8. Bought 2 lbs saleratus settled with [Anson] Northup[35] he is to pay McKusick for a plow lay I bought of him last summer price 4.37½ came down & stayed with E. A. Bissell Esqr. Clouded up & rained some J. S. Davis commenced work

Tuesday 21 I came to Haskells s[t]ayed untill after dinner. Came to Norris from there to Brawnes from there Home.

Wednesday April 22 I walked up to St Pauls from there to St. Peters[36] Stayed all night with Mr P. Prescott.

Thursday April 23. Steam Boat Cecilia arrived Doct. [George F.] Turner Requested me to catch him 2 or 3 Gophers[37] comeing home today I caught one on the ground or above ground the only one I have ever seen above the ground I took my gopher Back & gave it to a Naturalist at Mr Sibleys for whom I presume it was intended[38] he was very glad to get it. Then I came home

---

[35] Northup settled at St. Croix Falls in 1839 and in the spring of 1844 he removed to Stillwater, where he built a hotel and engaged in the lumber business. He subsequently built hotels in St. Paul, St. Anthony, and Minneapolis. Folsom, *Fifty Years in the Northwest*, 63.

[36] "St. Peters" was the earlier name of Mendota.

[37] Turner was surgeon at Fort Snelling. Return I. Holcombe, *Minnesota in Three Centuries*, 2:180, 250 (New York, 1908).

[38] The naturalist was probably Lamare-Picquot, a French scientist who was collecting specimens in the region in the spring and summer of

Friday 24 April   Clear & pleasant.   I worked on Esq Norris window Frames

Saturday 25th   I worked on Window Frames.   planted some garden seeds.   Lettuce[,] Cabbage, Tomatoes, & set out some Seed Beets & Parsnips and some Cabbage stocks also some seed Turnips

Sunday 26th April   Rather Cool & Harrison went over to Norris.   Martha & I walked down to the Claim Brawn was over but I did not see him.

Monday April 27   Harrison went ove[r] to Haskels & got 30 bushels of Blue Potatoes by the way of Brawnes & got one yoke of his Cattle.   Martha went over to Haskells on a visit.   Rained from 1 oclo[ck] untill nearly night.   Davis hewed out Timber for a Harrow   I worke[d] on Norris Window frames   Brissette brot home our large Iron Pot & 3 gal. of molasses

Tuesday April 28th   Harrison went over to Haskells to intercept Norris on his way to Still Water to get our plow brot. down.   he went on to Still Water & brot the plow.

Wednesday 29   I finished Norris Frames.   he came & took them away also his sash.   Harrison & I planted some Nishannock Potatoes[,] Carrot seed, Beet seed, Cabbage seed & Parsnip seed   Brissette came & got his Oats away he also got 5 lbs soap   Robert sent me word he wanted 20 Barrels of Potatoes   I sent a Note to Steel by Mr Mooers

Thursday April 30   Harrison took Mink up to Fords & had his shoes set, also he had a Bail put to a Kettle, one Trace chain lengthened, a hook put to the short Log chain

1846. He lived at Mendota during his stay in the Minnesota country, undoubtedly at Sibley's home. "Minnesota as Seen by Travelers," in *Minnesota History*, 6: 270, 277 (September, 1925).

&c &c   I worked on a Large gait [*gate*]. Harrison sowed some peas in the garden.

Friday May 1st   Weather most delightful. Capt Holcombe came & took the county Book up to Stillwater. I went up [to] Holtons & got 12 bushels of wheat. Harrison & [I] picked cockle out of the wheat   found it such slow work that I went over to Haskells & got his screen to run it through

Saturday May 2nd   Warm & pleasant. Harrison Riddled wheat. make good speed. I finished my gate. Commenced makeing a Large Harrow. Planted some bush Beans, Butter Beans & Speckled Cranberry Beans als[o] Cucumber, Musk & Water Melon seeds   Young Red River [heifer] took the Bull

Sunday May 3rd   Warm & pleasant   I sent over by Davis $1 00 to A. McHattie to pay for 2 steel Traps he brot down from Still Water

Monday May 4th   Harrison picking cockle out of our seed wheat. J. S. Norris here today. Haskell also here. I castrated 3 bull calves, & worked on my Harrow   Rained Very hard about 2 oclock   bot sundries for Harrison of Hopkins amounting to $1.00

Tuesday May 5th   Cloudy & warm. Harrison & Davis picked Wheat   I finished Harrow & picked wheat

Wednesday May 6th   Harrison mooved down on the Claim   bot of Hopkins 1½ bushels corn at 50 = 75   took 20 bushels Potatoes up to Hopkins for Steel to be shiped on Board Boat.

Thursday May 7   Harrison commenced Harrowing   I hung a Large gate down on the Claim. Sold Robert 7 Barrels potatoes.   *warm Very*

Friday May 8th   Charles commenced Traping for Gophers. *Very warm*   I commenced makeing a Roller.

Saturday May 9   Mail arrived on board the Lynx. I shiped 20 bushels Potatoes to F. Steel F[ort] Snelling Harrison Received a Letter From home.

Sunday May 10th   Very warm & pleasant   Harrison wrote a Letter home to Robert. I saw Mr Denton[39] a few minutes at Fords.

Monday May 11th   I worked on Roller. Sold 5 barrels Potatoes @ 1 25 = 6 25   Weather Very warm.

Tuesday May 12   Worked on Roller.   Rained a little. Steamer Cecilia arrived.

Wednesday May 13   Harrison got 27½ bushels oats for seed, also 4½ bushels to feed. he also got 8½ lbs pork & a pair of sheets & some Bread   I worked a little on the Roller

Thursday May 14th   I worked on the Roller. James Parker came over for Brawns oxen but did not bring an order so I did not let them go. Wind in the North & has the appearance of Frost

Friday May 15th   We had a heavy frost this morning. I fear the most is all killed.   I worked on the Roller.

Saturday May 16   Warm & pleasant somewhat Cloudy. I finished the Roller   Harrison got 4 lbs of Beef & 4 bushels of small Potatoes

Sunday May 17th   We had a very h[e]avy Rain last night together with a wind Storm & a little Hail   Today warm & pleasant   Davis took Mink went over to Haskells carried his Screen home also took Haskells & Bissells Cul-

[39] Probably Francois Denton, who is listed in the 1850 census schedules as a resident of Pig's Eye or Red Rock. The inhabitants of the two places are listed together.

tivators over brot over a skillet & Frying pan from Haskells.

Monday May 18th Morning quite Cool but no Frost. I sorted my potatoes those that were in the Root House. Martha had a mess of Turnip top greens for the First [time] I hoed my Peas for the first time hoed some of the small onions. Davis came up to plow the garden

Tuesday May 19th Davis commenced plowing the Garden. Charley went to the Fort I took up the balance of the Potatoes that Remained in ground Set out some seed Beets that I had buried with the potatoes in the fall, Sugar, Turnip & Mangel Wurtzel Beets they kept well in the Bottom of a Potatoe hole. hoed some onions &c &c.

Wednesday May 20 Davis plowing. Struck a Bolder & broke 2 inches off the point of the Boston plow ground it & went to work

Thursday May 21 Davis plowed untill noon did not quite finish. Mr Otis[40] came & took Brawns oxen away. Davis then went down to the Claim. Some days ago we missed one of our Pigs. Then yesterday another one. So I concluded to go up to the Slough where the Indians are fishing a good deal & see if I could see any sign of them. Ford went with me we found the one first missing shot as we suppose by the Indians out of mischief for She was shot just below the *arse* & they had not taken it away. The other one came home in the evening very lame haveing been hurt by some means in the hip. I made a Large box to keep grain &c in. We have shut our Pigs up in the calf pasture do not intend to let them run at Large any more untill the Acorns get ripe

[40] Brown may refer to Benjamin T. Otis, who settled at Taylor's Falls in 1846. In 1849 he removed to Vasa in Washington County. Warner and Foote, *Washington County*, 305, 477.

Friday May 22nd   We had a very fine Rain last night. it began to be needed   On Wednesday last H. Jackson Esq came down & was before me qualified as Post Master at St Pauls[41]   I rode over to see some of my neighbors, Lewis Hill, Furber[,] Norris & Rockwood. Rock. is not going to join Teams with me as we had been talking of doing   We have concluded that times are going to be rather hard this year[42]   in consequence of the low stage of the water the Lumbermen will not be able to get down their Logs, & too we both has [*have*] as much as we can do without breakin[g] Prairie.   I brot. home two large sacks from Rocks that I had left there in the spring.   Rock was Running out his corn ground to plant   Norris was behind with his work. I went on to Haskells & stayed all night.   saw his plowing   he is doing very good work of it   his fall wheat looks thin & very weedy   I fear he will not have much of a crop of it

Saturday May 23   Went from Haskells over to John Faulstrams[43]   saw Mr. J. Falstram   got some sugar for my services as Counselor in a suit at Law with Worth. took over to him a letter from D[avid] King.[44]   took over to Bissell his Cultivator   Came home.   Faylin came down & got 4 bushels of Oat[s] on A. K. McLeod's account.   got Cavileer 2 straps one for a Bell strap & one for a Belt   they came to .50

[41] A post office was established at St. Paul on April 7, 1846, with Henry Jackson the first postmaster. Williams, *Saint Paul*, 154.
[42] The depression did not come until the next year, 1847, although money may have become scarce even sooner on the frontier.
[43] John Falstrom was a son of Jacob. Warner and Foote, *Washington County*, 407.
[44] King was a missionary at the Methodist mission at Kaposia from 1837, when the mission was founded, until 1843, when it was abandoned. He remained at Kaposia for several years after that as Indian farmer. Hobart, *Methodism in Minnesota*, 14, 15, 22.

Sunday May 24th   Martha & I went down to the Claim. Harrison Finished sowing his oats yesterday. his wheat looks rather thin in places.

Monday May 25th   Steamboat Heuer arrived bringing D[avid] Wentworth & Family [Hilton] Doe sent up 2 stone jars for butter. I hoed out a part of our small onions.

Tuesday May 26th   Harrison got 128 lbs Flour 11 lbs pork & 3 lbs beef. Martha & I finished weeding & hoeing the small onions   Davi[d] Holton got a bottle of Bitters & box Pills[45] paid 1.20   I bot. for Harrison 1 lb saleratus at Hopkins .13   I bot at Hopkins 1 oz of Wafers 13 cent[s] Commenced makeing for Holton a waggon body or box

Wednesday May 27th   Mail arrived. Holton & his son-in-Law Wentworth came over to see us. Davis Harrowed the garden. I worked on Holtons Waggon box. Heard of the War.

Thursday May 28th   Finished Holtons Waggon box. Robertson Heiffer took the Bull.

Friday May 29th   Put up 2 Barrels ashes for soap makeing   hoed out the Cabbage plants Beans & vines. Yesterday we heard of the war with Mexico. Planted the balance of our garden Peas   We had a gentle Rain 2 oclock An excellent Rain. Sat out 340 Cabbage plants   Drumhead Dutch Red Green Savoy Early york & Sugar Loaf. Also Tomatoe plants. Harrison stayed over night

Saturday May 30   Morning warm & Rainy. River has risen some 2 feet in the last 3 or 5 days & still on the rise. yesterday Harrison commenced plowing for potatoes & Rutabagas   plows 10 to 12 inches deep. Davis came up & assisted me plant Beans. We finished planting the

---

[45] David Holton was a son of John Holton. 1850 census schedules.

garden by the house. I planted Melons Cucumbers & Pumkins. We hoed the Beets parsnips & Carrots. I planted a few horse Beans also a few lima[?] Beans

Sunday May 31st It Rained a good deal last night & is still Raining. River still on the rise. Mail by Cecilia

Monday June 1st Rained slowly all night & Still raining Harrison stayed over night with us We heard some War news by the Mail & Boat yesterday. Davis went away yesterday morning & has not yet returned. Sold my Large Prairie Plow to B. L. Rockwood he agrees to Break next year between the 20 of May & 20 June 8 acres for me for the Plow Harrison & Charly present he got 1 lb Rutabaga seed [and] 2 boxes Pills Rock paid me 5 Fra[n]cs or 95 cents James S. Norris Esqr came over & measured the Lumber that I bought of him early in the Spring. he was here nearly all day as it rained hard all the day Rockwood came over to see if I could take the plow that I sold him over to Brawnes Harrison stayed over night with us

Tuesday June 2 I spoke to Wentworth for his small Waggon to go to Haskells with. Cecilia went down. Davis worked here after dinner to day geting Bean pol[e]s &c I. sawed out some door stuff Esqr Hone came with 2 Horses & stayed over night

Wednesday June 3rd I went over to Haskells, borrowed his small plow. got 10 bushels seed Potatoes took Rocks. Prairie plow over to Brawns. Returned home.

June 4th Thursday Returned Wentworths Waggon

Friday June 5th Charley & I went to the Fort in Fords Canoe. Stayed over night at Prescotts.

Saturday June 6th Came home. bot of Steel goods & some groceries. traded some at Roberts

Sunday June 7th   Very pleasant   Steamer Falcon went up.

Monday I made a door & window shutters for a Shantee dow[n] on the Claim   also set glass in a sash for the Window

Tuesday June 9   Worked at Shantee down on Claim

Wednesday June 10   Worked at Shantee, & Finished

Thursday by noon   the Steamer Lynx came along & I went up to the Fort on her

Friday   I made a bargain with Captain [Samuel M.] Plummer to lay Flooring at $2 75 pr square in the Fort.[46]

Saturday June 13th   I Fixed up a place to work in Made a work bench got some boards under Shelter & came home.

Sunday June 14th   Very pleasant.

[46] Plummer, a captain in the First Infantry Regiment, was stationed at Fort Snelling from 1844 to 1846. Cullum, *Register of the Officers and Graduates of the U. S. Military Academy*, 614.

THE DIARY OF
MITCHELL Y. JACKSON, 1852-63

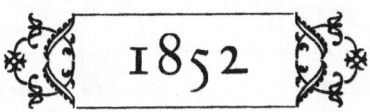

Wabash August 8th 1852   Partly for its convenience partly to save buying a new book and partly on account of sund[ry] memorandums already made in the forepart which already begin to be ancient   This little book is taken for a Diary

M Y Jackson

Wabash August 1852 Sunday 8th   Warm   This day fills up the measure of 36 years that has been allotted to the writer having been born in Knox Co Ohio Aug 8th 1816   I am this day 36 years old   In the prime of life   What the afternoon of a life—Spent I should think so far rather pleasantly [—] may be is all wrapped up in the mysteries of the future   The forenoon has not passed without its share of clouds   But the intervals have been filled up with many spots of fine sunshine and upon the whole I conclude that I enjoy this life upon an average full as well as the rest of mankind   Bro D I Jackson & sister Ellen are with us today having stopped last evening on their return from a land journey into Ohio[1]   They will remain till morning

Monday 9th   Expect to take the packet at three oclock in the morning for Toledo to complete some money ar-

---

[1] D. Imlay Jackson and his wife, Ellen Jane, lived in Delphi, Indiana, and later removed to Rensselaer.

rangements with P[hilo] Buckingham & Co and some other business Matters

Toledo Ohio Aug 12 1852 Thursday having arrived here last evening without any thing of particular interest transpiring by the way and not being able to finish my business in time for the mornings packet I have the day before me Weather warm Some cholera in the city as well as at Fort Wayne & many other towns. I am ready for the morning packet with 5000$ Dollars in N. Y. Drafts to advance on wheat & other property for shipment to Buckingham.

Wabash Aug 1852 Sunday 15th Reached home last night about midnight in good health find my little family in good health Sister Prudence who was sick with flux when I left is better[2]

Wednesday 18th Having some business at Marion I invite Mrs. Jackson to ride out with me in a carriage and after a very pleasant drive our little party consisting of myself wife & Preston[3] take dinner at the Indiana which is kept by one of my old school boys Mr Williams

Wabash Aug 1852 Thursday 16th After having staid over night with our respected Uncle D Imlay we drive home this morning against 10 O clock

Sunday 22 Warm Our Sunday School is dismissed this morning without going through the lesson on account of two or more funerals which take place this forenoon There is a good deal of sickness in town at this time Mostly Flux of which some 10 or 12 have died lately mostly children

[2] Prudence, a sister of Jackson's wife, was married to Jackson's brother Alexander.
[3] Jackson's second son, born in 1850.

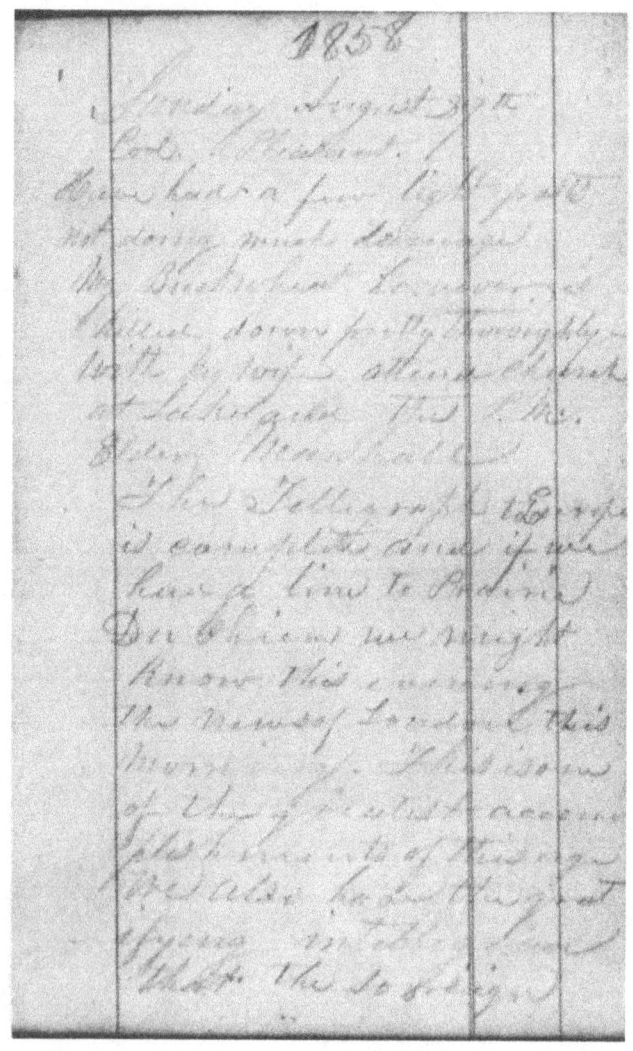

A Page from Jackson's Diary

Wabash Nov 1852 Tuesday Nov 2   Presidential Election Gen Winfield Scot[t] & Graham are the Whig candidates   Pierce & King Locofoco   Hale Abolition   I vote for the Whig of course and feel proud to loose my vote upon Winfield Scott

Wabash Decr 1852 Sunday Morning   We hear this morning the ringing of the last packet bell for the season   The canal has not been frozen over yet though the ground is frozen pretty hard this morning and this is the second time this fall that our streets have been hard enough to drive over   The last ringing of the packet Bell for the season will bring up some rather melancholy feelings— 4 or five months of winter must now elapse before its merry notes will again peel upon the air and gladden the hearts of the citizens of Wabash   But the Citizens of Wabash—who will they *then* be   During the reign of Winter for whose Grave must the icy earth be penetrated. Who will have gone to that "Bourn from whence travelers never return["]   Who of our happy and long life expecting Citizens hear this morning for the last time the lively peals of the packet bell   A Long tedious winter is upon us.   And who is to care for the poor For the Widow & the fatherless For the afflicted and the unfortunate who under ordinary circumstances are able to provide for them selves and families the necessaries of Life   Who and how many will live to be gladdened by the appearance of our Packets in 1853

Wabash Dec 1852 Tuesday 14th Navigation closed Canal frozen over   We have had no boats for several days but canal has not been completely frozen over at this place till this morning

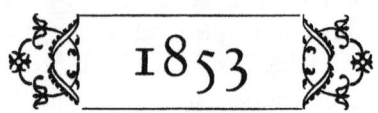

Wabash Jany 1st 1853 Saturday Another New Year has come upon us Finds us in the enjoyment of good health and as I think a full share of contentment and our [full]¹ as much happiness as falls to the lot of Mortals on an average

Jany 25 Tuesday Receive from the bank at Logansport for a/c of P Buckingham & Co of Toledo 500$ to be advanced as we suppose on property for shipment to them This is not of its self of sufficient importance to be noticed here only on account of the circumstances under which it is sent This being the second time that they have sent us money without our having solicited it goes to show that they have full confidence in us as prompt and faithfull business men

Thursday 27 Receive a letter from Philo Buckingham dated at Delphi Containing full authority to draw at 4 Mo on their house in N. Y.

Wabash Feb 1853 Sunday 6 Cold freezing with some snow on the ground Afternoon with little Oscar for company—walk down to Fathers who has been quite sick for some two weeks.² Find him somewhat dis-

¹ The word enclosed in brackets is crossed out in the original diary. Jackson undoubtedly meant to cross out the preceding word instead.
² Oscar was Jackson's eldest son, born in 1846. The diarist's father was Daniel Jackson.

couraged and under the impression that he would not likely recover Quite satisfied to die if that was to be the result With perfect composure gave directions about being buried The Doctor ([James] Ford) however thinks he will recover He is quite feeble being quite old (65 next July 17) Says he has lived as long as any man ought to want to live

Wabash Mar. 31 1853 Thursday 31 Received some goods from Toledo by Boat Patriot Navigation is fairly open East of this. Will not open West for several days yet Winter has been unusually mild, but a very unpleasant winter on account of the rain & mud

Saturday April 8 We learn that Philo Buckingham of Toledo died at Zanesville on Wednesday morning 6th

Wabash May 1853 Thursday 5th After a very dark and rainy night with a good deal of tramping about through the mud our domestic relations were extended lengthened & strengthened by the birth of *another boy* which important event took place at about 4 o'clock this morning[3]

Sunday 8th Offered to our church a protest signed by myself and fourteen other members protesting against what we understand to be an improper course of proceedure in matters of church discipline which the Church refused to receive

Tuesday June 28th W. P. Walker returns from California

Wabash. July 1853 Sunday 3rd Bro John O'Kane is with us and preaches in the presbyterian Church which has been obtained for our meeting to day After preaching a lengthy report is received from our Elders in which

---

[3] The boy was Jackson's third son, Frank.

among other things they report that they have urged A[lexander] E Jackson[4] and all the witnesses they knew of to prosecute and testify as to the guilt of Elder B[enjamin] Whorton That they set a time to hear and determine upon the charges preferred against him by A E Jackson But that not only A E Jackson but his witnesses refused to appear. Report wound up by recommending that Prudence Jackson and Miss S J. Walker be dismissed from the fellowship of the church for insubordination in refusing to attend and testify when called upon by the officers of the church I felt it my duty to state publicly that the report just received from the Elders abounded in misrepresentations and false hoods An additional report was offered and approved recommending the dismissal of myself and some 8 or 10 other members for disorderly conduct in signing and presenting a petition asking the church to dismiss us from its fellowship and setting forth our reasons for making such request A copy of this petition also a copy of the protest mentioned May 8th will be found among my private papers if the original papers should be lost or destroyed—and I think very likely they will for I have very little confidence in the men who have the management of what is *called* the *Church* of *Christ* at *Wabash*[5] I think no less of Christianity than before— and feel determined to live and die a consistant Christian But want no fellowship with such men and women as a part of our members have shown themselves to be

Wabash July 23rd 1853 We this day convert our warehouse property into Stock in the Cincinnati Newcastle and Michigan Rail Road at 2700$ We do this believing

[4] The diarist's brother.
[5] The petition is not with Jackson's papers.

that when this Rail Road with the valley & Eell [*Eel*] river Roads are completed our business must be greatly injured, and consequently the value of our property be diminished. But as the R R is to be the cause of this expected depreciation we think it but fair that it should own the property thus depreciated[6]

Wabash August 3rd 1853 Wednesday At 1 oclock start out with two teams and an extra hand with a Threshing Machine of Townsends Patent Intending to test its qualities by thrashing a few days and sell the machine At sunset find ourselves some 3 or 4 miles beyond the Eel river bridge at the house of Mr Alex Flora a very clever appearing Dunkard whose better half would weigh about 300 lbs. Mr Flora had a small crop of Wheat that he was anxious to have thrashed and was not only willing but anxious that we should stay over night with him and thresh out his crop which we concluded to do To me there was a kind of Novelty about this adventure that was rather agreeable than otherwise Our machine had been sold twice and returned on account of not performing to the satisfaction of the purchasers. Had been com-

[6] The editor has found no mention of the Cincinnati, Newcastle, and Michigan Railroad. Jackson probably refers to the railroad which was at that time building northwestward from Richmond toward Newcastle, and which later reached the Wabash River at Logansport. It is now part of the Pennsylvania system. The "valley road" was probably the Wabash, which was completed from Fort Wayne westward to the state line in 1856. The "Eel River road," known originally as the "Logansport and Northern Indiana" and later as the "Detroit, Eel River, and Illinois," was projected in 1852 to parallel the Eel River. It is now part of the Pennsylvania system. Frederic L. Paxson, "The Railroads of the 'Old Northwest' before the Civil War," in Wisconsin Academy of Sciences, Arts, and Letters, *Transactions,* vol. 17, part 1, p. 259–262 (Madison, 1912); Logan Esarey, *A History of Indiana,* 2:730 (Indianapolis, 1918); Balthasar H. Meyer, ed., *History of Transportation in the United States before 1860,* 508 (Washington, 1917); Helm, *Wabash County,* 145.

missioned to us to sell by the Agent of Mess[rs] Marsh & Co of Pavilion Centre N. Y. who still insisted that it was a good machine but neglected to pay up its freight Commission Storage &C till our lien upon it amounted to some 90$ and to pay this lien we had advertised it for sale and no one bidding we had made a nominal bid of 50$ and bought it and this adventure was for the double purpose of testing thoroughly its qualities and disposing of it. It is not strange therefore that my sleep was not very profound but rather impatient till

Thursday Morning Aug 4 When we were all astir rigging up for threshing After setting and being disturbed several times through the day by showers of rain and oftener by the flying of belts and other troubles incident to the life of wheat threshers night came on and we had the consolation of knowing that we had threshed and cleaned handsomely almost *twenty three bushels of wheat* Mr Flora however as well as his wife were fortunately possessed of a good stock of patience and good nature as well as the necessary quantity of Bred and Butter Pork & Beans &c to feed us with and as we had been disturbed by rain no complaint was heard although we had already detained him and his hands longer than would have been required to finish his whole crop with a good machine But on

Friday 5th the weather was fine and we commenced early and Oh if my go[o]d patience should ever be put to a more severe test than this I am fearful that I should loose my reputation as a man of patience But about sun set we passed the last sheaf through having threshed some 20 Bushels before noon and 49 bushels after noon Completing 93 Bushels in *two* days. This would have been no extra ordinary work for a good machine to do in half a day

Saturday 6th Fine summer morning Settle up with my friend Flora by charging him nothing for his threshing and paying nothing for our board This did not seem much like making money at the new business in which I had so recently engaged. But we packed up not seeming to be discouraged any *more* than we realy were And started North ward determined to get out of the range of the Pitts and Massiton [*Massilon*] Machine[s] and get if possible into some neighborhood where they had not been used to better threshing than it was possible for us to do[7] Drove on by way of Gilead to Newark which we reached about 3 or 4, oclock Saturday evening—rather discouraged with the adventure. Found several persons that could tell us where there was plenty of threshing to do and thought if our machine on trial would perform well that there would be a good prospect to sell. But no *bidders* I had now been out 4 days and made nothing but expended upwards of 20$ besides my time[,] and my men who were experienced threshers assured me that it was utterly useless to attempt to introduce the machine by setting it up again Being satisfied that we were perhaps in as good a neighborhood to sell as could be found I determined about tea time to put up for the night and if

---

[7] The Pitts threshing machines were made by the Pitts brothers—the "Buffalo Pitts" by John A. Pitts and the "Chicago Pitts" by Hiram A. Pitts, at Buffalo and Chicago respectively. The brothers in 1837 patented a combined threshing machine and fanning mill with an "endless apron," the original principles of which, with minor improvements, were used in threshing machines for over half a century. See R. L. Ardrey, *American Agricultural Implements*, 105 (Chicago, 1894). A drawing of the Massilon machine, made by Russell and Company at Massilon, Ohio, may be found in the *Northwestern Farmer and Horticultural Journal*, 5:343 (September, 1860).

no bidders could be found against dark to unload and send my men and teams home in the morning

Sunday 7th Feeling quite unwell as well as quite discouraged I concluded to go home with the teams leaving Mr Richards our feeder to sell or barter the machine as best he could. Gave him seven Dollars for expense money and directed him to come home when he had boarded out that whether he sold or not but urged him to sell or barter for something

Wabash August 1853 Thursday 11 Went up to the burget [sic] farm to set up for Mr Blocher a Pitts Machine that we had sold him the day before on condition that it would perform to please him *Very hot day* Worked all day helping to make his levers and get the machine under motion which we accomplished just at dark But quit without being satisfied as to its performance and came home greatly fatigued and with a bad head ache Found that Mr Richards had returned from Newark with 175$ worth of notes running mostly over two years with interest for the old machine that I would have been glad to have taken most any kind of a hundred Dollar horse for

Friday Aug 12 Went up again to Mr Blochers to see his machine perform but found his grain in such bad order that we could not tell much about its qualities for working

Wabash August 1853 Tuesday 16th Went out to Mr Cox's near Gilead to set up another Pitts Threshing machine. reached there about 1 o clock Staid over night found Mr Cox a good clever kind of farmer

Wednesday 17th After noon start home after putting the machine in good working order leaving it threshing 1 Bushel of wheat per minute of sheaves requiring two

Dz to a Bus. And seeming to give entire satisfaction to the purchasers

Wabash Oct 1853 Sunday 9th Weather fine and has been for several days past indeed I do not recollect ever to have seen so much fine weather in one full season Leaves mostly green yet which is quite unusual for that climate Indeed we had no killing frost till about the 1st of this month We have abundance of fruit particularly Peaches* Never saw as fine a corn crop Wheat good but average yield light Wheat is now worth 100 c Flour 5 & 550 pr Brl Common Labor 100 c per day or 75c and board

Wabash Oct. 1853 every description of property seems to be advancing except Warehouses

Thursday 20th Weather still continu[e]s fine. Leaves not yet thoroughly killed though they are mostly frosted and fallen. weather dry and roads very dusty My wife's uncle Simpson Alexander accompanied by his wife and little Daughter Martha is here on a visit from Fayette The first Wabash County agricultural fair opens today. Exhibition rather *slim* but when we considder that this county has been organized but about 18 years we are well satisfied with the opening of the fair

Friday 21 Fair opens out rather better. And upon the whole is full as good as I expected to see in this new county A light sprinkling of rain disturbs the exhibition somewhat There is a very respectable display of Cattle Horses Hogs Sheep Fowls Wheat Corn Potatoes & Fruit Particularly of Apples of which there is a good variety of the finest I ever saw Some weighing as high as 20 ounces

* good peaches still hanging on our tree in our garden peaches have sold from 100 down to 18c

(it is said) Agriculture is beginning to receive the attention which it deserves And when our farmers shall have succeeded in removing the forest from the rich lands of this County it must stand high as an agricultural county

Wabash Dec 17 1853 Cold & *snowy* Brother Alexander sells out his house hold goods with the intention of going to Oregon

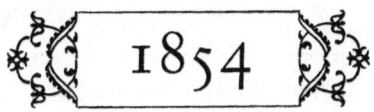

1854 Jany 1st Sunday   Another year numbered with the past

Jany 13th   Sell out our house & furniture, with the intention of emigrating to oregon the coming Spring

Wabash Feb 5th   Sunday   pleasant winter   Am preparing to start *West* tomorrow morning   But as *West* is now rather indefinite I should say that I design to start on horse back & alone go North to the Rail Road—Sell my horse if I can and think best—Thence to Galena—thence to St Paul Minnesota thence somewhere else perhaps return and perhaps have my family come on with that of A E [Jackson]

Gilead Ind[1]   Tuesday Feb 7   Morning snowing   hav-

---

[1] In the margins of the original diary Jackson gives the distances between the places at which he stopped on his journey as follows: Wabash to Gilead, 15 miles; to Newark, 5; to Rochester, 10; to the Smith House, 12; to Judge Pomeroy's, 11; to Laporte, 29; to Currier's, 29; to Osterhaut's, 26; to Chicago, 16; to Oak Ridge, 8; to Cottage Hill, 8; to Babcock's Grove, 4; to Wheaton, 5; to the junction, 5; to Wayne, 5; to Clinton, 4; to Elgin, 3; to Gilbert's, 8; to Huntley, 5; to Union, 7; to Marengo, 4; to Garden Prairie, 6; to Belvidere, 6; to Cherry Valley, 6; to Rockford, 8; to Winnebago, 7; to Pecatonica, 7; to Nevada, 8; to Freeport, 6; to Warren, 25; to Chapman's, 4; to Shullsburg, 10; to Platteville, 20; to Cumberland (Lancaster), 16; to Underwood's, 8; to Patch Grove, 10; to the Wisconsin River, 6; to Prairie du Chien, 6; and to St. Paul, 226. On a page of the memoranda preceding the diary proper he gives a table of distances between Prairie du Chien and St. Paul, which may be found in the Appendix, *post*, p. 223.

ing lef[t] home yesterday morning on a long journey I am here this morning at Mrs Orstotts [?]   2 Yorkers here from Wisconsin 55 m. West [of] Milwauke[e]   Speak well of that Region   Prairie best for corn but the right kind of openings best for wheat   Sowed about 40 acres in a very careless manner on sod and raised a little over 400 B.   Good water & stone (lime) Not much snow in winter but little mud   Market Milwauke & Chicago hawl[ed] 80 Bus to former place with 2 horses   plank road most of the way   pine 75 or 100 m north affords good market for farmers near.   Get my business with Mr Dowd settled about 10 and start to Newark which I reach about noon

Wednesday morning 8th   having bought a Canadian Pony last evening of Mr Carpenter partly to arrange up a claim against him and partly because I found that my horse would not answer to travel I arrange with Mr Curtis to return the old horse to Wabash.   Write home and take an early start on my long journey

Smith house or Lion 8 m. south of Plymouth 3 oclock Wednesday 8   Stop here to feed Mainly to rest my Pony who is making better time than I had reason to expect having traveled from Mr Curtis's where I staid last night 10 m E. of Rochester to Rochester in 1¾ hours   delayed fully an hour and reached here before 2   This is a fine farm in the thick woods   Worth 25$ pr Acre   South bend for market   passed over some Barrens to day that deserve the name.   Saw one farm with some 80 to 100 Acres cleared & fenced & had evidently been cultivated some years but was deserted and looked as though it had not been tended for 2 or three years and so thick were the Oak Sprouts that in a few more years it will look like the ballance of the land about it excepting a good assortment of old Oak Stumps that look as though they might last till the owner could travel all over the globe in search of a more sensible location and *still* stand a memorial to mark the scene of his folly

Laporte Ind Feb 1854 Thursday evening Pleasant day Snow nearly gone quite sloppy Staid last night with Judge Pomeroy 3 m this side of Plymouth having traveled 33 m yesterday & twenty [*sic*] nine to day write home expect to take R R to Chicago in the morning

Porter County Friday 10th evening After a pleasant winter day and hard traveling find myself at the house of Mr Currier 7 miles west of Valpairaso [*Valparaiso*] & 29 miles from Laporte. Was unable to get my horse aboard the cars this morning so I take the old fashion. From Laporte to Valpairaso is twenty two miles and is south of west The country for 5 or 6 miles before reaching Laporte and for say 10 or twelve miles on my rout[e] to day is the *very finest* I ever saw and that is saying a good deal for I passed through the Beckner & Mount farms on Eel river on my way and thought it would not be beat on my tour But these quarter, half & whole section Wheat fields and Corn Cribs by the Dz rather beats [them] But timber water & stone are short. From Westville 11 miles south west of Laporte on to Valpairaso the land is more variable, some very fine and some marshes or wet prairie with openings and some groves of fine timber Red oak ash, Cherry Blue ash, Hickory, Whitewalnut Red elm Honey Locust Hawthorne &c. Valpairaso I should think was rather hard at any rate the "American["] at which I stopped is *decidedly* so The country through which I have traveled this afternoon is of the kind you could not give me—sand ridges and scrubby oaks with occasionally a slough or pond   very little settled—a few starved looking cabins and log & Brush fences   Mr Curr[i]er is from Massachusetts and has a new farm on the 20 Mile Prairie   That is[,] it is 20 miles from Michigan City which by the way is about the distance I have been from that place all day and will be about the same distance most of the day tomorrow

Chicago Sunday evening 12th   Warm for the season   wind has been from the south for 2 days   Left Mr Curr[i]ers yesterday morning with a cold wind blowing from the South west   chilly & cloudy   ground frozen hard   roads quite Icy in places but against noon the Ice begins to give under the continued South wind   Ride 17 miles through a barren region (after leaving the 20 m Prairie) much the same as yesterday only more sandy and larger marshes and Oak more scrubby   passed the village of Hobart this morning 3 or 4 miles after starting remarkable for nothing but a nice mill upon a lake stream (some of the head waters of the Calumet) and a nice park   After feeding & dinner (at a tavern with its sign torn down) ride on cross the Calumet river running to my left through a beautiful Prairie or marsh say from one to 10 miles wide   Think this prairie might be easily reclaimed as it is not one of the deep marshy kind But sandy with rather light grass partly burnt and partly not.   After crossing for about a mile or a mile & a half the road runs through this low prairie in all directions with new tracks cut out on the fresh sod till it is about as wide as it is long   Then comes the sand ridges again with prairie on either hand stretching out almost as far as the horizon with short scrubby timber of the poorest kind   These ridges are peculiar in being straight and uniform as to height & width—look as though they had been thrown up by nature to build railroads upon

Cross the State line shortly after crossing the Calumet and near sunset re-cross the Calumet and put up at the house of Mr Osterhaut 26 miles from the 20 m prairie Landlord not at home but accomodations good Sleep fine for the first night in Illinois & in sight of a burning Prairie which continues to burn all the night Start early this morning and travel through a beautiful prairie country but not of the best quality of soil to this place which is quite a City Incorporated in 1837 with a population of some 4 or 5 thousand and now numbering 61000 having increased some 22000 within the last year There is no telling where the corporation line of this mighty young City is to be. The plat of ground on which it stands seems to extend west and south as far as we can see perhaps to sundown Write home

Monday 13th Rained last night Is quite muddy and looks like a general break up Go to the Depot the first thing Cannot get my horse on till evening to start tomorrow morning have to remain all day and all night Step into the office of a Real estate Commission Merchant. Speculating in *Dirt* is one of the most active branches of Chicago enterprise find a quarter 7½ M south of the City limits and about 10 or 11 M from the City proper for sale at 20$ per acre and 40 acres joining at 25 terms ¼ down Bal 3 annual payments with Interest this I set down as a good speculation for somebody Lands can be bought within 2 miles of the limits at from 500$ to 2000$ per acre. land all much the same as to quality a level second rate Prairie a few poor groves in the distance say 8 10 & 20 miles distant   City property worth from 75 to 300$ pr foot   A farm of 400 acres 22 m. n. west offered at 7000$ pretty well improved good water not much timber   good house barn &c   This is a regular *Steam* City. Several fine steam boats and any quantity of sail vessels in the harbor   Steam cars steam mills steam warehouses steam water works and any quantity of steam shops

Chicago Feb 14th Tuesday Morning Cold Snow Wind from N. E.   find my horse in the Accommodation train which will lay over at Freeport all night and be taken on to Warren by the express train to morrow morning this is a vexatious and unexpected delay   But Rail Roads will have things all their own way and I go aboard and start at 8.10

At Oak Ridge
Cottage hill
Babcocks Grove
Wheaton or Warren
Junction 11^{10} off at 1245
Wayne
Clinton at 1.15
Elgin is a fine looking village on the north side of Fox River and 42 m from Chicago   off at 3.15
Gilberts
Huntl[e]y
Union at 5
Marengo   quite a nice little Prairie village   new
Garden Prairie Station   This is indeed a Garden prairie with fields say from 80 Acres to ½ Sec laid off in regular order evidently by the genius Yankee
Belvidere at dusk   Go out to procure some horsefeed
Freeport Wednesday morning   After a tedious days

travel yesterday through a Storm of Snow & Sleet we reached Belvidere 78 miles at dusk and whilst out getting some oats & Hay for Fred the train drove on Then had to wait for the Express train which passes at 10.40 and overtakes *Fred* at Freeport

   passing Cherry valley
   Rockford
   Winnebago
   Pecatonica
   Nevade [*Nevada*][2]

to this place [*Freeport*] in the night   Reach here at 12[.] 55M   Find and feed my horse and go up to the promonade which is full—then on to the Stephenson which is also full and already some two or three guests snoozing round the Barroom for want of Beds   This being the best chance left I turn in and sweep a berth on the soft side of the floor lay down the broom for a pillow and about 3 get to sleep   Against 5 the crowd had reached 6 or 8 and the broom had been taken from under my head to sweep a place for some one else   This morning is a beautiful clear cold morning   looks like thawing But continues cold only thawing where the sun strikes fair

   Warren Ill Feb Wednesday 15   Left Freeport at 1.45 reach hear [*sic*] at 4.10   Get out my horse and start for the North West   Put up at Mr Chapmans   find small tavern with 25 guests a perfect crowd   The country through which we have passed from Chicago has been mostly fine   Wide spreading Prairies with but little tim-

---

[2] Nevada was on the Chicago and Galena Union Railroad in Ridott Township in Stephenson County, Illinois.   When the railroad removed its station in 1860 the town went out of existence.   Addison L. Fulwider, *History of Stephenson County, Illinois*, 1:374 (Chicago, 1910).

ber unfortunately passed Rockford in the night This is my first night in Wisconsin nice farm & nice country Stone barn Limestone at that

Platt[e]ville Grant Co Wisconsin Thursday Evening 16th Feb Left this morning traveled over a beautifull rolling Prairie to Shullsburg this brings us into the Lead mining Region and to the right may be seen some of the most beautifull farming Prairie and to the left poor looking Ridges all dug up for Lead this Shullsburg is the capitol of Lafayette Co.[3] Thence to this place is nearly all Prairie with at least 15 miles without a *riding switch* Blue Mounds to the right and have been in sight all the after noon. cross no water from near Shullsburg to near this place Land beautifully undulating Soil good fenced with sod & Ditches no timber Saw sun set in the wide prairie Could not see a house at Sun set and roads kept forking without guide boards till I found myself upon a very dim track in deep snow & bad traveling Think I will not forget my first Prairie Sun set but I am here and safe at the house of Mr Boynton the shrewd and gentlemanly proprietor of the Platteville Hotel

Underwoods Grant Co Friday evening 17th Rigged a Cutter this morning and have traveled this day with much more comfort to my self & Fred over a broken country partly and mostly timbered Hills bold & Romantic scenery bold and picturesque. cross fine spring streams with lime stone bluffs Some pine. to Cumberland the County Seat of this county is better timber than thence

[3] The county seat was removed in 1856 from Shullsburg to Avon, later named Center, and in 1861 it was removed to Darlington, its present location. John G. Gregory, ed., *Southwestern Wisconsin: A History of Old Crawford County*, 1:611 (Chicago, 1932).

here but scenery not so grand[4] The Sun Sets in the great west over a distant plain without a shrub to disturb the view

Pra[i]rie Du Chien Wis. Saturday Evening 18th Pleasant & has been thawing since about 10 oclock this morning Left Mr Underwoods or Little Grant House this morning at 9 Pretty good snow to Patch Grove through a fine Country. Some of the finest Rolling prairie interspersed with midling timber Near Patch Grove is some farms that would come as near filling my fancy as any Dist[rict] I ever saw laying to the South[,] of the best quality of soil with good water and good Bur oak rails with a fair view to the South west clear across the great Mississippi for forty miles Land worth from 4 to 15$ Market this place

This afternoon the Snow is almost gone having been but little. Drive mostly among hills & Bold Bluffs [of] Limestone & Deep ravines with beautiful springs of water and some pretty good timber Bur Oak Linn. [*linden*] Whiteoak and in the low grounds Black & White walnut Linn Sugar, red elm with Grape & green Briar vines, Raspberries &c bottoms too narrow to be valuable Cross the Wisconsin Six miles from here and Six mile[s] from Patch Grove Bottoms low and badly overflowed. Rafts of Saw logs laying beside the road must have been floated here when the road was entirely impassible This Bottom is partly timbered with valuable timber both for wood & Lumber But must produce Billious Diseases Prairie Du Chien is situated on the East or Wisconsin

[4] Jackson was mistaken about the name of the county seat. Lancaster, which was on his direct route from Platteville to Prairie du Chien, has been the county seat since the organization of Grant County.

side of the Mississippi say 6 m above the Junction of the Wisconsin on a high bottom but lower back toward the bluff than toward the River   from here to St Paul is 226 m

Prairie Du Chine Sunday Feb. 19th 1854   Spend this Sunday at this uninteresting town of about 1500 inhabitants   Cross the river on the Ice and ascend the Iowa Bluffs and take a view of this old village and fine Bluffs on the east or Wisconsin side

Lansing Iowa Monday Feb. 20   Reach this place at 3 and put up   This is a pleasant landing in Allamakee Co near Columbus a rival town one mile below

Brownsville (or Wild cat)[5] Minnesota Tuesday 21 Reach here between 3 and 4 P.M.   Wind from the South and thawing very fast   Indeed the Ice is about half covered with water   I intended to drive to La Cross[e] 12 mile[s] above but find that it would have taken hard driving to reach it at dark and I feel decidedly disinclined to be found driving alone upon this mighty sheet of Ice & water after dark   so I put up and resolve to stay off the Ice unless the prospect is better for sound going tomorrow or at most to go no further than Lacross on the Ice

Brownsville Feb 22 1854 Wednesday 22   If ever I was cheered—yes made glad by a Northwester it is upon this very morning   It is freezing like bones   The water and snow of last evening is a perfect glare of ice but not hard enough to bear a horse but soon will be at this rate

Red wing Minnesota Saturday evening Feb 25   Very comfortably quartered in a nice new hotel in this nice

---

[5] "Wild Cat" is the name of a creek that empties into the Mississippi at Brownsville, as well as of a high bluff near by.   Upham, *Geographic Names,* 241.

Jackson's Sketch of Prairie du Chien

Jackson's Home at Lakeland

new town (commenced last spring)⁶ The Capitol of Goodhue County But I must give some account of the Journey from Brownsville Well there being no blacksmith in that town (a county seat Houston County about 48 hours old)⁷ I purchased a file and sharped [sic] my horses shoes the best I could and at 10 started upon the new coating of Ice Dine at Lacross 12 miles and have my horse well *sharped* and drive on to Hammonds at the upper mouth of Black river 15 miles above La Cross which claims to be at the Junction I guess it does not empty at the same place more than one year

Thursday 23 Drive on by Monteville a nice place for a town 4 miles Bunnells landing⁸ 7 miles and dine at Winona 6 m and drive 3½ miles out and stay over night with my old friend J[ohn] Iams⁹

Friday 24th Drive (by land) through Minnesota City 3 miles See Mr [Edward B.] Drew¹⁰ and Mr Hotchkiss Dine at Mt Vernon 12 m and then by land to Wabesha [Wabasha] village 20 miles which I reached after dark And that I reached the village and avoided Camping was owing to the disinterested friendship of some natives

⁶ The first hotel in Red Wing, the Red Wing House, was completed in the spring of 1853. Red Wing was surveyed and platted the following summer. *History of Goodhue County*, 338 (Red Wing, 1878).
⁷ Houston County was established by an act of the Minnesota legislature approved on February 23, 1854, and Brownsville was named the county seat. In April, 1855, the county seat was removed to Caledonia, where it has since remained. Minnesota Territory, *Laws*, 1854, p. 70; *History of Houston County*, 283, 308 (Minneapolis, 1882).
⁸ Bunnell's Landing, named for Willard Bunnell who settled in Winona County in 1842, is now called Homer. *History of Winona County*, 577 (Chicago, 1883).
⁹ Iams, who came from Wabash, Indiana, was a member of the Rollingstone colony. He was the first sheriff of Winona County. *History of Winona County*, 255, 558.
¹⁰ On Drew, see *ante*, p. 8, n.

whom I found camped near a slough upon which I was traveling and which was leading me off from the right track. this they knew and was good enough to hail me and by signs to put me right   I was shown the right road by a fine specimen of the natives who walked out with a conscious rectitude of person as well as purpose   I shall ever feel gratefull to this unfortunate race for this act of pure kindness done by a barefooted *savage* as he would be called in polite circles

To day 25th   I have passed Reeds [*Reads*] Landing traveled the whole length of Lake Pepin—Saw the Maiden Rock or bluff from which the Constant Winona leaped down into eternity rather than wed another than her lover [11]

Prescott Wis. 1854 Sunday evening 26th Feb   Left Red Wing at 10.30 this morning & Reached here at 3   distance 24 to 26 miles   Ice good   day Cold & Clear   Thaws some on the land   This young little town is located on rather a broken site just below the outlet of the St Croix and Douglass [*Point Douglas*] is upon the point above, Both claiming to be great towns in the future and both rather advantageously Located and surrounded by good Country But they are booth [*sic*] too near Saint Paul (22 miles) to ever make any great things   But Prescott I should think destined to make a good town.

SAINT PAUL (Minn) Monday evening Feb 27th Sold my Cutter to Mr Foster [12] at Prescott this morning and rode from there here.   15 mile[s] out of 22 being

---

[11] For this well-known Indian tale, see G. Hubert Smith, "The Winona Legend," in *Minnesota History*, 13:367–376 (December, 1932).

[12] This may have been Joel Foster, who settled at the falls of the Kinnickinnic River in Wisconsin in 1848. His reminiscences may be found in Warner and Foote, *Washington County*, 198–214.

overland I thought best to travel in this way About ⅔ of the Portage however would have been good sleighing Ballance rather bare and somewhat sloppy From Douglass the first 3 or 4 miles is mostly up hill and over a prairie beautifully undulating and mostly facing the South Many beautifull farms look as though they had been cultivated for many years and the many Piles of straw and stacks of Oats & Wheat fully confirm the stories we read about the productiveness of this neighborhood Large *farms* are still laying *out of doors* and look very inviting to the enterprising husbandman Some good locations are said to be vacant and yet subject to entry at 125c per Acre plenty of timber on the Islands of the Mississippi which is in sight and within from two to five miles but some 300 feet below. This timber can be had for the stealing though it is not very good rail timber but valuable for fuel being mostly White Elm, Cottonwood Maple, Blue, white and black Ash, red Elm Butternut, Hackberry &c Plenty of scrubby Black oak interspersed among the prairie for posts and a few that would make a whole rail cut. Further up this way we find the prairie more extensive and more level but not so good being altogather [*sic*] too sandy Cross one nice Creek and one that might be Called a Creek, Slough, or string of little lakes or ponds. Otherwise water is scarce Saint Paul looks just about as I expected to see it. Narrow Crooked streets some being dug down but many more that have yet to be dug down Houses of all grades & sizes and shapes

    The bench or table land of the main Plat is very similar to the Table land about Wabash. The same kind of Shelly Lime stone and a building stone underneath just like that found in the Wabash quarries   This City must be an exception to the great generality of this Country. When the frost leaves it must be muddy   But upon the uplands and even the low table lands we will not be troubled much with mud   The weather for the past week has been mostly delightfull winter   On Tuesday evening at Wildcat or Brownsville it grew rather muggy and threatened rain and on Wednesday morning it was pretty cold. But since then and particularly today has been delightfull   Sky perfectly clear and sunshine without the shadow of a cloud—The citizens at Winona as well as here say they have had no rain since last Nov

Saint Paul Tuesday 28   Weather still fine and snow going off   Met Mr [James M.] Winslow of this city whose acquaintance I had made on the cars west of Chicago—find him to be a man of some consequence in point of capital[13]   Also deliver an introductory letter from Mr Connell to Col Robinson who seems to be much of a gentleman[14]   Through his politeness I was introduced to Gov [Willis A.] Gorman and several others of more or less distinction   I conclude that in point of talent and shrewdness that this 5 year old City will compare favorably with any other City

Afternoon   write to A. E. and also to my wife   Postpone going to the falls [of St. Anthony] till tomorrow

Wednesday March 1st   Morning rainy   the first rain of

[13] Winslow settled in St. Paul in 1852. He built large hotels in St. Paul, St. Anthony, and St. Peter, and he introduced telegraph service into St. Paul. Upham and Dunlap, *Minnesota Biographies*.

[14] It is probable that Jackson refers to Daniel A. Robertson, the founder and editor of the *Minnesota Democrat* at St. Paul, who, like many newspaper editors of the time, was called "Colonel." The only Robinson listed in the first *St. Paul Directory*, that for 1856–57, is Thomas Robinson, a carriage maker.

the season too bad a day to visit the falls Afternoon walked up on the hill to see the City which looks quite scattering but the surrounding Country looks grand— Rolling Prairies interspersed with scrubby Oak groves with the Mississippi winding its way through the valley below I think a country residence might be built in sight of this City and yet be 20 perhaps 30 miles distant

Saint Paul March 1854 Thursday 2nd According to an arrangement made yesterday I accompanied Mr Winslow (today) some 17 miles up the river by [way] of St Anthony. Saw the falls and the City. The falls do not exhibit to much advantage at this season of the year particularly upon as blustry a day as this. The site for a city however is beautifull and who lives to visit this place 20 years hence must see an immense city spread out in every direction from the falls If navigation extended to the falls there would be but little chance for a city at St Paul But as Saint Paul is virtually the top of Steam boat navigation it must be the City of *fact* and St Anthony the city of *fancy* The country between the two cities is delightfull some beautifull farms that look at a distance like old farms But when we approach them we find that what we took for an orchard 30 years old is nothing but a grove of dwarf oaks The buildings are new commodious and tastey and indicate a thrifty set of farmers The country above the falls so far as we went (8 miles) is sightly but not so good as below

Capt Bennetts Mar 1854 Friday evening 3rd Notwithstanding the cold I determined to leave the City and ride out into the country somewhere. find myself here a little before sunset The Capt very kindly consents to entertain me as well as they can in back woods style

Saturday 4th Spend the day looking round in this neighborhood Capt Bennet owns & occupies the Brophy farm[15]—Is from Wheeling Va. Is an old steam boat Capt a M.M. [*Master Mason*] and much of a Gentleman to all appearances and Mrs. Bennett a matron much to my liking—a "Female Woman" of the right kind and her Daughter Miss Dora is a lovely girl of *sweet* fifteen— sings sweetly and plays upon her Piano This is a novel entertainment A piano Forte in a Log cabin The whole family seem to take particular pains to make me feel comfortable In short this is one of the "first families of Virginia" and no mistake—one of the most agreeable and hospitable I ever met with

Sunday 5th Weather more pleasant but still somewhat cold Ride out a few miles North with the captain who could not go out with me upon yesterday Return in the afternoon

Mar 1854 Monday 6 Evening At the house of Mr Finch 3½ M East of St Anthony Left the House of my new friends (Capt Bennets) this morning and have traveled say 3 miles today besides looking at 3 or four beautifull farms in this n[e]ighborhood worth from 900 to 2300$

Tuesday evening Mar 7th 1853 [*1854*] find myself at the house of Mr [John S.] Mann about 3½ miles S. W. of the falls. Have had a very pleasant day The ground is mostly clear of snow. find some beautiful Prairie this side the river A fine Town or City in prospect is springing up on this side called Minneapolis Have

---

[15] The Brophy farm, first occupied by Michael Brophy in 1850, was near Lake Johanna. J. W. Bond, *Minnesota and Its Resources*, 362 (New York, 1853).

examined the claim of Elder [Edwin W.] Cressy.[16] like it well

Mendota Mar 1854 Wednesday evening 8 Have traveled today from the house of Mr Mann by way of the falls of Minne Ha ha through this place and out some 5 or 6 miles South East through a beautifull Prairie interspersed with groves of scattering Bur Oaks & small Lakes and french cabins then turned about and returned Stop at the Mendota house[17] Ascended a hill just below this village this afternoon from which I had a full view of Saint Paul 7 mile[s] down the Mississippi—Saint Anthony 9 miles up the river—the Fort (Snelling) just across the Minnesota and its bluffs for a great distance up to the S. West—The bluffs of the Mississippi away to the South North and East. In fact look which way I would the view was grand beyond any Landscape I ever beheld This hill should be the site of an observatory How magnificently grand must be a view from this point in the blooming Spring the verdant Summer or golden Autumn And as if to add a melancholy interest to this enchanted spot, upon the very summit is an ancient as well as modern burying ground where the natives have perhaps for centuries deposited their dead[18]

Snelling house St Paul 1854 Friday Morning 10th Made

[16] Cressey, who came to Minnesota from Wabash, Indiana, lived near Lake Harriet. He organized the first Baptist church in Minneapolis. *Minutes of the Twenty-fourth Anniversary of the Minnesota Baptist State Convention, October, 1883,* 25 (Minneapolis, 1883).

[17] This was probably the stone dwelling built by Jean Baptiste Faribault at Mendota in 1837. It was used as a hotel for a time. George E. Warner and Charles M. Foote, eds., *History of Dakota County and the City of Hastings,* 513 (Minneapolis, 1881).

[18] Jackson's lookout point was undoubtedly Pilot Knob, which was used by the Indians as a burial ground and council place and is now included in Acacia Park, a Masonic cemetery.

the acquaintance of Mr [Henry H.] Sibley yesterday morning at Mendota and went out to see a very new claim belonging to him Also some other claims owned by Mr Faribault & his son[19] and reached hear [sic] after dark last evening. visited the Lodge[20] Bound for Hudson today

Stillwater Friday 10 Evening Stop at Minnesota house[21] This is quite a stirring Village and never can make a City for want of room [below the] hills Two beautifull Spring Brook[s] [put in] here from the Minnesota side

Stillwater Friday 10th Mar Land office & Territorial Prison Located here. Head of Lake St Croix

Lakeland Saturday evening 11th Left Stillwater this morning Crossed on Ice to Hudson on the Wisconsin side and recrossed and put up with Mr [Freeman C.] Tyler This beautifull place is a village, Town, or city in embryo Mr [Moses] Perrin Proprietor[22] situated nearly opposite Hudson I have deliberately concluded not to cross the Ice any more This place will probably be the crossing of the Green Bay & St Paul R. R. Also the Madison & Saint Paul R. R.[23]

Lakeland Mar 12 1854 Sunday Beautiful day I remain at Mr Tylers and rest over Sunday Afternoon walk

[19] Jean Baptiste Faribault, who was for many years a well-known fur trader in the Minnesota region, had several sons.
[20] Probably the Masonic lodge, since Jackson was a Mason.
[21] The Minnesota House, which stood on the corner of Main and Chestnut Streets in Stillwater, was built by Elam Greely in 1846 for a private residence. It was sold in 1847 and was used as a hotel for many years. Warner and Foote, *Washington County*, 526.
[22] Tyler and Perin had a sawmill at Lakeland. Perin platted the town in 1849. Warner and Foote, *Washington County*, 417; Folsom, *Fifty Years in the Northwest*, 372.
[23] These were two of the many railroads of the time that were projected but not built.

out on the hills far enough to see that this was a beautiful location

Monday 13 beautiful morning Walk out with Mr Perrin four or 5 miles west find some fine country and some vacant Lands After noon Rains a little Evening Rain & snow

Tuesday 14th Beautiful morning Only snow enough to whiten the Roofs a little which melts soon after sunrise Ride up to Stillwater again to mark my Plots and return

Lakeland Mar 1854 Wednesday 15th Dine with Mr [Samuel P.] Bonsell whos[e] wife is the Daughter of Aaron Perrin (Mary) of Fayette Co [*Indiana*] and a school mate of my wife

Thursday 16 Weather continued dry & very pleasant —just warm enough to be a little uncomfortable with active walking up hill on the sunny side and just cool enough to be a little more uncomfortable on the other side without exercise

Friday 17th *Cold* as *"bones"* Regular Northwester Drive with my Host Mr Tyler to St Paul & back wind blows like Jehu very cold

Lakeland Mar 1854 Sunday 19th Morning Cold & Clear Afternoon quite pleasant still dry & clear Walked up to Stillwater yesterday and back as far as Mr Greelys[24] where I staid all night and walked down over the hills this forenoon to my old stopping place Mr Tylers and by the way I should here remark that I have been fortunate in stopping here as Mr T. and his very amiable Lady & family have treated me with great kindness and

---

[24] This was either John or Himan W. Greely, both of whom are listed as farmers living at Lakeland in the 1860 census schedules.

attention for which they shall have a good warm place in some corner of my memory

Lakeland Mar 1854 Monday 20th Clear & pleasant went out surveying with Mr Perrin to assist in measuring

Tuesday 21st Bou[gh]t a claim of Mr Bonsall and looked partly over the farm of Mr Newell Has rained most of the day

Wednesday 22nd Cool & Pleasant Walk to Stillwater and make some Preemption claims

Thursday 23rd pleasant walk down to Mr Newells remain all day and in the evening conclude a bargain for the farm of Jonas and Amos Newell and sleep upon our own premises

Cottage Spring Mar 25 1854 Saturday The above is the name given by myself to our new residence (subject to the approval of my wife of course) Pleasant cool clear day Spend this day very pleasantly in performing my first days labor upon our new farm—Almost complete a cow Stable 12 x 16 ft. Am delighted with the farm Bought a plough yesterday of Mr Perrin but the ground is frozen too much to plough

Monday 27th Cold & clear Thermometer 4° above 0. Still too cold to plow Do some surveying

Tuesday 28th pleasant but co[l]d walk without regard to any road to St Paul

St. Paul Wednesday Mar 29 1854 draw my money and take the hack for Stillwater. Enter the Bonsall lands remain over night and on

Thursday walk down to Cottage Spring get a bond from Jonas Newall by being patient

Friday 31 *Snow* get my bond from Mr Amos Newell & T A Wood and feel like starting home after dinner

JACKSON'S DIARY, 1854   117

Prescot[t] Saturday April 1st Cold & mostly clear Started from Capt Tylers yesterday at 2 o clock. Staid with Mr. Furber Cottage Grove walked on here this morning Greek Slave not returned yet—no chance of getting below but to walk [25]

Wa Coota [*Wacouta*] April 1854 Monday 3rd Clear & pleasant Left Prescot yesterday morning in company with Mr Buckingham who lives on the Isabella [26] nearly opposite this and a young man from Wisconsin by the name of Cairnes and footed it down and staid over night with the Buckinghams and ferried over to this place this morning. Still no boat Afternoon tramp on Stay at a Cabin on the west shore of Lake Pepin in sight of "Maiden Rock" weather beautifull air warm but bracing Found a Tulip in bloom in a valley this afternoon

Wabashaw village Apr 4th Tuesday evening weather delightfull after a pretty tedious tramp reach this place feeling pretty well tired of tramping

Wabashaw Wednesday 1854 Apr 5 beautifull weather I am now below Lake Pepin and the river is free from Ice below this and I only wait for a Steam boat to go down. O this waiting

Thursday 6th 10 oclock A.M. on board Steamer Greek Slave and aground in sight of Wabasha where we have been for an hour ½ past 3 off again

---

[25] Joseph W. and Theodore Furber, brothers, both lived at Cottage Grove at this time. The "Greek Slave" was a steamboat in the upper Mississippi River trade. George B. Merrick, *Old Times on the Upper Mississippi*, 272 (Cleveland, 1909).

[26] The Isabel River. According to the *First Annual Review of Pierce County, Wisconsin, January 1st, 1856*, 14 (Prescott, 1856), in 1854 or 1855 one Buckingham erected a sawmill on the Isabel River in Pierce County, Wisconsin. This may have been John Buckingham, whom Folsom in his *Fifty Years in the Northwest*, 208, mentions as the first chairman of supervisors of Isabel Township.

Friday 7th   pleasant   nothing new

Saturday 8th   Beautifull day   We are so much behind our time that there is now no prospect of reaching Warren to take R R before Monday.   Meet the Steamer War Eagle in Galena river bound for S*t* Paul   Also meet Boat Julia Dean bound for Rock Island which boat I take in hopes to reach Chicago sooner that way than via Warren

Comanche Iowa Sunday Morning 9th April   find ourselves laying here where we have been most of the night on account of wind   9 oclock brings us to head of rapids La Clare [*Le Claire*] on Iowa & Port Byron on Ill[inois] side both nice locations 16 m above Rock Island   Here we waited for our Capt to procure a pilot till near noon then went by hack to Davenport and ferried over to Rock Island   Stop at the Graham house   don't like it

Monday Morning 10th   off at 8   About 1 Inch Snow up Rock River

Tuesday Morning Michigan City 11th Apr   clear with sharp frost & Ice   Tellegraph home   off for Lafayette 91 miles at 8   distance from here to Chicago 55

April 1854 Wednesday 12th Evening   reach home having reached Lafayette yesterday before noon   dined at the City Hotel   called upon N[oah] S. Thompson[27] was introduced to his wife and took tea with them.   Mrs Thompson makes a very favorable impression and I should think she is a very amiable Lady   Having been absent over two months I am greatly rejoiced to see my family and find them in good health

Wabash April 21 1854 Friday evening[28]   Rain with

---

[27] Thompson's first wife was Jackson's sister, Kitty Ann, who died in 1852.   Jackson Diary, May 31, 1852.

[28] This entry begins a new volume of the original diary.

thunder   We are at the Indiana house in waiting for the Packet expecting to start about mid night for our new home in *Minnesota*   our company consists of myself & wife, Oscar Preston & Frank[,] Sister Prudence and little George (Alexander remaining to come through by land with some cattle)   Oliver Caldwell & Milton Morgan having started through with horses on last Tuesday[29]   We are accompanied by Mr J. H. Ray & Lady & Child & Mrs Henry Ray & child[30]

I should here say that although I thought our business here *Closed* before leaving yet I have been very busy ever since reaching home and have only been able by a vigorous effort to shape up our finances and pack up our goods and be ready to start now having been at Wabash 9 days except last Saturday[,] Saturday night and part of Sunday which time I spent in going to Somerset arranging some business there and returning.   Found very bad roads with snow, rain & sleet going & returning

And now as I am about leaving Wabash very likely for ever I should say that I have lived here since November 1833 being over 20 years.   Have seen this country a wilderness and witnessed its gradual rise & progress, was here when it was organized for Judicial purposes attended its first election.   Saw this town (now numbering some 12 or 13 hundred souls) before the Stakes were driven to indicate the corners.

In short I have seen the day of small things here and it gives me pleasure to remember them

Here I have lived since a boy of 17   Here have I en-

[29] Oliver Caldwell was Mrs. Jackson's brother, and Milton Morgan was a son of Jackson's sister.
[30] For Jackson's estimate of expenses for four persons from Wabash to Lakeland, see the Appendix, *post*, p. 224.

joyed my youthfull aspirations Here passed from youth to manhood Here my schemes of youthfull ambition have been cherished—disappointed or accomplished I leave Wabash not without many regrets on account of being separated from my nearest surviving relatives

To make this permanent separation with my aged and venerated Father is indeed painfull. It is also painfull to part with my only surviving sister Mrs Morgan   We have also many other relatives and friends that we regret to be separated from Our wives also leave an aged Mother and Brothers & Sisters and other relatives and many valued friends and associates But we go with buoyent hope of future Happiness & prosperity Good health long life &c Yet we cannot but be apprehensive that *this* farewell may be "Farewell for ever" But the bell rings and we are off at one Oclock

Packet Saturday evening 8 Oclock At Lockport find we can go no further in this direction on account of Breaks between this & Carrollton 6 miles. This distance we could make in wagons but our goods are unloaded at Logansport on account of same break and no chance of getting them here or forward if they were here so we remain aboard and return to Logansport rather blue Capt Petree refuses to refund any part of our fare (to Lafayette) We stop at the Burnett house to *wait* and consult what further measures to pursue Think of re-shipping to Toledo and taking Rail road from there to Chicago

Logansport April 1854 Sunday 23rd   warm & Pleasant. have nothing to do but wait at the Burnet house at an expense of some 5 or 6 $ pr day with our Teams ahead and our harness & other household goods here behind a break that may detain us a week or two with 60 or 75 acres of Ground in Minnesota distant some 600 miles to be plowed and planted yet this spring I need not say that I feel *fidgety* decidedly

Afternoon—News from the break more favorable prospect of passing on Wednesday This is cheering and we think we will not attempt to escape at the "east gate" (Toledo) but wait as patiently as we can till we can go on Meet Mr Bird who thinks we can pass the break by wednesday evening without much doubt

Monday 24th warm & pleasant See the capt of Boat G H Standart who still has our goods aboard and gives us some encouragement that he will not unload our goods but wait and go on below as soon as he can pass

Delphi April 1854 Tuesday 25th warm & pleasant Left Logansport in hacks at 2 oclock and reached here about 8 last evening and stay at the Buford house. Call on D. I. [Jackson] this morning. Our whole crowd is here except Mr Ray who remained at Logan[sport] to urge forward the goods and come on with them. Walk over to Pittsburg with my Brother in the afternoon Meet Mr Aulds at Pittsburg who is recently from our neighborhood in Minnesota

Delphi April 26th (Wednesday) 1854. Lodged last night again at the Buford house where we took break fast on account of little Sarah Ellen being sick and Sister Ellen Jane being in rather bad health Walk over to Pittsburg with Mr Ray who reached here last evening with news that our goods would probably be here to day in which case we will be under headway again this afternoon At 5 oclock bid adieu to Bro. D Imlay and Sister Ellen Jane and take packet for Lafayette still ahead of our goods

Lafayette Thursday Apr 27 Cold & misty with very unpleasant north wind remain all day at City Hotel Our goods still behind the break. Call on N. S. Thompson at the Drug store A tedious long cold day

Friday 28th Severe frost ground frozen somewhat Afternoon more pleasant. put in part of the time gathering Locus [Locust?] seed. Evening just after going to bed the packet arrives when I get up & Dress & go down to Landing Hear that the water is let in that light boats may pass to night Supposing our goods would arrive before or about daylight I conclude to go by Packet and meet them to have them landed at the Railroad Meet our boat about midnight and return & receive our goods in person at the depot and on

Saturday morning 29th get our goods aboard of the New Albany & Salem R R and absolutely start again at 9 Oclock [31] pass Michigan City at six & reach Chicago at about 10 stop at the Merchants hotel where we must remain over Sunday

Chicago April 1854 Sunday 30th rather a pleasant day Frank is quite sick from having taken cold Mrs J. H. Ray is also complaining and none of us complain of being well though we do complain of being impatient to get away from this miserable old House By the way the Merchants Hotel is a great humbug Kept by a hard Yankee who claims to be all the way from Down East. He is evidently making money just now by crowding his house too full

Chicago May 1st 1854 Monday morning. pleasant Mr

---

[31] The New Albany and Salem Railroad traversed Indiana from New Albany on the Ohio River to Michigan City and thence westward to Calumet. Meyer, *History of Transportation*, 508.

Ray goes forward with the ballance of our Company except myself and I remain to get our goods from the depot of the Mich Southern R R to the Galena [and Chicago Union] Depo[t] which I succeed in doing by One oclock and in the afternoon see them aboard the cars and am now waiting for the night train[32]

Warren May 1854 Tuesday 2nd Meet my family and the rest of our company here this morning before breakfast Wait here all day for our goods which are to be here to night. Cool & Windy vegetation more backward here than on the Wabash

Wednesday 3rd Goods are here Packed up & off at 2 We take stage at 5 for Galena

Thursday 4th Galena Reached here last night at 11 stop at the Bradley Take Steamer Royal Arch for our destination to start at noon None of us well to day For myself I am down with Billious fever and taking medicine of my own prescribing Off at 4 P.M and on the Mississippi before sun set[33]

[32] The Galena and Chicago Union Railroad was completed to Galena in 1854. Paxson, in Wisconsin Academy of Sciences, *Transactions,* vol. 17, part 1, p. 260.

[33] In a letter dated January 30, 1898, Jackson related to his grandson, Raymond A. Jackson, the following incident of the journey to Minnesota:

". . . We reached Galena early in the morning by stage. I went aboard the 'Royal Arch' at once and learned that she was going up to Minnesota at 10 Oclock. I asked if he [*the captain*] could take us up. On learning that we wanted to go to Lakeland . . . he promptly answered that he could not take us as they were not going up the St. Croix this trip. That the other steamer the Lady Franklin would go up tomorrow and would make the trip up the St. Croix. The Lady Franklin was a hard looking little old craft, and I had already been delayed about a week. Had a farm in Minnesota to seed. My men & teams would be there waiting and my plows, harness and other supplies for housekeeping would be brought up on the steamer with us. . . . I claimed fraternal consideration and the captain . . . became affable . . . saying he would go out and see if there was anything else that wanted to go up the St. Croix. . . . In less than thirty minutes he

Steamer Royal Arch Mississippi Friday May 5   My health is much improved to day   fever broke up.   Feel weak.   Weather fine   Lowlands quite green with many new varieties of flowers in bloom

Lakeland May 1854 Saturday 6th   Weather has been fine to day   Reach this place about 3 this afternoon and debark and move our goods from the Landing to our own premises where we propose to sleep at home

Cottage Spring May 1854 Sunday 7th   pleasant day our furniture being partly packed up and partly open and piled round in our way we do not have a very comfortable Sunday for our first at our new home

Monday 8th   Haul a load of wood and in the afternoon start the plow   Rain with Thunder

returned, reporting that he could find nothing else for the St. Croix but he had made up his mind to take us aboard. We soon had our stuff several dray loads aboard and were wheeling up the great Mississippi on a fine large new side wheeler with a captain that seemed to understand his business as well as his fraternal duties. At Lakeland . . . he landed our property and ourselves on the sandy beach and without going on up to Stillwater winded his beautiful craft and returned, having made a run of about 40 or 50 miles to oblige us.

"I have never met the captain since, but have always felt that I owed him or some other Mason a large fraternal debt that I might never be able to pay. But the next day the old Lady Franklin which we had left in the harbor at Galena steamed up and followed us as far as Lake Pepin, where she sank in deep water. . . . Had we been aboard and been lucky enough to get into a life boat and all of us reach the shore, our farm tools and summer supplies and house furniture would have been a total loss. Our farm must have gone unplanted and our ruin complete."

According to Merrick, however, in his *Upper Mississippi*, 278, it was nearly two years later—in the fall of 1856—that the "Lady Franklin" sank. Russell Blakeley, in his "History of the Discovery of the Mississippi and the Advent of Commerce in Minnesota," in *Minnesota Historical Collections*, 8:401, 403, mentions the "Lady Franklin" among the steamboats in the upper Mississippi trade in 1855 and 1856. E. H. Gleim was the captain of the "Royal Arch." See Blakeley, in *Minnesota Historical Collections*, 8:394. A typewritten copy of the letter quoted above is in the Jackson Papers. The original is owned by Raymond A. Jackson.

Tuesday 9th Cold rain from the S. W. with stiff wind

Wednesday 10th Cool *Windy* Plant one acre of corn one half of the yellow dent and the ballance of the 8 Row and other early garden corn

Thursday 11th morning cool & frosty—very pleasant Plant our early potatoes. Set some Seed Onions Cabbage turnips &c also some Peas Lettuce Cucumbers Parsnips Onions & Parsley & Peaches

Sunday 14th Pleasant Write to Mother Caldwell and William [34]

Monday 15th Very pleasant go over to Hudson pay 16⅔ for Coffee and 90c for a hoe [and] 25c for brooms

Tuesday 16th Rains all day with stiff wind from E & N. E.

Wednesday 17 Rain again with wind same as yesterday a few short intermissions or rather remissions in the afternoon

Thursday 18th almost clear with light frost Beautifull morning Ground thoroughly wet with 2 days constant rain yet Mr Tyler is going to harrowing this afternoon Roads good

Friday 19th Showery with one shower of small hail. afternoon Pleasant. sow three acres of Oats between and after shower

Saturday 20th Pleasant—with rather too stiff a wind for sowing oats at 10. Afternoon pleasant Receive our Bedsteads—f[reigh]t. 1050

Sunday 21 beautiful Morning & day Walk down to the lake shore with the boys (Oscar & Preston) Prudence

---

[34] Elizabeth Alexander Caldwell, Mrs. Jackson's mother, was the widow of General William Caldwell. Their son William was Mrs. Jackson's youngest brother. Helm, *Wabash County*, 246; Jackson Diary, August 24, 1864.

& George both sick last night and still sick Martha is also complaining

Sunday 28th   weather fine   For the past week we have enjoyed *delightful spring* warm with fine breezes and occasional showers   Finished our Oats early in the week and commenced planting our Cornfield on Friday 26th (Eclipse)

Sunday June 4th 1854 For the past week the weather has been delightfull—would be hot if it was not for our fine breezes   Mornings & evenings cool & mostly still— with breeze coming up at from 8 to 10 oclock A.M.   The prairie is now a beautiful green interspersed with beautiful flowers in great abundance & variety.   The wild rose made its appearance yesterday morning and is welcome as well as beautiful   We are introduced to some beautiful stranger almost every day in some wild and rare flower.   Some of these flowers must be preserved—not that they can ever be made any more beautiful or arranged with any better taste than now   But this great Prairie flower garden as arranged by the hand of the Creator is now exposed to the plow & the lowing herds are already making their paths and selecting their shades and watering places and it is plain that the native beauty must give way to the artificial   we finished planting our corn at noon yesterday and went fishing—caught but one   Left our net with Miss Bonsell and Perrin

Monday 5th   Beautiful rain which is much needed. lasts most of the day   some thunder & a good deal of rain   We had 2 fine fish sent us last night as our dividend on net. weight 17^{lb}

Tuesday 6th   Cold Cloudy and Windy

Sunday 11th   warm & pleasant   The last part of the

week has been very fine spring or summer weather. Drove to Saint Paul yesterday with 2000 lb Flour and returned last night

Friday 16th Henry Ray arrives from Wabash Bro. Alexander has gone back after a stray animal will probably reach [here] tomorrow or next day

Saturday 17 Bro. A. E. reaches home for dinner. warm we have not seen him since the night of the 21st April when we started from Wabash He started with cattle May 11th We cannot ferry the lake to day on Account of Wind

Sunday 18th clear, warm and calm. The Ferryman are [sic] anxious and the boys are willing to bring the cattle over to day but I insist on respecting the christian sabbath or the first day of the week by our example and trusting to providence for good weather tomorrow

Monday 19th Morning too windy to ferry Thunder & Rain, Sunshine and wind. Evening Rain

Tuesday 20th pleasant Too windy to ferry Evening get a few cattle over

Wednesday 21 Undertake the getting over of Cattle in person and finish just after dark some 15 or 20 swimming after the last load Hard ferry and hard ferryman Mr Oliver the proprietor is certainly as near destitute of common politeness or common civility as he could well be[35]

Sunday 25 Pleasant. Mr J H Ray as well as his son and hands are with us expecting to go on up the Minnesota where he has located to morrow

Sunday July 2nd Weather excessively hot but tempered

[35] John Oliver with his family of sons settled in Lakeland about 1849. The elder Oliver and his son John had been harbor pilots at Boston. Warner and Foote, *Washington County*, 413, 422.

with a breeze that keeps us from suffering Beautiful corn growing weather Never saw crops come forward so fast

Sunday 9th Cool enough to be pleasant. Most of the time since last Sunday has been hot. Beautiful thunder shower friday and quite cool saturday

Friday 14th Receive a letter from Bro D I Jackson also one from H[ezekiah] Caldwell[36] also one from W. I. Ford Esq also a funeral notice all announcing the death of My Father at Wabash on the night of the 26th June This announcement though I cannot say it was altogether unexpected was startling and the bereavement seems to fall the more heavily on account of the great distance we are from him He is reported to have died of Cholera. Taken suddenly on Monday evening 26th June and died about midnight at the house of Jas Langhery[?] in Wabash.

This is my second parental bereavement and it is perhaps not improper here to reaffirm what I have frequently said before that to their care during my youth & the good example they have constantly set before me and for the good moral and religious training received from them during my youth I am indebted for what of usefullness I possess. I have this comfort however that I have no recollection of ever speaking an unkind word to either of them But to the day of their decease I should have considered a request or reasonable command as binding upon me as though I was still a boy and subject to their control

Sunday 16th Warm but pleasant Mr W. Sweetser of Wabash is here and seems well pleased with the country

---

[36] A brother of Mrs. Jackson. Helm, *Wabash County*, 247.

Sunday 23rd warm pleasant attend preaching at Lakeland by Mr Gibson the first we have attended in the territory[37]

Cottage Spring Aug. 1854 Sunday 27th weather beautiful Finished our Oats harvest yesterday. gathered a grist of Corn during the week within 90 days from the time it came up Our dent corn continues to grow rapidly and fill heavily but I have fears of its ripening

Cottage Spring Sept 1854 Sunday 3rd Pleasant. during the past week we have had heavy rains say Wednesday Thursday & Friday Drove to Saint Paul on Thursday with a load of Potatoes got good and wet staid all night peddled out my Potatoes and returned on Friday through the rain again accompanied by Mr [Lemuel] Bolles Miss [Harriet A.] Newell & Oscar.[38] home after dark

Sunday 10th weather continues rainy went over to Mr Fowlers near Red Rock yesterday[39] returned late last night with the Bull Zac Taylor

Sunday 17th Still continues rainy[,] that is unsettled Has rained [not] less than half the time for the past week Commenced our threshing yesterday but did not get done owing to rain in the evening

Sunday 24th Sept weather settled and pleasant Milton & I Finley Morgan[40] left for Wabash day before yesterday. No frost yet

[37] The Reverend A. Gibson was pastor of the First Baptist Church of River Falls, Wisconsin.
[38] For Bolles see *ante,* p. 11. Miss Newell taught the first school in Lakeland Township at the home of Elias McKean. Warner and Foote, *Washington County,* 413; *post,* p. 162.
[39] Biographical sketches of the brothers William and Giles H. Fowler, who are listed in the 1860 census schedules as farmers living at Newport, are given in Warner and Foote, *Washington County,* 374, 383. Jackson, *post,* p. 204, mentions a Seymore Fowler.
[40] Jackson's nephew. See *post,* p. 143.

Sunday Oct. 1st Morning partly cloudy & foggy, But soon clears off and is a beautiful and pleasant fall day Or indeed more like a summer day. As we have had no frost yet and but for our Almanacs we might suppose it still summer The weather for the past week has been delightful excepting yesterday when it rained nearly all day. We have been engaged mostly cutting corn & Hawling Oats to Stillwater Our Corn is ripening beautifully notwithstanding the long spell of warm wet weather beginning late in August and continuing some 3 weeks when our corn seemed as though it never *would* ripen. There has been no trouble about corn *growing* But the trouble seemed to get it to *ripen* And if frost had have come at the fifteenth of Sept. Our corn would have been almost ruined. But thanks to a good overruling Providence Our crop is now safe from frost and is a heavy yield

Sunday 8th mostly cloudy Past week mostly delightful fall weather. Our first frost was on Wednesday morning 4th when we had a sharp frost since which the weather has seemed like autumn Attended Lodge at Stillwater on Monday night (2nd)

Monday 9th Surprised this morning by the appearance of Bro. D. Imlay from Delphi

Friday 13th Bro Imlay left for Ind. last night as we suppose, having gone over to Hudson yesterday and several steamers having passed last night.

Sunday 15th several sharp frosts during past week with cold rain Mr. A. Newell started below yesterday

Saturday 21 Rain Receive Threshing machine from Piqua for Mr Edwards and ride up to give them notice. Home after night

Sunday 22nd Pleasant Attend Preaching at 3 by Mr

Gibson at Lakeland Past week has been rough weather in the main

Sunday 29th Past week has been mostly pleasant Oct. weather. Was out to Mr Edwards' on Thursday Returned about Midnight saw several Prairie fires Rode near one late in the night with plenty of Darkness to exhibit its frightful beauties to good advantage

Cottage Spring November 1854 Sunday 5th Cool Most of past week has been clear & cold fall weather Ice ½ inch thick friday & saturday morning Been engaged setting up a Moffitt Threshing machine for past 3 days [41]

Sunday 12th Cold Worked with machine till Thursday noon when we were stopped by rain with thunder afternoon chilly & rainy and on friday morning the 10th we find about an inch of snow with strong symptoms of approaching winter. On Friday night the quantity of snow was doubled with pretty fair winter on Saturday This morning was almost clear with signs of thawing but the snow has not gone yet (evening) clear & frosty

Sunday 19 Killed our hogs on Tuesday & Wednesday Thursday went to Stillwater Friday & Saturday cold

Sunday 26th Cold Clear & windy a light snow fell yesterday which gives a little when the sun shines a good deal like winter

Sunday Dec 3rd Beautiful winter day some 3 or 4 inches of snow Lake froze over during the early part of the week Write to William & Oliver Caldwell

Sunday 10th December fine winter day past week Do. Walk up to the post office at Lakeland We have already had a good many days that would pass for cold weather

---

[41] See *post*, p. 194.

in Indiana, though we lack the rainy muddy sleety weather of that latitude

Sunday 17th Wintry. During the past week the weather has been warm for the season. snow mostly disappeared under the influence of south winds and sun shine. But yesterday we had a regular snow storm which lasted all day & till bed time This morning we have some 4 inches of snow But the north east wind of last evening has ceased and it is winter but not very cold

Sunday December 24th Pleasant winter — sunshine and thawing even in the shade. On Monday of past week went down to Mr Fowlers and returned on Tuesday and on Friday drive a load of flour to Stillwater for Mr Bolles Mostly cold clear frosty weather till yesterday with pretty fair snow which has disappeared on the south hillsides in the roads so that our sledding is spoiled except upon unbroken tracks Tomorrow is to be Christmas but we see no signs of it yet We tell the boys that "Santa Claus has not learned the way up to Minnesota yet["] We dined with Capt Tyler on Thursday (Thanksgiving)[42]

Sunday 31 Pleasant On Monday Tuesday & Wednesday of past week the weather continued to grow milder. And on Thursday morning it was *very* cold clear & frosty. Clear all day with but little wind and but little snow yet no signs of thawing Friday — cold south wind Saturday warmer but not as warm as we would expect from the continued south wind

[42] Before Lincoln appointed the last Thursday of November, 1864, as Thanksgiving Day, a precedent followed by presidents ever since, a day late in December was usually named as Thanksgiving Day by the governors of Minnesota.

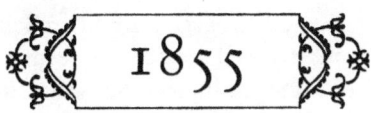

1855

18 and 55 Monday Jany 1st   Newyears day in Minnesota I suppose is cellebrated at the towns where there is plenty of whiskey by some noise and fun   But in the Country — in the quiet country where we have the good fortune to live there is no extraordinary doings   The day is mostly cloudy with south wind warm enough to husk corn from the shock with bare hands

Tuesday 2nd   find the snow and ground thawing before day light under the influence of the continued south wind. continues warm all day and as muddy as it ever gets in Minnesota

Wednesday 3rd   A Rain of last night wound up with sleet and snow this morning   Indeed yesterday and to day have been regular Indiana days

Sunday 7   More moderate Thursday Friday & Saturday having been stormy & wintry

Sunday 14th   fine winter weather   write to William & Oliver

Sunday 21st   very cold — almost clear with gentle wind from the North   good sledding since this snow fell say about 5th

Sunday 28th   cold   The past week has been Minnesota winter *I reckon*   cold — mostly clear with occasional light snows. Walk over to Hudson with Mr. Martin[1] to meeting — (Methodist) congregation numbered 22 ½ males & ½ females. mostly well dressed and respectable appearing Preaching rather ordinary Ice seems sound Recd a letter from Bro D. I. yesterday

Sunday Feb 4th Attend church at Hudson with my wife & sister Prudence hear elder Gibson preach to a respectable appearing congregation. hear much better singing than we commonly hear. Afternoon — write to Bro D. I. A E with his wife & Martha attend church at night

Tuesday 6th   visit at Mr. [Sterling] Jones[2] fine winter a little snow Mr. Jones is a Delphi man We sold 200 Bus corn yesterday at 80c for the Woods[3]

Lakeland Minnesota Feb 1855 Sunday 11th Snow Sledding still good write to M. Whiteside

Sunday 18 Pleasant winter. Preparations made for starting to Lake Superior on Tuesday morning next with a load of pork for Mr. Bowles [*Bolles?*]. Learn that he has given up the trip and I am not much sorry. I was to have been "Supercargo" for two sled loads & drive one myself

Sunday 25th Real Minnesota winter I think Friday night, yesterday last night and to day so far (3 Oclock) the coldest weather I ever experienced. Having no thermometer I can only guess that it is at least 30° below 0. perfectly clear with a light breeze from the N. W. Altogather [*sic*] too cold and dry for the frost to stick to our

---

[1] Probably Albert Martin, a farmer at Afton. Census schedules, 1860.
[2] Jones came to Wisconsin from Indiana, and in 1850 settled near Hudson. Folsom, *Fifty Years in the Northwest*, 169.
[3] This corn was sold to lumbermen for use in the woods as feed for oxen or horses.

whiskers. Never saw the air look more clear   Light not intense but bright   Sun shines perfectly clear and yet no signs of thawing

1855 Minnesota Mar. Sunday 4th   after steady winter ever since the 3rd of Jany, it now seems spring   The wind turned south upon the very night dividing Feb & Mar. on winter & spring Since which it has gradually grown warmer.   Yesterday the snow failed fast under the influence of pure sunshine.   To day is mostly cloudy but wind in the south & still thawing gradually   write to I Finley Morgan

Sunday March 11th   Cloudy with cool N. E. wind though not cold enough to freeze yet it does not thaw much   past week has been *spring*—weather mostly pleasant for the season   snow has nearly all disappeared   Had a little rain one night which is the first since about the first of Jany.   Frequent freeze & thawing with *mud* & melting snow   Mr Martin returned yesterday from the woods

Sunday 18th   Past week has been winter again.   The cold N. E. wind of last Sunday continued all day Monday with increased severity shifting a little more to the east in the evening and snowing.   continued to snow all day Tuesday and against Wednesday morning we had some 6 or 8 inches of good sollid snow but not very cold.   Too cold to thaw much however   Thursday about the same   Friday mostly clear with fair prospect of thaw during the forenoon but afternoon is colder   Saturday 17th was mostly clear with sharp N. W. wind which drifted a light snow of last night into the tracks that had been pretty well beaten during the past few days   The roads may now be considdered *good*   Met with the district school trustees yesterday to designate a site for a school house (Having been chosen a trustee at the annual meeting on the 1st Tuesday of the present Inst) The other members being Mr Perrin & Mr [George W.] Leach. To day is mostly cloudy with south wind and a little snow

Sunday 25 mostly cloudy rather pleasant Past week has been emphatically Winter: especially the forepart sledding continued good till Friday when it was spoiled by sun shine & south wind Saturday mostly clear but cold. Today the prospect of spring seems doubtful—does not thaw as much as it froze last night

Monday 26th The rain of last night at dark ceased soon after dark Then came a violent wind storm accompanied with light snow Today is blustry & cold with occasionally a little fine drifting snow.

Tuesday 27th Morning cold & clear with stiff north breeze decidedly winterish

Sunday April 1st Pleasant clear rather cool for the season snow all gone except the banks. ground not thawed through yet Write to S. P. Bonsall

Sunday 8th April 1855 Easter sunday fine weather Clear—dry—windy Spring is gradually creeping upon us. ground not thawed through yet—Though the surface is settled & dry Fire on the prairie occupies our attention to day Ploughing next week

Sunday 15th Spring comes in fine first thunders on thursday. Have 5 acres of Oats sown & some wheat ground plowed finished marketing our corn at Hudson at 90 c a few tulips have made their appearance upon the dry looking prairie These welcome harbinger[s] of spring are cheering after six months of Winter Lake is still closed against steam boats but must open in a few days if the weather continues as warm & fine as at present

Sunday 22nd   delightful spring weather   Past week has been mostly warm dry & rather windy though not unpleasantly so   The lake is clear of Ice and on Wednesday (the 18th) The steam boat *Excelsior* came puffing up perfectly crowded with passengers bound for *Minnesota*   Mr. Martin left us on Tuesday   I have been engaged most of the week getting in logs   Had a letter from Will also one from Milton.   Rather windy for comfort to day

Sunday 29th   Warm—beautiful spring weather. Have been harrowing in wheat and ploughing for oats during the past week.   Oliver & *Will* Caldwell reached here from Wabash on Tuesday with D[aniel H.] Tyner[4] & Geo. Hoover   Spring is coming forward rapidly.   Sold some Oats & corn during the week at 70 & 100 at the barn

Cottage Spring May 1855 Sunday 6th   Weather still continues beautiful.   Indeed I never saw spring come in so rapidly as for the last 4 weeks   A light rain of last Sunday night brought out the Plum blossoms and many green things   Apple blows are now coming out   I have finished sowing oats (unless we sow a few acres above the meadow) and been hawling lumber most of the week   Mess[rs.] Tyner[,] Hoover & McKackum are with us.   Write to Milton

Sunday 13   Warm—pleasant—Dry   Had some pretty sharp frosts during the week—but it is now warm and very dry   We commenced planting corn yesterday (12) which is full two weeks earlier than we commenced last

---

[4] Tyner settled at Mankato, where he engaged in the livery business. In 1860 he was elected sheriff of Blue Earth County.   *Mankato, Its First Fifty Years, 1852–1902*, 319 (Mankato, 1903).

year. Corn planted now cannot grow till we have rain
We have now lived in this climate one year and can say
I like the climate well. Dont owe a dime in any store
nor have we bought any goods on credit Have had no
Doctor upon the premises ex cept one who came to buy
a horse He presented no bill, nor had he bank bills
enough to buy a pony—(Hard times)

Sunday 20th Warm and *Dry* We are still without our
spring rains and suffering for rain. dont see how any
thing can grow yet the wild grass looks fine & flourish-
ing. pasture good flowers abundant but *flour* scarce and
held at from 10.50 to 14 $ pr bbl Meal Corn & Oats scarce
and high Oats could be sold at 1.00 potatoes 1.00 Corn
100 to 150 Wheat 2.00 and this with steam boats passing
daily from the lower Mississippi. We have 18 acres of
Corn planted and 15 acres more plowed but it is too dry
to grow Looks like rain to day however and I still have
faith that if we plant in season we shall reap at harvest

Sunday 27th Done planting corn except about a dozen
rows. A beautiful thunder shower of last Sunday night
with a hot sun shine on Monday (90 degrees in the shade)
and another good rain last night makes things look *green*
Write to Will. Expect to enter upon the duties of Assessor for the 2nd district of this county this week

Lakeland June 1855 Sunday 3rd Pleasant. Friday &
Saturday mornings were frosty Mr Sargent & family are
boarding with us weather continues dry

Sunday 10th Weather pleasant but still continues dry.
I have been travelling over the country most of the past
week and never saw a poorer prospect for crops especially
corn. Wheat looks midling well but corn & Oats must
fail unless we have rain *soon*. Our corn is badly cut by

the worm and squirrel[5] not more than half of a 33 acre field standing. must go to replanting tomorrow

Sunday 17th But little rain yet Think the corn & Oats of this district may be set down at less than half a crop with all the rain needed from this on And as almost a failure without rain soon Have finished replanting our corn but it looks distressed

Sunday 24th June Attend meeting at Afton a new town laid off by Messrs Getchell[,] Thomas & others 3 or four miles down the lake shore.[6] Attend the burying of a child of Mr Stouffer which is the second death in his family within a week from *Putrid sore throat* This is the first funeral I have attended since settling here. It seems pleasant to meet with a congregation of Christians and I should think that most of those assembled this afternoon are professors of Christianity. It also seems pleasant to witness the studied concealment of sectarian names open avowals of Christianity. An Episcopalian Minister from Saint Paul was to have preached but did not come. Bro Putnam filled the place as well as his health would allow[7]

Wednesday 27th Had a good heavy thunder show[e]r last night which wet the ground thoroughly this with a few light showers last week will start the green things up rapidly Met the other assessors at Stillwater on Monday 25th[8] Staid over night on Monday night

Sunday July 8th On last Sunday (1st) I attended meet-

---

[5] Jackson probably refers to cutworms and gophers.

[6] Afton was platted by Ralzaman and Joseph Haskell, Hewitt L. Thomas, and Charles S. Getchell in May, 1855. Warner and Foote, *Washington County*, 402.

[7] The Reverend Simon Putnam was the first pastor of the Congregational Church at Afton. Warner and Foote, *Washington County*, 403.

[8] The other assessors were W. H. Johnson and J. C. Mason. Warner and Foote, *Washington County*, 323.

ing at afton at 3 P.M. Thence in company with Mr Martin drove to Stillwater where it was necessary for me to meet the board of Co Commissioners I remained at Stillwater till Thursday when I returned by steamer Regulator For nearly two weeks we have had frequent abundant rains and great growing weather. I have not yet completed the work of assessing & returning my list. had a letter yesterday from Bro D. I. the first for a long time

Sunday 15th Very warm with thunder Have had frequent rains during past week. Cut our Rye must cut early oats within a week. shall wind up my labors as assessor about Tuesday next when I expect to go to the plow or cradle with all the vigor at my command Have not had good health for the past week Improving the last 2 or 3 days. My old lung dificulty has troubled me somewhat with Billious symptoms I am in hopes that plenty of out door work will straighten me up again. I feel quite anxious to quit these books & figures (assessment papers) and get hold of the plow again I should not have engaged in it in the first place if I had not been poor I would much rather plow

Sunday 22nd During past week we have had some hot weather A great time for corn & weeds to grow. Finished my assessment duties & made my report on Tuesday returned home on Wednesday and plowed corn the rest of the week Like this better than assessing

Sunday July 29th Weather for past week has been delightfull summer Have been engaged in haying Our hay owing to the Drought in the spring is quite light I stand haying mutch better than I expected—for I was not stout by any means at the commencement But am evidently improving Atended meeting this forenoon at Afton with Mrs Jackson Alex & Lady attend at Lakeland this afternoon. first meeting held in our district school house which is in sight though distant near 2 miles Harvest this week.

Minnesota August 1855 Sunday 5th In company with my wife attend church & sunday school at Lakeland

Wednesday 8th Was sick with billious fever yesterday & day before. am well enough to drive with Martha & Frank to Stillwater to day. This is my birthday (39) Only one year this side of 40 is it possible a mear boy. can hardly appreciate that I am a man grown and responsible for my own actions till I am forty

Sunday August 12th Attend Meeting at afton in the forenoon with my wife & in the afternoon at Lakeland with the boys (Oscar & Preston) & Mr Putnam. Weather fine Eat bread to day made from wheat of our own raising ground yesterday at Bolles Though I have kept house for eleven years I never have eat wheat bread of my own raising before. we raised our corn bread last year I of course eat wheat bread of my own raising when a boy at home. But have bought all the bread stuff for our table ever since we have kept house. This seems an Epoch of some importance in my history, and realy seems quite a comfort. Especialy as money is growing somewhat scarce

Sunday 19th Write to *Will* & Mother do not go to meeting

Sunday Aug 26th Cool. Afternoon attend meeting & S[unday] S[chool] Pleasant

Sept Sunday 3 Mr Baker & Mrs. Sargent are with us do not go to meeting today

Sunday 9th Pleasant Attend (with Oliver) meeting

at Afton. Finished our grain harvest during the past week. Have a pretty fair crop all stacked in good order Have some hay to cut yet for our cattle Corn appears quite backward being now in good order for roasting

Sunday 16th Attend Sunday School with the boys (Oscar & Preston) get there too late

Sunday 23rd Cloudy & Rainy. We have had a week of very wet weather A very heavy rain last night accompanied with thunder Corn continues to grow green We have been trying to make some wild hay but make a bad out getting it dry

Thursday 27 frost in the neighborhood but none here. Mercury stood at 39 at day light.

Minnesota Oct. 1855 Friday 5th Sharp frost—the first killing frost. Mercury stood at 27° at sunrise Morning clear afternoon cloudy with light squalls of dry snow from the N. W.

Sunday 21st Beautiful day smoky sunshiny & windy Ride out to the *Mounds* neighborhood with Martha & the children in the P.M.[9] find the ground *grey* with snow this morning which soon melts off Day rather dull & chilly mostly cloudy. Our Corn is much injured by frost. Had plenty of time to ripen But the cold & wet weather of August & Sept prevented it from ripening Since the frost the weather has been mostly fine We had rain enough in Sept to make up what we lacked in May & June I should think. I am not well suited with Minnesota weather this season

1855 Minnesota November Sunday 4th Weather fine

---

[9] Jackson probably refers to the conspicuous mounds in section 8 in Afton Township, southwest of Lakeland. They were sometimes known as "Bissell's Mounds," named for Elijah Bissell, who made a claim near them in 1842. Warner and Foote, *Washington County*, 399.

Mostly clear with pretty sharp frosty mornings Some fires in the Prairies Have been gathering corn during past week. finished that *standing* on west side of field Corn only *tolerable* as to quality and yield *light* say 20 bus. pr acre Our hogs have done well upon acorns

Sunday 11th Misty cloudy rainy. Most of past week has been fine weather for harvesting corn

Sunday 18th Cold. Mercury 12 at sunrise Walked down to Daytons with Oscar J Holton Helm is with us to dinner

Sunday 25th Past week has been mostly winter Some 2 or three in of snow fell last night which added to what we had before makes some 4 to 6 in snow. Sledding good. The lake is pretty well closed in front of us—no boats for more than a week. The last boat of the season probably left Saint Paul on Monday or Tuesday for down river Navigation is now closed and we are shut out from the southern world for the coming five months. Alexander sets house keeping in the north wing on friday of the past week. Our families having kept but one table since living in the Territory

1855 Minnesota December Sunday 2nd cool windy past week mostly pleasant winter. Rather warm for snow to last—indeed our sledding is fairly spoiled till we get some more snow I sold a load of corn at Stillwater on Wednesday at 100c This opens high for corn in the ear and rather an inferior article. Chickens 4 $ pr Dz Had a letter from my Nephew I. Finley Morgan. Dated at Winona. Learn that his father & mother & Milton & his wife and C [*etc.?*] are all there. answer this evening

Sunday 9th Blustry past week mostly pleasant commenced snowing yesterday about noon with wind in the north—snow wet as water and came endwise like pitch forks. Helped Mr [A. D.] Kingsley thrash[10] did not get done We are to thrash the coming week

Sunday 23 Mercury stands at 24 below 0 this morning This is one degree colder than I ever saw indicated Past 2 weeks has been mostly good winter weather Have had a tedious time thrashing—the threshers having come on Monday evening the 10th and staid till Friday 21st after noon—(eleven days) threshing

480	Bushels of Oats	
121	"	Wheat
20	"	Rye
30	"	Barley
651		

Sunday 30th fine winter During past week the Mercury has stood most of the time below 0 and was down on Monday morning 30 degrees below This I am willing to admit is cold enough to satisfy me Walk down to Catfish[11] Cross on the ice which is now very sound

[10] Kingsley was postmaster at Lakeland from 1855 to 1858. Warner and Foote, *Washington County*, 418.
[11] Catfish Bar extends out from the east shore of Lake St. Croix near Afton. Upham, *Geographic Names*, 571; Merrick, *Upper Mississippi*, 192.

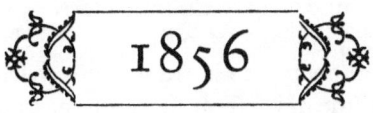

Sunday Jany 6 1856   Wintry.   Have spent most of the past week cutting wood down to Catfish mound   New years day not excepted   Upon that day Oscar (now 9 years old) accompanied me.   staid all day with Mercury at 20 below 0 at sun rise.   this is good grit   write to R. D. Helm also to D. M. Cox

Sunday 13th   Cloudy with a little snow   The past week is spoken of by old settlers as the severest weather ever experienced.   Indeed for the last six weeks the winter has been considered unusualy tight   Tuesday (8th) was particularly severe—Mercury standing 30 below 0. at daylight and holding down to about 20 with a pretty stiff Northwester.   I walked to lakeland and froze my face   On Wednesday I drove to Stillwater with Mr Bonsall to attend the Commissioners court

Sunday 20   Attend church at Lakeland with Martha (Elder Gibson.)   Sleighing bad on account of drifting last night.   Had a letter from Bro. D. I. Jackson at Renssellaer a few days since—the first for a long time—which I answer to day

Sunday 27th   clear—cold.   went to Kinnik-kinnik [*Kinnickinnick*] yesterday with the bobs.   Had to stay over night & return to day with part of a load of lumber. The small pox is in Kinnikinnic

Feb 1856 Sunday 3rd Cold & clear. yesterday was severely cold—mercury standing at 26 below 0 in the morning 10 at noon & 12 at sunset with sharp W. N. W. wind most of the day. This morning the mercury stands at 26—4 at noon & 5 at sunset but it is pleasant compared with yesterday being nearly still both days clear & dry. write to John U. Pettit M. C.[1] We visited at Mr. Jones[s] on Thursday. Mr J is a good Wisconsin farmer and well fix'd up every thing comfortable only *Water*

Sunday 10 Hazy but pleasant day Snow gives a little to day the first since winter commenced Had a visit from Messrs Jones & their ladies on friday accompanied by Mr & Mrs Perrin & Mr & Mrs Bonsall

Sunday 17 Some faint signs of spring Found a hens nest Was over to Mr Jones[']s one day during the week and exchanged some seed wheat

Sunday 24th Morning frosty—beautiful day. Snow begins to show signs of spring. Attended the Lyceum at Lakeland last evening. had quite an interesting meeting of Gents & Ladies Question Is the Liquor dealer the bigest scoundrel in the world Affirmative carried

Lakeland March 1856 Sunday 2nd Cool last week has been mostly fine weather yesterday morning however was cold Mercury standing 8 degrees below 0. but the sun soon came up with power enough to thaw the snow that was exposed.

Sunday 9th Cold Mercury stood at 18° below 0 this morning. Write to Will

Sunday 16 Attended Lyceum last night with Martha Weather keeps cool

[1] Pettit was a representative in Congress from Indiana.

Sunday 23rd Clear pleasant Had a very disagreeable Equinoxial snow storm last evening which disappears under the influence of the genial sunshine of today and leaves with perhaps less snow than we had yesterday morning The sledding may now be considered broke up. Though some sleds are still running The ground is nearly half bare

Sunday 30th Write to Will not to start as early as the 15th as the ice will not likely be out by that time Also write Mr. [J. R.] Moffitt with liberty to ship 2 machines

Cottage Spring—Lakeland April 1856 Sunday 6th The past week has been our break up. Having Rained on Tuesday evening with wet snow and continued thawing ever since except Saturday morning when it was frosty Mercury being at 24° but reached 56 during the afternoon

Sunday 13th Fine sugar day as we would call it in Indiana But we have no sugarmaking here. No making of sugar troughs—spiles—furnaces camps &c My boys will know nothing of the pleasant excitement of the hurry & bustle of the "sugar making" Sugar camps are perhaps the strongest marked localities of my boyhood. So indellably is the "sugar making" of my boyhood days fixed upon my memory that I can scarcely realize that more than thirty springs have blended with as many summers—ripened into as many mellow autumns, and been succeeded by as many frosty, blustry, ice bound, winters: since my first "sugar making" And now at this distance I can almost smell the smoke and see the blazing fire as it used to shine upon the huge forest trees through the thick black darkness of an Indiana sugarmaking night With equal distinctness can I see the pearly drops and hear the peculiar trickling of the sacharine fluid as it flows from the spiles upon a bright, frosty, sunshiny, morning—such as this

Past week has been mostly spring weather with not very distant thunder on Friday followed by a little rain in the evening. But on yesterday morning a few large drops of rain was followed by quite a shower of small hail about as big as buck shot. and that by the *steepest* kind of a north East snow storm which lasted till nearly noon. Something like 2 inches of snow must have fallen. but it mostly disappeared during the afternoon. No plowing done yet. Begin to be anxious to *tare up the ground*

Sunday April 20th Pleasant Spring weather after a pretty rough week except yesterday The lake opened about friday (17th) but as yet we have had no steam boats. Commenced plowing yesterday. ground full wet but cannot wait. As I have the whole place to manage this season with but one team, I shall have to keep moving. Write to J H Ray The early spring flowers are out in abundance

Monday 21st First boat up last night

Sunday 27th Past week has been exceedingly wet Have five acres of Oats & Grass and four acres of wheat sown the latter not harrowed on account of rain Mother Caldwell and Will arrived yesterday from Wabash I am quite unwell today with an attack of Billious fever

Cottage Spring May 1856 Sunday 4th Clear—cool—frosty Past week has been almost without sun shine. Except Monday and yesterday, I think the sun has not been seen. Every appearance now indicates fine weather Have 10 acres of wheat sown

Sunday 11th Past week has been mostly good weather Have 26 or 28 acres of wheat sowed

Sunday 18th Weather fine attended church at Lakeland Finished seeding hill field on Friday and commenced plowing in lower field Planted some small pines yesterday

Sunday 25 Weather fine Had a fine thunder shower on Friday night which made the ground rather wet to work We however go ahead with the corn ground. I commenced laying off yesterday[2]

Minesota 1856 June 1 Sunday Quite warm and pleasant. Every thing looks fresh and green The air is loaded with the fragrance of many flowers. The trees are out in their best regalia and the hills are dressed in the brightest green We drove to Afton this morning but learned that meeting had been changed to half past 2 Came home and returned again at that time heard Mr Putnam preach Finished planting corn (except the ground about the house) on Friday 30th having commenced on Monday 26th The same day that we finished last year and commenced the year before Corn planted on monday and Tuesday (soaked) is coming up handsomely I have to enter upon my duties as assesor the coming week Jonas Newell returned a week ago

Sunday 8th Walk to church at Lakeland Weather fine and has been during past week. Have been engaged partly in assessing and partly in trying to arrange a settlement with old Jonas Newell who is acting as ugly as he knows how

---

[2] Jackson evidently refers to the practice of measuring a cornfield for the purpose of setting the seed at an even distance. Since corn is seeded in rows and in separate hills, it was not easy to get a machine which would do the work, and much had to be done by hand.

Thursday 19th Went to Stillwater to procure money to pay Jonas Newell Balance on farm not being able to execute a satisfactory mortgage without a quit claim from A E returned home to go again tomorrow

Friday 20th Go again to Stillwater Mortgage my part of the farm to Mr Strong for 850$ with interest at 3 pr c pr mo and pay old Jonas up all that is due and to fall due and take a deed

Tuesday 24th in company with Mr Bonsall go to Saint Paul to witness the ceremonies of laying the corner stone of the Historical Societys building also the corner stone of the Masonic building[3]

Wednesday 25 After participating in the interesting ceremonies of yesterday and joining in a procession of (I should think) two or three hundred Masons and having a good time staid at the American and return home doing all the assessing I could on the way going & coming[4]

Sunday 29 Staid at the "half way house"[5] last night and come in this morning & attend preaching by Mr. Putnam at Afton in the afternoon Have to meet the other assessors at Stillwater tomorrow to Equalize &c

Sunday 6th July Walked down from Stillwater last night after dark after working hard there most of the week rumaging over the records. Hard work this assessing. No rest or fun for me on the 4th

Sunday 13th Worked hard at Stillwater till Thursday

---

[3] Neither of these buildings was constructed beyond partial foundations. Williams, *Saint Paul*, 363; Charles E. Mayo, "Homes and Habitations of the Minnesota Historical Society," in *Minnesota Historical Collections*, 8:106.

[4] The American House, built in 1849, was on Third Street, near Exchange, in St. Paul.

[5] The "Half Way House" was a hotel on the stage road between St. Paul and Stillwater kept by John Morgan. Folsom, *Fifty Years in the Northwest*, 63.

evening. came down in Mr Haskells wagon Went to Saint Paul on Friday bot a reaping machine and returned. rigged it up and cut some light grass yesterday. Grass is very ripe and a part of my meadow should have been cut a week or two ago The best part however is just about ripe enough

Sunday 20th Haying mostly done and in very nice order. crop good

Sunday 27th Went to Stillwater on Monday (21.) to make my return and settle with the board but there not being a q[u]orum returned without a settlement. have cut 5 acres of light wheat and as much light Oats Hay all in the barn in nice order. Weather has been very warm and mostly dry for the last month or 6 weeks Small grain must be light. Corn looks well

August 1856 Sunday 3rd Beautiful cool summer day as has been many other days though we have had a good proportion of real hot days mostly tempered by a pure breeze This is the midst of Minnesota harvest. My grain is mostly cut there being but about 12 or 13 acres of wheat yet standing and 5 or 6 of Oats. My health was somewhat impaired by the close application necessary to complete the assessors duties in time for harvest My old cough returned and has been quite annoying though I think it is now wearing off and my general health improving

Sunday August 10th 1856 Pleasant cool Summer weather During past week—have wound up harvesting except a small piece of oats too green to cut Commenced stacking Friday P.M. but was interupted yesterday morn by rain The fortieth anniversary of my birthday went off without any extraordinary commotion on Friday the 8th

Here I am forty and can scarcely believe that I am grown. can it be that Twenty years have come and gone. That twenty years have passed from the unwasted future and been enjoyed each their full number of days and then numbered with the eternal past since I was in my "teens."

But it cannot be otherwise *I am forty* and yet how little have I accomplished: Though I have never been idle— cannot endure idleness The stream of time flows with accellerated velocity as we grow older. Forty years! How long when looked at from the head of the stream and yet how short when viewed from the other end. How vividly and how indellibly is impressed upon the tablet of our memory all the windings and ripplings and little eddies of the miniature stream of our childhood We can almost feel the cool refreshing shad[e] of the bending bushes and inhale the fragrance of the tempting flowers that grew in such profusion upon its banks and were reflected in such confusion by the dancing limpid water upon which our tinny *barque* bark [*sic*] was gliding

Sunday 17th Weather continues fine Spent most of the past week in stacking. William Caldwell is going to Wabash tomorrow

Sunday 24 Fine weather. with Martha & Frank attend church at Afton

Sunday 31 Weather continues fine very dry. expect to Thrash this week

Sept 1856 Sunday 7 weather fine a little rain yesterday. Finished Thrashing Friday evening and helped Mr Kingsley yesterday Wheat turns out very poorly. Have off of 30 or 32 acres only 326 bus Oats no better. Some 260 bus from 15 acres

Sunday 14th Weather dry & warm Mercury up to 100° in the shade on the south recess With Martha & Frank attend church at Lakeland P.M.

Minnesota Sept 21st 1856 Sunday Cool cloudy pleasant. *First frost* yesterday morning Write to Will Corn ripe

Sunday 28th cool Write to I Finley Morgan from [whom] I had recd. a letter during the week (at Chatfield)

Sunday October 5 beautiful fall day have had some pretty thorough frosts and the weather is now decidedly autumnal. Dry—Windy—Smoky

Sunday 12th Beautiful day—warm—dry—Smoky, Minnesota Autumn With Martha—Mother Caldwell & Frank attend church at Afton

Sunday 19th Our beautiful autumn weather is still continued Our first election in Lakeland precinct came off last Tuesday I had been appointed one of the judges Moses Perin & Capt Tyler the other two We appointed R[euben] H Sanderson[6] & S. P. Bonsall as clerks. Votes polled 51 I vote with what is now called the republican party—in favor of J. C. Fremont for president at the coming presidential election which goes off in the States next month. As we are still under Territorial government we have no voice in that election But had I a vote I should take great pleasure in voting for Fremont and Freedom in Kansas

Sunday 26th After a rough rainy week it is rather pleasant to day Going to Stillwater tomorrow with a load of Turnips &c

---

[6] Sanderson, who settled in Lakeland in 1855, was a representative in the territorial legislature in 1857. Upham and Dunlap, *Minnesota Biographies*.

Minnesota Nov. 1856 Sunday 2 Rather winterish
Sold my Turnips last Monday at 50c except 10 bus at 40c
to close Attended Mr Perins sale yesterday

Sunday 9th Rather winterish most of past week Mercury was down one morning to 6° No snow yet. Roads fine

Sunday 16 Have been to Stillwater twice during past week with flour & Corn meal Sold the former at 4 & 4.25 & the latter from 125c pr bushel down to 2c pr lb William Caldwell returns from Wabash

Sunday 23 Snow nearly ½ inch and snowing Attended the funeral of S. P. Bonsall on Friday He was buried with *Masonic* honors. In which I joined Navigation closed Monday or Tuesday

Sunday 30th Snow about 4 inches & snowing roads good winter mild

December 1856 Sunday 7th Beautiful winter For the last 3 or 4 days the weather has been cold clear & still. Mercury has gradually run down to 14° below o at which it stood this morning walked across the lake day before yesterday. Ice sound but rather smooth to drive on

Sunday 14 Thermometer indicates o Weather for past week has been mild Butchered on wednesday. Got up a Farmers club[7] met for the first time at the school house Wednesday evening Also made up a Club of subscribers for the Northwestern Farmer & Horticultural Journal[8] My 4 hogs weighed 1023 lb Sold the best one

---

[7] These farmers' clubs did not take part in politics, according to the recollection of Preston Jackson, but merely discussed the technical problems of farmers.

[8] The *Northwestern Farmer and Horticultural Journal* was published at Dubuque, Iowa.

weighing 300 lb for 30$ to Sanderson & Bailey[9] at Lakeland

Sunday 21st Snow with wind from the south east. quite stormy afternoon the wind tacks round to the Northwest and gives us a terrible snow drift

Sunday 28th Cloudy snowy Helped Mr Wilson Thrash on Tuesday Wednsday & Thursday till noon and on Friday went to Hudson marketing Sold chickens at 3 & 4$ pr dz Lard 20c Butter 40c Eggs 50

[9] Probably Oliver Bailey, who is listed in the 1860 census schedules as a farmer of Lakeland.

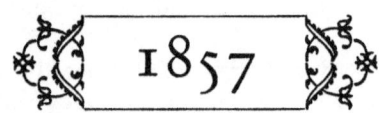

1857 Thursday Jany 1st   New Years again. nothing unusual going on.   Thrash some corn

Sunday 4th   Cloudy dull   Have had an unusual amount of cloudy weather this winter   Snow 10 or 12 inches deep   We were visiting at Mr Leaches on Friday

Sunday 18th   The coldest day I ever enjoyed or endured the mercury falling to 36 this morning[,] clear—still write to Bro. Imlay at Rensselaer also to Bro N. S. Thompson at Lafayette   To Milton M Morgan at Chatfield

Sunday 25 January   Still tight winter   Sold my lakeshore fraction on Friday to Mr Douglass at 15$ pr acre. Cost 5$ less than 3 years ago.   Mr Douglas also takes my black horses   Prospect good for selling the ballance of my farm at 40$ pr acre   More than a hundred percent above cost

Sunday Feb 1st   Cold & clear   Mercury 12° below zero Martha has been for several days and is still confined and suffering greatly with Rheumatism

Sunday 15th   Winter is softening up a little   Having thawed a little yesterday & today   Last Tuesday was a *singer*   The mercury standing down to 34 below zero This has been a terible winter.   The most rigorous I ever witnessed

Sunday 22nd   Pleasant.   Past week has been mild with

evident signs of spring I drove to Saint Paul on last Monday remained over night returned to the half way hous[e] and staid Tuesday night, and drove home by way of Stillwater & Hudson on Wednesday Paid 587.25 c upon the money hired last June to pay old Newell

March 1st 1857 Sunday Cold & Windy—clear. Have had a week or more of fine weather but March comes in like a Lion Sold out the hill field during the week for 1800$

Sunday 8th Past week has been sharp winter Mercury down yesterday morning to 15 below 0. wind south today with some signs of spring Spent most of past week in assisting Mrs Bonsall to administer on the estate of her husband Received a letter from Bro. N. S. Thompson

Wednesday 11th Walked to Saint Paul yesterday and returned today quite tired Finished paying off the Mortgage given to Mr Strong last June for 1079.50 c This with 1200$ that will be due me from Mr Goss[1] will clean out all the back payments upon this farm I hold my remaining part now at 4,500 and have personal property worth at least 1,000. Came to this Territory 3 years ago worth about 1300$ Have not made this 3,700$ by farming but by the rise of real estate.[2] Thus much for a judicious purchase. I should say here however that I went quite too extensively in debt to feel comfortable and consequently have not spent the past 3 years as pleasantly as though I had been out of debt This is the second time in my life that I have went largely in debt and fought it

---

[1] A Joseph Gosse is listed in the 1860 census schedules as a lumberman living in Stillwater.

[2] Fortunately Jackson sold this part of his land during the high prices of the land boom and before the panic which occurred in the autumn of 1857.

through successfully. But I dont consider it safe and think now that I will take no more such risks I have now a nice little farm of 67 acres all under fence a good house, Barn & spring And if the soil was as good as I should like and I had some wood I think I should call this Home. It makes a man feel very comfortable to be out of debt

Sunday 15th Weather rather rough Messrs Winslow and Miller of St Paul staid with us last night They propose interesting themselves in the sale of my land by having a part of it laid out into village lots[3]

Sunday 22nd Evident signs of a thaw Rains nearly all the afternoon seems odd to see rain having had none for some 5 months Returned from St Paul in the afternoon through the rain having driven out there with sleigh yesterday by way of Stillwater Gave Mr Winslow a plot of my ground for sale

Sunday 29th Pleasant spring weather snow going off rapidly under the influence of warm sunshine Lake still frozen up—might cross on the Ice opposite this The winter has been very severe and protracted but we have now had two days of fine weather A few wild geese flying to the north and the crowing of the prairie chickens makes us feel confidence in the present indications of spring

Sunday April 5th After a few days of good spring weather the wind struck up from the south on Thursday morning and continued cold and strong for 48 hours when it commenced snowing (Saturday yesterday morning) against noon yesterday we had some 5 or 6 inches of heavy

---

[3] This was the eastern part of Jackson's land, which later became Jackson's Addition to Lakeland. *Plat Book of Washington County, Minnesota,* 27 (Minneapolis, 1901).

snow winding up by rain which continued most of the afternoon settling the snow to about 2 inches and the wind in the mean time having shifted from the south by way of the East to the North N. W. and rather gaining than loosing in force. This morning and all day the wind continues with unabated fury from the N. W. The Mercury standing on an average at about 20 above 0. Mostly cloudy. Evening nearly clear

    Sunday 12 Wind south with a driving snow storm. The past week has been much like several of its predecessors alternating every two or three days from sunshine and North winds to cloudy, rainy, and snowy, with south winds Never endured so disagreeable a spring Went to Stillwater in a cutter on Monday 7th sleighing pretty good though not lasting We begin to Long to see the ground thaw out. ground that froze up early in November still remains so and seems likely to so remain One consolation however—we have but little mud

    Sunday 19 Pleasant—clear and still would be beautiful weather for the fore part of March Past week has been decidedly winterish Monday morning clear & cold with another snow storm in the afternoon ballance of the week has been mostly clear with a sharp North & North west wind. thawing a little during the middle of the day I crossed Lake St Croix on the Ice on Friday (17) with entire safety and it looks as though the bridge might last for a month Received a letter from Bro. D. I. at Rensellaer on Wednesday & answer today Thermometer down during past week to 8 degrees above zero

    Sunday 26th Find myself at the Winslow house St Paul where I have been since thursday evening except that I staid with Mr Winslow on Friday night Spring seems gradually creeping on   Though it snows this morning and winds up with rain   Bought a bay mare last evening and ride home on a buffalo blanket   I should perhaps here say that from my short stay at the house of Mr Winslow I am favorably impressed with the hospitable and real lady like appearance and conduct of his matronly wife and interesting Daughter

One little incident might be mentioned illustrating his hospitable disposition   Just before dinner Mr W. invited me into an adjoining room to see a map of West St Paul but instead of a map I found upon a table a *bottle* of what he said was good *Gin* with two glasses   This was a stumper   To decline to drink with my distinguished and gentlemanly host seemed an impossibillity an absurdity   But my duty seemed to stand right out before me. Intemperance in every shape and any use of spirituous [liquor] that might lead to intemperance either in low or high places *must* be discountenanced.   and decline I must and did giving the true reason for asking to be excused and pleading that I was consci[e]ntiously temperent upon which he removed the poison without himself tasting

Sunday May 3rd   At last it seems to be spring   past week has been mostly fine weather   Made a hot bed and in the afternoon yesterday concluded to see if every thing was ready to start the plow on Monday   Arranged the harness &c &c and struck in to see if the ground was dry enough.   plowed about half an acre.   ground rather wet but will be in good order tomorrow unles it rains   First Steamboats made their appearance last evening but encountered ice down near Catfish and laid over but to day the fleet some 8 or 10 boats broke through and reached the open water at Lakeland and Hudson. Mother Caldwell and Will are fixing to leave

Sunday 10th Past week beautiful spring weather up to Friday when we had a gale from the south which tacked to the south west and give us a very unpleasant day yesterday with a little snow and this morning we have half an inch of ice with cold wind from the North Mother Caldwell and Will started home on Monday by steamer Montauk Have some two acres of wheat sown and six acres ready for corn Health bad to day Lake clear of Ice Spring very backward

Sunday 17th pleasant. Most of past week has been cold & disagreeable today is clear & pleasant — cool for the time of year indicated by the Almanac. The plums are not yet out nor have the leaves made their appearance on our crabs

Sunday 24 Last snow bank disappeared fore part of past week weather fine. A beautiful Thunder shower last night, which was much needed Had a visit by Mr. & Mrs. Perin on Wednesday (20th). Plum blossoms begin to appear. spring very backward

Sunday 31 Rain without intermission with N. E. wind. chilly — damp spring crop in. went fishing in the afternoon yesterday in the afternoon, with the boys Outside pasture begins to be pretty good. Wild flowers out in abundance. fish none Tomorrow is our election for delegates to the constitutional convention[4]

[4] Washington County elected seven delegates to the convention, all of them Democrats. The story of the two rival conventions, Democratic and Republican, which met in St. Paul in July, 1857, held separate sessions, and produced two constitutions nearly identical, is told by Folwell in his *Minnesota,* 1:393–421.

Sunday 7th June Past week cold up to yesterday when it grew warm and today it is hot. mercury runs up to 90° in the shade Attended the election on Monday and voted the republican ticket. Balance of week assessing

Sunday 14th Rainy fine growing weather. Grass, Wheat Oats &c fine. Corn backward but promising. Been assessing past week

Sunday 21 Pleasant. Attend church at Lakeland at ½ past 2 Elder [Lemuel] Nobles afficiates[5] The rain of Last sunday continued over Wednesday and taken together was the heaviest rain I ever saw. corn looks bad

Sunday 28th Pleasant Wrote most of the day to be ready to go to Stillwater tomorrow to attend the equalization board

Thursday July 2nd evening attend the school exhibition and was much interested. Think Miss Newell a good teacher

Sunday 5th Warm Attend church at Lakeland and Afton both

Sunday 12th Warm Been at Stillwater all the week assessing. very hot.

Sunday 19th An uncommonly pleasant day. Though the weather has been mainly pleasant for six weeks. Sun shines hot with a pleasant N. W. breeze Accompany my wife to church at Lakeland this afternoon. Hear a new minister from Hudson (did not learn his name) — read a good sermon tolerably well. Rye & Hay ready to harvest tomorrow

Sunday 26 Pleasant Been harvesting rye & grass weather hot & dry. looks like rain today

[5] Nobles was a Methodist minister at Hudson. Folsom, *Fifty Years in the Northwest*, 133, 161.

August 1857 Sunday 2nd Dry & hot. Feel decidedly inclined to rest. Been haying all the week

Sunday 9th Pleasant. Have had several fine showers amounting to an abundance of rain. Attend church at Lakeland with Martha & Frank P.M Rev. [Charles] Thayer.[6] yesterday was my birthday — 41 years old

Monday 10th Meet the County Commissioners at Stillwater to return my assessment They express themselves well satisfied with my work and allow my bill 170$

Sunday 15th Cold rain from N. E. Finished haying yesterday Harvest done all but stacking First green corn & squashes today Write to Bro D. Imlay

Sunday 23 Pleasant. Weather for past week has been quite cool Finished stacking Met Capt. Tyler & Mr. Sanderson last evening to adjust claims against the Bonsall estate

September Sunday 6th Pleasant. With my wife drive down to Cottage grove to church hear Mr. Putmam [sic] address a very respectable appearing audience. Return by way of Afton and attend service in the afternoon

Sunday 20 After Several days of cold cloudy rainy days it is clear and pleasant again, having cleared off last night without frost. Attended a mass nominating Republican convention at Stillwater yesterday Expected to receive the nomination for the senate or house but did not. Feel well satisfied to vote for Judge [Hewitt L.] Thomas instead of myself[7]

Sunday 27th Attended church at Afton P.M. with my wife weather delightful

---

[6] Thayer was pastor of the First Presbyterian Church of Hudson. Warner and Foote, *Washington County*, 413.

[7] Thomas was one of the proprietors of Afton, where he settled in 1855. Warner and Foote, *Washington County*, 400, 402.

Sunday 4th Oct. 1857 weather dull but not disagreeable. Our first sharp frost *here* was on *Wednesday morning 30th Sept* which cut down the vines and tender things pretty generally But we have not yet had a dead killing frost

Sunday 11th Rain with cool wind from the South and west. Alex commenced Threshing yesterday. I do not help being fearfull of the dust. My lungs being rather delicate I feel a good deal enlisted in the Election which is to come off on the coming Tuesday Hope to see This county republican and Minnesota Do

Tuesday 13th *The* Election of Minnesota takes place to day. Attended at Lakeland early. was chairman of a Republican committee made during the past week to *try* to keep illegal voters from the Ballot box. But this was impossible as the new constitution allows all whitemen that have been here 10 days to vote And the way the *"dear Irish"* are marched up to vote the *Dimmicratic* ticket is a sin against heaven & Earth It is distressing as well as disgusting to see the poor ignorant—bigoted Irish who if left to their own reflections long enough to learn something of our institutions would be disposed to vote right led about by their love of Whiskey and their worst passions stirred up by a set of demagogues calling themselves *National Democrats* But *really Northern Doughfaces* who for the love of Office are willing to betray the best interests of their country to the great Slave power of the South I think there were from 50 to 100 votes polled here by persons having no interest in the affairs of Minnesota

Sunday 18th Cool cloudy dull Election news favorable Washington County is Republican by from one to two hundred notwithstanding the frauds perpetrated not only here but in other precincts. State still doubtfull. Hardly dare hope that we have elected Alex Ramsey and a Republican legislature[8]

Sunday 25 Self & wife attend church at Afton. Cool —pleasant

Nov. Sunday 1st Cool. All ready to go to church at Lakeland when Mrs Bonsall came and we gave out going

Sunday 8th Nov. Find ourselves in the midst of a big *snow storm* this morning which lasts till about noon. giving us from 4 to 6 inches of heavy snow with wind N. W. Should think this is the beginning of winter

Sunday 15th Have had just one week of winter. weather pretty rough but not very cold

Sunday 22nd Winter still holds was at Stillwater Tuesday (17th) and found people crossing the lake upon the Ice. Lake was still open to Bay town But navigation may now be considered closed Have had no boat for 4 or 5 days. The Mercury reached zero this morning for the first at day light and an hour later 4° below

December Sunday 6th after a rain & almost a general thaw which turned again to winter last Sunday night it is again moderate winter. Write to Will

Sunday 13th Mild clear Thaws freely Was at St Paul & back Friday brot home a cutter & Harness

Sunday 20 Mild winter The thawing of last Sunday continued from day to day till it wound up with rain and that with snow

Sunday 27th Mild winter. But little snow Going has

[8] Ramsey was defeated by Henry H. Sibley, the Democratic candidate, by a small margin. The Democrats also elected majorities in both houses of the legislature. Folwell, *Minnesota,* 2:2–4.

to be done on wheels   Christmas passed off quietly   Was at Stillwater Wednesday   Business very dull. all complain of hard times   Since 1836 there has been no such Revulsion in money affairs[9]   Fortunately for myself & family I am "out from under"   Owing nothing that I have no certain means of paying, and having plenty of the substantial comforts of life we ought to be thankful & happy

Thursday Dec. 31   This winds up the year 1857   We have this evening a beautiful snow storm which is much needed as the ground has been almost bare for some time so that all the going had to be done on wheels.   The winter has been very mild.   The Mercury not having been below zero but once or twice   Amongst the hopes for the coming year prominent is the hope that it will be as happy as the past has been

M. Y. Jackson

[9] This is the first mention in the diary of the hard times that descended upon the country in 1857. It shows how long it took for the repercussions of the panic caused by the failure of the Ohio Life Insurance and Trust Company in August, 1857, to reach the frontier.

1858

Friday January 1st[1] This little book has at least this advantage It commences with the year And upon a beautiful bright clear dry Minnesota winter day with about 4 or 5 inches of new clean snow which fell last evening. Drove to Stillwater with a cutter to day Business dull It is difficult to sell even Farm produce for money. Traded some Eggs at 37½ c pr. dz. for good Sugar at 16⅔c pr lb

Sunday 3rd Beautiful winter day. with my wife attend baptist meeting at Hudson during the afternoon. visited Mr. & Mrs. Sterling Jones yesterday

Sunday 10th Attend service at Lakeland P.M. Elder Thayer Good sleighing

Sunday 17th Fine winter with Martha attend church at Afton P.M. Elder Putnam Attended Lodge at Hudson last evening in company with Bro. [Lucius A.] Huntoon[2]

Sunday Jany 24th Cloudy—Thawy—rainy Had about five days of the most beautiful winter weather during the past week that I ever enjoyed But it looks like we

---

[1] This entry begins a new volume in the original diary.
[2] Huntoon was a merchant in Lakeland and was postmaster for many years. Upham and Dunlap, *Minnesota Biographies;* Folsom, *Fifty Years in the Northwest*, 374.

should loose our snow now   Attended Lyceum at the school house on Thursday eve.

Sunday 31st   Mild winter   Attend church P.M. at Lakeland   Rev. [C. H.] Marshall (I believe was the name)³   My wife accompanies me   Find schoolhouse very dirty and cold   Attended Lyceum Thursday evening

February 1858   Sunday 7th   After a few days of sharp cold weather it is again mild winter   With my wife attend church at the school house P.M.   Mr Thayer was not able to attend and the little audience dispersed without service   Attended Lyceum on Tuesday also on Thursday evenings of past week   First discussed the Kansas question the latter the [Commodore Hiram] Paul[d]ing & [General William] Walker question   I took the affirmative of the following resolution   Resolved that Com. Pawling discharged a high duty to his country & the civilized world by arresting General Walker⁴

Sunday 14th   Remained at home and let Alex & Prudy have the horse & cutter to go to meeting

Sunday 21   winterish   Too cold to go to meeting

Sunday 28th   After some fine warm weather which took off our snow it is again cold   Was at Stillwater with my wife on Thursday.   found pretty good sleighing   Was present at a *post mortem* examination of Mr Robertsons boy on Friday and at his funeral on saturday

1858 March Sunday 7   Signs of Spring

Sunday 14   Winter is gradually yielding to spring   Write to N. D. Myers & M. C. Baker

³ Marshall was pastor of the First Congregational Church at Hudson. Warner and Foote, *Washington County*, 233.

⁴ Walker, who had become dictator of Nicaragua after aiding revolutionists in 1855 and who had been forced out in 1856, was arrested by Commodore Paulding of the United States navy when he landed at Grey Town with a second expedition in 1857.

Sunday 21st after a week of Spring it is a little cool to day We commenced plowing on *Wednesday 17* on Alexanders low prairie Find the ground full wet but stick to it. and he & I togather [*sic*] have plowed about 10 acres. On Friday we were greeted by our old friends the Robbins and larks mixed with Geese Ducks & Blackbirds The Snow birds mostly disappeared the day before. So that if we are not to have Spring early the birds are to be disappointed as well as ourselves Write to the N. W. Farmer and Stillwater Messenger

Sunday 28th Good sugar weather With my wife & Bro Alex & his wife attend church at Lakeland both A M & P.M. services by Elder [Enos] Munger Baptist[5] Having been chosen one of the Trustees of the baptist church I met the others at the house of Esqr. Morgan[6] on last evening to organize. The other trustees are Judge Thomas of Afton, Elias Dagget[t,][7] A. D. Kingsley & G. W. Leach. Also attended a political meeting last evening at the School house for the purpose of opposing a proposition to so change the constitution of Minnesota as to loan the Bonds of the state to the amount of 5.000.000$ to R R Cos[8] The Lake opened yesterday (27) though we have had no boat yet

Monday 29th Pleasant weather *First Steamboat* up

---

[5] Munger was pastor of the First Baptist Church at Lakeland from its organization in 1858 to 1862, when he enlisted in the army. Warner and Foote, *Washington County*, 414.

[6] Probably W. W. Morgan, who is listed in the 1860 census schedules as a "notary and conveyancer" at Lakeland.

[7] Elias Daggett is listed in the 1860 census schedules as a farmer at Lakeland.

[8] The story of the "Five Million Loan," whereby the Minnesota Constitution was amended so as to permit the loan of the credit of the state to the amount of five million dollars in aid of railroads, is told by Folwell in his *Minnesota*, 2:37–58.

Attend an anti loan meeting at Inv[er] Grove 6 miles below Afton evening

Sunday April 4th Past week mostly fine spring weather Find some early flowers on the 1st Attend and preside at an anti loan meeting at the school house last evening meeting addressed by Dr [J. H.] Reiner[9] & Maj Vanorks

Sunday 11th Cloudy and has been cloudy and rough weather most of past week Wind N. E. Thunder—rain—small hail—winding up with heavy snow—awful. We must have some 2 inches of the wettest kind of snow And on the mantle piece bunches of flowers gathered by the children some days since

Thursday April 15 Clear cool morning frosty This is the election day which is to determine by direct vote of the people whether we loan the state credit to the amount off [*sic*] $5,000,000 to the land grant companies for the purpose of assisting to start our railroad system This measure I think will be carried At the same time I think It is the measure that will involve Minnesota in a debt of that amount for I have no confidence in the companies that they will ever pay a dollar except a few installments of interest that will fall due before they can draw the full amount My belief as to the course the companies will pursue is this They will do only the amount of work necessary to enable them to draw their 500,0000 [*sic*] bonds Then very likely without a mile of R. R. completed ask an additional loan and unless we give it to them or release our mortgage so that they can mortgage to others they will abandon the work—forfeit their charters—go down—fail Then re organize a new company made mostly of the

---

[9] Reiner was a physician at Marine. *Stillwater Messenger*, September 24, 1861.

same men and ask at our hands a new charter   And having pocketed about $3,000,000 clear in the first operation they can afford the next time to obligate themselves to *complete* and *equip* at least a few miles of Road[10]

Sunday 18th   Cloudy dark day   much of the past week has been cloudy & cold   with my wife & Preston attend church at school house A.M. Elder Munger   Afternoon at Afton Elder Putnam.   Rain

Sunday 25th   Cool for the season   With Mrs. Jackson and Alexander & Prudence attend meeting at Afton A.M. Elder Putnam   and at the Lakeland school house P.M. Rev. Marshall

Sunday May 2nd   Cool but Pleasant   With my wife & Frank attend church at Lakeland   A.M. Elder Munger P.M Rev. Caldwell of Stillwater

Sunday 9th   Cool Mostly clear   Bad weather still predominates   Attend church at schoolhouse P M. Rev. Marshall

Sunday 16th   Cool.   P.M. rain with a little snow or hail mix^d   Past week mostly good working weather, but cold with wind mostly from North & N. E.

Wednesday 19   commenced planting corn yesterday believing that it was too early by every thing but the almanac   To day my corn planting is suddenly stopped by a cold rain from the N. E. which soon ripens into a thick heavy snow storm and now at noon the snow is falling terribly

[10] Jackson was among those whom Folwell calls the "remnant of conservative men who did not lose their heads," and who "pointed out with unerring foresight the weaknesses and vices of the bill, which experience later revealed to the mass of the voters." Jackson's predictions concerning the bond issue were, in the main, correct. Folwell, *Minnesota*, 2:47.

Sunday 23rd Cloudy Stay at home A.M. for fear of rain P.M. attend church at Afton. Rain. Elder Munger preaches

Sunday 30th Pleasant. With my family & that of A. E. attend church both A.M. & P.M. Elder Munger A.M. & Elder Thayer P.M.

Monday 31 Pleasant finish planting corn except the South garden Grass is growing rapidly owing to the great amount of wet weather By the almanac this is late corn planting But judging from other vegetation it is early enough

Sunday June 6 Pleasant Attend church at Lakeland A.M Elder Munger. Was at Stillwater Friday Recd a letter from D. I. yesterday Answered to day

Sunday 13 Pleasant Attend church at Afton A.M. Elder [William T.] Boutwell[11] and at Lakeland Elder Thayer P.M. Have been engaged past week in making the assessment again weather mostly pleasant but cold for the season Pigeons are taking up the corn

Sunday 20th Since Thursday the weather has been excessively Hot with pleasant stiff breeze from South & S. E. Neglected to go to meeting to day Write to Mrs. Bonsall, D. M. Cox, M. C. Baker & Mr Wood. begin to need rain

Sunday 27th very hot attend church forenoon at Lakeland Elder Munger

Sunday July 4 1858 Attended a Picnic with the school children yesterday Near capt Olivers Another is arranged

[11] Boutwell accompanied Henry R. Schoolcraft's expedition to Lake Itasca in 1832 and for many years thereafter was a missionary to the Chippewa at various points in the Minnesota region. After 1847 he lived on a farm near Stillwater. Folwell, *Minnesota*, 1:175–177; Upham and Dunlap, *Minnesota Biographies*.

for tomorrow in the grove below us Have to be at Stillwater most of the coming week

Sunday 11th Fine weather for crops we have had a fine and very heavy rain I went to Stillwater on Tuesday and returned late last eve.

Sunday 18 Warm—fine growing weather. rigged up my reaping machine on Monday. Set the boys to cutting Rye on Tuesday (13) then left for Stillwater. returned last evening attend church this P.M Elder Marshall

Sunday 25 Warm & Rainy. have had an immense amount of rain during the past week. Returned from Stillwater on Friday by foot mostly This winds up my work at Stillwater except to make my report on the first Monday But It will require hard work to complete my list by that time

Sunday August 1st Another hot rainy week. Bad for haying & Harvesting. Had to foot up the totals of my Tax list to day to be ready to submit it to the commissioner tomorrow

Monday August 2 Hot with appearance of rain. Take Boat Equator for Stillwater arrive at noon

Tuesday 3rd Heavy rain last night return home this PM by Mr Allibones wagon [12]

Sunday Aug 8 Past week has been hot with a heavy rain about every other night Dreadful bad weather for haying. This is my birth day again. 42 years old to day

Sunday 15th Horses not able to drive to church Weather continues hot with frequent rains. The grain is already seriously damaged At the request of the

---

[12] The census schedules for 1860 list John Allibone, an Episcopal minister, and William Allibone, a farmer, both of Denmark Township, Washington County. John Allibone settled in Denmark Township in 1851. Warner and Foote, *Washington County,* 354.

County Commissioners I as well as each of the other assessors have undertaken to re-appraise all the property charged in the assessment roll for this year: reducing the valuation about one third This we can do conscientiously, as owing to the pressure of hard times there seems to be but little *value* in *money* attached to *any thing*

Sunday August 22 Cool for the season Have had no rain for about a week Returned my corrected assessment Roll to the Commissioners on Tuesday (17) Walked to church with Oscar to day at Lakeland Elder Munger[.] Finished Stacking on Friday & helped Alexander hawl oats yesterday the air feels like we should have frost. It is said that the Atlantic Tellegraph Cable is laid and that we are to be in communication with Europe in a few days

Sunday August 29th Cool. Pleasant. Have had a few light frosts not doing much damage My Buckwheat however is killed down pretty thoroughly. With my wife attend church at Lakeland this P.M. Elder Marshall The Tellegraph to Europe is complete and if we had a line to Prairie Du Chien we might know this evening the news of London this morning. This is one of the greatest accomplishments of this age We also have the gratifying intelligence that the sovereign people of Kansas have rejected by an overwhelming vote the Slavery constitution framed by a Convention of unprincipled and reckless slavery propagandists. Elected by fraud and force and upheld by the present corrupt South fearing and South obeying administration of James Buchanan

Sunday Sept 5th Pleasant With my wife & Frank attend church A M At Lakeland and at Afton P.M. Hear Elder Munger at both places

Sunday 12th Pretty sharp little frost this morning but it does not cut down my squash vine in the east garden Sowed 6 acres wheat yesterday up on the hill

Sunday 19 Beautiful warm day Write to William Caldwell Also to John Iams

Sunday 26 Pleasant Autumn With my wife attend church at Afton A.M. Elder Putnam. P.M. Drive on down to Mr Allibones and return Was at Stillwater yesterday to meet the Republican Central Committee of which I am a member Called our precinct conventions for next Saturday and the County convention for Monday following

Monday 4th October Pleasant but cool Drive to Stillwater with Martha who needs the services of Dr. Newell (Dentist) and I wanted to attend the Republican county convention[13]

Tuesday 5th pretty sharp frost this may be called our first killing frost A fine Squash vine in my garden is killed down. also my Tomatoe vines are somewhat nipped

Sunday Oct 10 Fine fall weather The frost of Tuesday morning was followed by rain on Wednesday night and by a "black frost["] on Thursday night which with another on Friday night has pretty well killed down all green things

Tuesday Oct 12 General Election day We (the Republicans) carry Lakeland precinct by 15 majority

---

[13] Dr. George C. Newell, according to his advertisement in the *Stillwater Messenger* in 1858, "plugged in" decayed teeth "in the most approved manner," mounted artificial teeth "on gold or silver by the latest improvements," and extracted teeth "with neatness and despatch." An account of the Republican convention is given in the *Stillwater Messenger,* October 5, 1858. Jackson was nominated for assessor of the second district.

Wednesday 13th Republicans have the county except Judge Thomas who is beat for Senate [14]

Sunday 18th Oct Pleasant Autum With my Wife attend church at Afton A.M. P.M. at Lakeland No service. Got home just in time to avoid a heavy rain and wind storm took shelter in the barn

Wednesday 20 Our first Town Election Under the new Town law [15]

Sunday 24 Cool—Pleasant Martha & Oliver go to church at Lakeland

Sunday 31st Oct Go with Oscar to Dr [Edward W.] Johnsons for a prescription for an obstinate cough with which he has been troubled for a week or more with cold & fever [16] Weather cold wet & disagreable

November Monday 15 Lake closed over in places last night The Fred and also the Alhambra break through and are undoubtedly making their last trip for the season. I had my horses shod at Afton to day

Wednesday 17 Attend a sheriff sale at Mr Bolles's[.] cool. ground pretty well frozen with say two inches of snow Winter sets in rather moderately The weather during the fall was mostly bad[,] cold—cloudy rainy— with N. E. wind More N E winds this fall than altogather since I have been in Minnesota

[14] The results of the election are given in the *Stillwater Messenger*, October 19, 1858.

[15] The law to which Jackson refers was the act passed by the first state legislature providing for township organization. The act was approved on August 13, 1858. Minnesota, *General Laws, 1858*, p. 190–227.

[16] Johnson practiced medicine in Lakeland from 1855 until 1864, when he removed to Owatonna. Warner and Foote, *Washington County*, 418.

Wednesday 24th   Send my team to the woods with Mr. Downing[17] & Mr. Young

Sunday 28 Nov.   mild winter. 2 or 3 in snow. cloudy and has been all fall

Wednesday 8 December   Clear which is rare   The sun looks like an old friend that had been traveling in foreign lands   But with the sun shine we have the mercury down to 22° below. went with M̲r̲ Young to Hudson

Thursday 9th   Clear with mercury at 32° below and yet the weather is quite endurable being still

[17] This was probably either David Downing, who is listed in the 1860 census schedules as a farmer living in Denmark Township, or the James Downing mentioned by Jackson, *post,* p. 180, 196, who is not listed in the census.

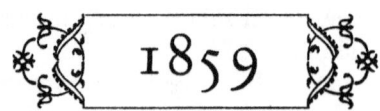

1859 Jany 6th Thursday   Start to the *woods* with C. H. Rice & Spoffords team[1]   Stop at Marine   find my left Ear frozen

Friday 7th   Evening at Taylors falls   Cold clear day mercury at 15° this morning with pretty stiff breeze from the north   will be colder in the morning

Jany 9 Sunday evening   at the camp   Staid last night at Kanots and reach here about 2 Oclock this P.M. and am to lodge for the first time in a lumbering camp   From Stillwater to Marine 12 Miles the road is from rolling to hilly—country rough and mostly poor   From Marine to the falls 18 or 20 Miles the road runs mostly through timber from brush up to trees   not very valuable   A few tolerable sugar orchards.   At the falls there is a good prospect for a fine Manufacturing town   at the falls we crossed to the East or Wisconsin side and continue up along the river through rough stony & mostly timbered ground some 12 miles and cross Wolf creek out some 2 or 3 Miles from its junction and 12 miles above the falls   Thence 14 miles

---

[1] A Charles Rice appears in the 1860 census schedules as a laborer living at Lakeland, and one Jacob E. Spofford is named in a list of letters uncalled for at the Stillwater post office, in the *Saint Croix Union*, January 9, 1855.

mostly through Pine barrens to Kanots Thence mostly through a fine young forrest East to Wood lake cros[s] big Wood lake on the ice and find the camp south side of little Wood Lake say 10 Miles from Kanots in sec. 36 T 38 N.—R 18 W

Monday 10 & Tuesday 11th Crooss [*sic*] the little lake on the ice go down past the dam & ramble out a few miles north in quest of game and to see the country

Wednesday 12th assist about the camp & in the woods

Thursday 13th fine day Ramble all day south west from camp. Land is better than to the North Best timber is already cut and much of the ballance destroyed. Evening learn that a team is going down from the other camp in the morning and decide to go down

Sunday Jany 16 At home. Missed the team friday morning and had to foot it home which I did in two days reaching home last evening about 8 or 9 having staid at the falls on Friday night. The distance to our camp must be near 80 miles

Monday 24 Write to Mr Baker at Concord N. H. Find that more than half of his corn has been stolen from the crib

Sunday 30th Evening with my family attend the wedding of Oliver Caldwell at the house of Mrs Bonsall the bride

February 1859 Sunday 6th Beautiful winter. real Minnesota Winter Mercury down to 12 below 0 and we would think it 12 above so still dry & clear is the atmosphere Walk to church hear Elder Monger

Sunday 13 Lovely winter weather mercury 6 below this morning. walk to church hear Mr Monger. With my wife attended a donation party on Thursday evening

10th at Afton for benefit of Mr. Putnam   very pleasant assemblage

Sunday 20   The weather has been a little too fine to hold out

March Thursday 3rd   A very disagreable snow storm prevents us from attending a donation party at Lakeland for the benefit of Mr. Marshall of Hudson

Monday 7th   Sloppy. snow nearly all gone. The Teams come down from the woods this P.M.

Wednesday 9th   Muddy. Drive to Stillwater with Jas Downing   First appearance of wild geese

Sunday 27th   We have had more snow during this month than all winter besides   The ground though nearly clear from snow is not thawed through   With Martha, Sister Prudence &c went to church.   heard Mr Monger. (Robison Baptized)   And again in the P.M. heard Mr Marshall on baptism.   Heard the first *larks this* morning.   Also Prairie Chickens

1859 Minnesota April Sunday 3rd   we are all April fools this time.   The clouds had been thick & lead colored for a week or more, and on yesterday morning the snow commenced sifting down fine and soon growing thicker, with a howling raging wind from the north and I think I never saw so violent a snow storm   To day we have a driving drifting wind from the west   Write to Will

Tuesday 5th   Town Election   Republican ticket carries by 23 & under

Wednesday 6th   Evening attend a meeting of a Library association that is forming in Lakeland   We propose to form a Circulating library by requiring each member to contribute as an initiating fee 3⁰⁰ worth of Books or 2⁰⁰ in money

Sunday 10th weather continues decidedly bad Lead colored clouds—Snow & mud with faint streaks of sunshine crossed the Lake on ice yesterday

Thursday 14th another snow storm last night with a driving cold west wind this morning Looks like winter Mercury 26 above 0

Sunday 17th weather continues disagreeable

Sunday 24th For two or three days it has looked like spring Steam Boats reached St Paul on Thursday and we shall expect one here every day. Lake has been closed a little more than 5 Mo.

Tuesday 26 First Steam Boat up late this evening. The past has been a long though mild winter. Spring seems now to be here in earnest. Plowed & planted my Pea ground to day

Sunday May 1st We have now had a week and a few days over of real spring Commenced plowing for wheat & Oats on the high prairie with a snow drift along the north fence

Sunday May 8 Spring comes on rapidly sowed 2¾ acres of tea wheat yesterday. Our driving crew came down from the Woods and report our logs "hung up" for the season Both dams having "blown." This is bad news and will be quite embarrasing to me as I have contracted some 200$ of debts expecting to pay with the proceeds of these logs

Sunday May 15th 1859 Weather past week has been from showry to wet Sowed my Siberian Wheat on Monday (9) and finished harrowing oats yesterday

Sunday 22nd Past week has been showry & cold Planted 2 or 3 acres of corn on north new ground yesterday Oscar keeps the plow going while I & an Irishman plant

Thursday 26 5 years ago to day we commenced planting our hill field with corn commences raining before breakfast and continues all day with a driving wind from the North west. North N. E. & N. N. W. again At Sunset we have a gale of wind & rain from the N. N. W. that drives a steamer to the opposite shore of the lake where she blows her whistle for a signal of distress as I suppose But it would be impossible to render any succor from this side The passengers must suffer from the storm if they are forced to leave the boat

Friday 27 Fine day after the storm which continued nearly all night The Steamer blown ashore turns out to be the Equator, Capt [Asa B.] Green and is pretty thoroughly wrecked[2]

Saturday 28 Beautiful day Go to Stillwater with some beets & Parsnips which I sell at 60 & 75c. pretty readily. Oscar accompanies me. [John] Carmoody plants the North meadow field with corn

Sunday 29 Pleasant Rather cool for corn

Sunday June 5 Past week has been rainy & *cold* Finished planting the south meadow field Thursday (2nd) Had a sharp frost yesterday morning which does up the Tomatoes Cucumbers &c

Sunday 12th Weather continues cold and wet

Sunday 19 Weather continues cold & wet. Took my boys to Stillwater on Friday 17 to witness the military

---

[2] Merrick, in his *Upper Mississippi*, 190–195, describes the wreck of the "Equator." The versatile Captain Green was at various times during his life a lawyer, sheriff, probate judge, and steamboat captain, and in 1860 he was ordained a minister in the Baptist church. Folsom, *Fifty Years in the Northwest*, 374; *post*, p. 203.

cellebration of the anniversary of the battle of Bunker hill.
A. E. & family left for Indiana on Thursday 16th

Sunday 26 Warm—pleasant looks like rain Past week has been pretty fair spring weather P.M. very hot

Tuesday 28 Morning rain with thunder & wind P.M. *Another Boy* is added to our little family This is the 4th boy in succession.[3] Our youngest being 6 years old on the 6 of May just past

Sunday July 3rd Weather warmer but still wet. Write to Mother Caldwell & Prudence

Sunday 10th Weather warm. But little rain for a week Thursday was the hottest day I ever experienced and friday was about Do. except that we had a breeze

Sunday 17 Past week mostly hot with showers Had first green peas on Thursday Last half of the week very hot. Corn & weeds grow beyond all precedent

Sunday July 24th Real summer Winter wheat is ready to cut also the hay. Must finish my corn tomorrow and go into the harvest next day

Sunday 31 Summer weather with copious showers Never saw things grow so Have 6 or 8 ton of nice hay out bleaching. Had heavy rain Friday night. Showry Saturday. Sun shines to day. must rake up some hay this evening. I never saw the Wheat & oats finer than they must be if we have one more week of good weather

Sunday August 7th Fine summer weather We set our Reaper last evening preparatory for harvesting Monday morning. The harvest looks very promising. Indeed I think I never saw so fine a harvest. Grain is heavy and stands up well we shall commence on Oliver Caldwells

---

[3] The boy was William. Census schedules, 1860.

wheat which ripens first but is full green yet Tomorrow is my birthday when I shall be 43 years old

Sunday 14 Have had a week of good harvest weather shall nearly finish tomorrow if we have good luck

Sunday Aug 21st Finished harvesting on Tuesday 16. Have not commenced stacking yet Weather for past 2 weeks has been favorable for corn

Sunday 28 Rained Monday & Tuesday Ballance of the week good weather for hawling in grain Not near done

Sunday 4th Sept a little frost Friday morning also this morning weather cold for the season. A E Jackson & family returned from Indiana on Wednesday

Sunday 18th Attended our primary Republican meeting at the school house last evening at which Carlos Clement[,] Jacob Lowell & Elias McKean were chosen to represent this Town at the Co Convention on tomorrow. This delegation will go for D[aniel] T Watson for representative[4] On Tuesday (13th) I drove to St Paul in search for a girl to do housework Stay at a Dutch boarding house & return on Wednesday with Miss Hettie Hoffstrom quite a nice appearing little Sweedish maiden of 16 years

Monday 19th Attend the nominating convention at Stillwater with Mr. Stearnes.[5] nominations much as I expected. Watson, [Andrew J.] Vanvorhes [*Van Vorhes*] & [Orange] Walker for representatives [Granville M.] Stickney for Sheriff—[Thomas J.] Yorks for Register

[4] Clement was a Lakeland merchant, a partner of Lucius A. Huntoon. Lowell and McKean were farmers and Watson was engaged in the lumber business at Lakeland. Upham and Dunlap, *Minnesota Biographies*; Warner and Foote, *Washington County*, 415, 416; census schedules, 1860.
[5] The 1860 census schedules list George H. Stearnes, a lumberman, and Charles E. Stearnes, a farmer, as residents of Lakeland.

[F. A.] Haskell for Treasurer [Rudolph] Le[h]micke for Auditor &c⁶ I received 12 votes out of 29 for Auditor Dont like the ticket but expect to vote it except Mr Stickney whom I *must* reject on account of his increasing intemperence & immorality Dislike his prodigality in particular

Minnesota Oct 1859 Thursday 6 Drive to St Paul with Miss Hettie Hoffstrom. return late in the evening cool chilly but pleasant Autumn weather

Sunday 9th Had a dead killing frost Saturday morning which killed down our tomatoes which had been in good order up to this time Though the corn &c on the low ground has been killed down several weeks and is now dry enough to gather

Tuesday 11th Election. Democrats are again cleaned out almost 2 to 1 I Believe they are beaten through out⁷

1859 November Saturday 5th Drive to St Paul with Hettie & Prudy leave the *former* & return with the latter at 9 PM

Sunday 11th Cold—Snowy—wintry Steam boats howl as if they were frightened

Sunday 20th Winter has given back a little. Lake is still open here but remains closed at Stillwater Went to mill on Friday Staid over night at Mr Rutherfords⁸ & returned yesterday

⁶ The proceedings of the convention are printed in the *Stillwater Messenger*, September 27, 1859. All the candidates mentioned by Jackson were elected. *Messenger*, October 18, 1859.
⁷ The Republicans were victorious in the state election as well as in the Washington County election. *Stillwater Messenger*, October 18, 1859.
⁸ Jackson probably refers to James Rutherford, who had a flour mill on Brown's Creek in Greenfield, now Grant, Township. A William Rutherford also lived in Grant Township, where he owned several farms. Folsom, *Fifty Years in the Northwest*, 66, 369; Warner and Foote, *Washington County*, 457; census schedules, 1860.

Sunday 27th Freezing again we had a heavy rain on Friday night & yesterday till noon when I went to the field to bring in the plow preparetory for Winter. Plowed an acre & brought down the plow Write to Rouser Evans Daniels & Co Piqua. Cold

December Friday 2nd This is the day appointed by the authority of the old State of Virginia for the execution of old John Brown[,] Old Osawatomie Brown sometimes so called from the active part he took at that place in Kansas in repelling the "Border Ruffians" This man Brown is to figure somewhat in the history of this country And especially is he to figure when the history of the "Irrepressible conflict" that is now waging between slavery and freedom in this country is acted and ready to be written out This Conflict is to be settled by the American people but in what way God only knows It is a conflict for the suprenacy [*sic*] and control of the federal government, between two antagonistic parties viz. the *free* laborers of the Northern & free states and the slave owners of the southern & slave states In other words it is a conflict between the owners of the mussels [*sic*] of the North and the claimants of the mussels of the South John Brown very naturally believed that Slavery was a great wrong ang [*sic*] honestly believed that it was the *duty* of every lover of freedom to do all in his power to abolish it. And especialy was he impressed with the belief that he had a duty to perform in the matter of liberating the oppressed. The history of Kansas already knows *John Brown* of Osawatomie, where he with a few brave lovers of freedom rolled back the tide of mercenary ruffians whos[e] business in Kansas was the establishment of Slavery.

But for the determined resistance of a few such brave hearts & stout arms assisted by heavy contributions from the North and New England states and a good supply of Sharpes Rifles Slavery would this day have existed to blacken and curse the lovely prairies and fertile valleys of that young and promising territory.

In this struggle John Brown lost two *noble boys*—one was murdered unarmed and another taken prisoner and driven with heavy chains before these merciless slavery extensionists for 30 miles through the blistering sunshine and choking dust which cruel treatment ended in his death. Not the strangest thing in history will be the fact that John Brown after this merciless destruction of his sons to make room for slavery should become a *Mono Maniac* and conscientiously battle against it wherever found And that contrary to the wishes and counsels of the more prudent and cautious of the free state party he crossed the Missouri line and actualy liberated about a dozen Slaves by capturing their masters and holding them as prisoners till the Slaves were run across the line. Then liberating their masters, without harming them (except in one instance where resistance cost a slave holder his life) led them Moses like through Iowa and several other states to Canada And now for attempting to repeat this daring deed in the state of Virginia on a much larger scale he is overpowered, falls wounded by government soldiers and surrenders. and having lost about 15 out of his party of about 20 he is to be hung to day charged by the grand jury of Charlestown with Murder, Treason and causing an insurrection His remaining conrades [*sic*] are to follow in a fortnight

Saturday 10th   Hawl a load of corn from Mr Gages for Charlie Bonsall [9]   24 10/70 Bus

Monday 12   Butcher day   PM a little snow.   cold

Saturday 17th   Hawled another load of corn from Mr Gages on Thursday 25 4/70   Hawled Wood for Mr Martin on yesterday and another load of corn today 26 9/70 bus

Sunday 18   Cold with a little snow with wind from the N. W. West   Walk up to Meeting.   hear Elder Monger

Sunday 25th   Cool quiet Christmas   We are having some good sollid winter but little snow

[9] B. F. Gage is listed as a farmer at Afton and Charles Bonsell as a laborer at Lakeland in the 1860 census schedules.

1860

January 1st 1860 Sunday   Mercury down to 30 below 0 and yet it is a pleasant winter day

Sunday 8th   With Preston & Frank Drive up to church   Elder Monger   Pretty fair sleighing   Pleasant day

Sunday 15   Pleasant winter weather   With Martha attend church at Afton P.M.   Elder Monger   Snow is going off   Roads much damaged

Sunday 22   Warm & Pleasant   Snow mostly gone   Prospect of a January thaw

Saturday 28th   Bring home a new set of bob sleds that I have been helping Mr. Gage to iron most of the week   Snow nearly all gone but weather decidedly cool

Sunday Feb 5th   Been having some very cold weather and bare ground.   A little snow last night, and weather moderate to day.   Called Dr Johnson on Wednesday (1st) to see Oscar who had been suffering for a week with Rheumatism and fever.   Yesterday and to day he is worse, his fever having assumed the Typhoid form

Tuesday 7th   Oscar is worse. Rheumatism having attackd his heart.   He suffers much and the chances seem dreadfully against his recovery

Wednesday 8   Oscar seems better but is very helpless

Wednesday 22nd Rain last night and today. snow nearly all gone P.M. Windy, snowy, freezy Oscar is much reduced but the prospect now is that he will recover

Friday 24th Oscar has a return of his rheumatic dificulty to his chest which came on last night and he is in much distress as well as great peril to day Write to Mess[rs] O Ferrall Daniels & co of Piqua

Sunday 26 Pleasant Oscar seems to be improving again

March Sunday 4th Weather mild and spring like. Oscar has improved much during the week. Is entirely free from fever and excepting his right hip nearly free from rheumatism. But this right hip Oh! how dreadfully he has suffered with it for nearly six weeks. And to day what a dreadful discovery Dr. Johnson makes—namely That this right leg which has given him *so much* pain—so many sleepless nights, has *shortened up* by the displacement of the hip joint till it is something like an inch and a half shorter than the other. That in a word Our noble boy—our heroic boy—our active stirring energetic—life loving and life enjoying boy is at best a cripple for life Oh! how this announcement seems to take hold of me—how it depresses me—and how the hot tears do flow from my eyes and how I could weep and how I *do* weep And Oh! how I dread to make this disclosure to him How can I make the dreadful announcement. and how must it crush his buoyant young spirit—Heroic as he is How small would seem the sacrifice if by giving what property I possess I could restore him to soundness. And how cheerfully could I and how cheerfully could his mother go to work and how we would delight to struggle against poverty if by so doing we could but avert this calamity

Monday 5th Beautiful Spring day See a flock of Wild Geese going North If this is to be Spring we are being cut short of our usual amount of hard winter.

Sunday 11th Beautiful Spring weather Dr [Otis] Hoyte [*Hoyt*][1] was here with Dr Johnson on Friday and agrees substantialy with him that oscars hip Joint is used up They made quite a thorough examination but could find no matter ready to be discharged

Sunday 18th Our Spring weather continues. We have the finest weather I ever enjoyed for the Season Hitched up my team yesterday (St Patricks) and plowed up about a quarter of an acre of ground for early potatoes & Peas I finished my fall plowing on the 27 of Nov. Since then we have had 111 days of weather unsuited to that useful and health giving exercise

Saturday 24th cool. ground frozen somewhat. Sowed a few peas. About 10 Oclock to night I am frightened by symptoms about Oscar that leads me to fear—indeed to believe that his remaining hip (left) is unjointed If I could only *hope* that I am mistaken I might sleep. But so deep is my conviction that I cannot sleep. And now at two Oclock [A.]M. I have not closed my eyes. Oh! my noble boy my heroic boy, my patient boy my little comread [*sic*] How can I remember your fleetness—your extreme activity—your love of field and flower The patter of your little feet always at my heels. O how can I remember all that you *were* and survive the shocking clatter of your cumbrous unwieldy crutches—henceforth an indispen-

---

[1] Dr. Hoyt lived in Hudson, Wisconsin. Warner and Foote, *Washington County*, 227, 241; Folsom, *Fifty Years in the Northwest*, 165.

sible appendage   O why is this cruel calamity fallen upon my darling boy

Sunday 25th   Dr Johnson thinks I was mistaken in my supposition about Oscars right hip joint last night

Thursday 29th   Cross the Lake to Hudson and have an interview with Old Dr Hoyt   He says frankly that Oscars case is doubtful.   But thinks we may keep him.   makes some suggestions for Dr. Johns[on's] consideration   He assures me that he has great confidence in the capability of Dr J. and has been aware of his treatment and thinks it the best that could be done[2]

Sunday April 1st   Weather continues fine & Spring like. Planted my early Potatoes on Tuesday & Wednesday (27th & 28th) also planted my early Peas   Started my team to plowing on the high prairie on Friday 30th   Mornings frosty   Oscar seems decidedly better to day   Found a little yellow flower on the 29th   Flowers & Larks plenty today

Tuesday 3rd   Weather continues beautiful Spring[.] Election—I am a candidate on the Republican ticket for county commissioner.   Had nothing to do with my nomination which took place at our county convention last Wednesday I believe   I learn that I am complimented by some 22 votes above my party ticket at Lakeland.   this is rather gratifying and makes me feel proud of my vote at home[3]

Sunday 8th   Weather continues fine   First Steamboat up on thursday (5th)

Tuesday 9   Commence sowing wheat

[2] Oscar lived through this trying time, but remained a cripple for life.
[3] Jackson and the other Republican candidates for county commissioners were elected. *Stillwater Messenger*, March 27, April 10, 1860.

Thursday 12th   Finish sowing 25 acres wheat
Sunday 15th   Weather continues fine
Sunday 22nd   A few rainy days wound up last night by a snow storm and the ground is white this morning with nearly an inch of snow which mostly goes of[f] through the day
Sunday 29   Fine weather mostly.   sharp frost last night with prospect of another to night   Spent yesterday with Preston down at Afton digging up trees

1860 May Sunday 6th   Delightful spring weather. Almost finished sowing my oats yesterday   Oscar seems to be improving a little in his general health   But his hips and left elbow are bad—useless   It has been more than one hundred days since he has been able to turn himself over in bed.   And during most of this time compelled to lie square upon his back   He now sits part of the time in a rocking chair which is a great relief

June 1860 Sunday 10th   Spent from Monday to Friday inclusive at Stillwater in attendance upon the commissioners court, of which body I have the honor to be a member.   Mr. J[oseph] W. Furber of Cottage Grove, Mess[rs Louis] Hospes & [John] McKusick of Stillwater & Mr [Asa S.] Parker of Marine constitute the balance of the board   Mr Furber was chosen chairman.   A very good choice.   Write to Will Caldwell   Have a mess of New Potatoes for dinner   Think we will have Peas next Sunday

Sunday 17   Have a mess of new Peas & Potatoes

Wednesday July 4th   Take Dinner with Bro A. E. Oscar is able to be with us by being carried to the carriage and lifted out.   He is still perfectly helpless

Friday 13th Commence the new harvest by cutting my Rye The old familiar clatter of the reaping machine sounds quite natural Though there is nothing about it that reminds me of harvest as conducted in the days of my boy hood. Then the old simple crooked sickle[,] then the more formidable looking cradle were the only implements known. Now the machine drawn by 2 or 4 horses cuts its throng of four to six feet as fast as the team can walk, and from four to six men are busy binding and setting up the sheaves The wheat will be ready for the reapers in say 2 weeks. I never saw crops look more promising. The season since corn planting has been rather wet for that crop and also rather cool for Corn

Sunday 15th   very warm   Have New Cucumbers

Sunday 29th Mr J R Moffitt of Piqua Hailed me last evening in the street and enquired if I knew whether M. Y. Jackson was in town. When I informed him that I was the man he answered that his name was Moffitt Then I knew him I have been in correspondence with him for some six or 7 years but never saw him till now He remained with us over night. I buy a Threshing machine of him agreeing to pay on receiving the Machine at St Paul   100.00
Cash in 6. mo   100 00
Do   " 18 "   100 00
3 lots   135.00

Sunday August 5 Commenced Harvesting my Wheat 25 acres on Wednesday (4th) finished last evening except setting up about 10 acres. we are to commence on Olivers tomorrow

Sunday 12th Cool for the season with my Wife & Willie drive out to Mr Fowlers in quest of a wheel for my reaping machine. finding none at Mr Fowlers drive on to Hastings where we arrive a little after dark. Put up at the Burnett House[4]

Monday 13th Find a wheel which I purchase of Mr John C Meloy agent for Mannys Reaper[5] Call at the foundry of A R Morrill and make some effort to introduce the building of the Moffitt Threshing Machine.[6] Drive home about 5 P.M.

Tuesday 14th Receive a note from my friend A. J. Vanvorhies editor of the Stillwater Messenger informing me that I had been elected a delegate to the State convention (Republican) to assemble at St Paul tomorrow and asking as a personal favor that I meet him and our county delegation this evening at St Paul This I can not do as my team must work in the harvest and I cannot get another in time

Wednesday 15 In company with Mr Watson Drive to St Paul to attend the convention and assist in forming an electoral ticket for the election of Ab Lincoln to the presidency Also in nominating Mess[rs] Aldridge [*Aldrich*] & Windon [*Windom*] for re election to congress and Mr McElrath [*McIlrath*] for State Auditor and A. J. Vanvorhies for Clerk of the Supreme court[7]

[4] The Burnet House was operated by William E. Allison, according to an advertisement in the issues of the *Hastings Independent* for 1860.

[5] See *ante,* p. 17, n. Meloy was auditor of Dakota County from 1859 to 1862 and, later, vice president of the First National Bank of Hastings. Warner and Foote, *Dakota County,* 224, 227, 315.

[6] Morrill established his "Hastings Foundry and Machine Shop" in the spring of 1860, according to his advertisement in the issues of the *Hastings Independent* for the summer of 1860.

[7] Cyrus Alrich was representative in Congress from Minnesota from 1859 to 1863, and later became postmaster of Minneapolis. William Windom was a representative in Congress from 1859 to 1869, a United States senator from 1871 to 1883, and secretary of the treasury under

Friday 24   with my team Preston & Jas Downing start for St Paul for Threshing machine. Camp at Tanners lake and drive in

Saturday 25   Load our Machine & start home. Camp at our last nights resting place and drive home on

Sunday 26   weather fine but cool for the season

September Saturday 1st   Meet Mess[rs] McKusick & Furber (Co Commissioners) at the house of Mr. Getchell to hear an appealed road case

Tuesday 4th   Attend the regular sitting of the Commissioners

Minnesota 1860 Sept 8 Saturday   Walked home from Stillwater last night through a very wet rain having been there since tuesday boarding at the "Putnam"[8]

Wednesday 12th   Walk over to Mr Hills beyond Hudson to see some cattle. trade for a nice young bull & 2 calves & return

Sunday 30   Drove to Hastings for some Machine repairs on Wednesday (26) Finished my threshing on Friday morning

October Wednesday 10th   Bought Downings interest in threshing machine last night agreeing to pay upon our lumber joint indebtedness 80.00 The loses or gains of the machin[e] thus far to be equal. I to pay all back payments and release downing from any further liability on a/c of our notes given to Mr Moffitt   Let my threshing machine last night to Mess[rs] Fowler   they to furnish

President Harrison. Charles McIlrath was state auditor from 1861 to 1873. Van Vorhes was clerk of the Minnesota supreme court from 1861 to 1864. Upham and Dunlap, *Minnesota Biographies*; Minnesota, *Legislative Manuals*.

[8] The Putnam House was on Second Street in Stillwater. E. B. Whitcher was the proprietor. *Stillwater Messenger*, September 11, 1860, advertisement.

teams & run it at their own cost except Oil and repairs about machine and give me half its gross earnings[9]

Sunday 14th Pleasant fall weather after a few sharp frosty nights. we have had a full month of rainy weather a prospect now for some good weather It seems pleasant to see the sun shine

Sunday 28 After two weeks of good weather we had a cold wet rain yesterday Cloudy muddy & gloomy today Had a letter from Mr Moffitt yesterday

Saturday 3rd November Drove to Stillwater with wagon to attend the sitting of the board of Commissioners A very wet—cold muddy disagreeable day drove home after dark

Minnesota Nov 6th 1860 This is our great Presidential Election day (see ticket) I vote the Republican ticket with a very little scratching In addition to the republican ticket Lincoln & Hamlin there is three others viz Douglas & Johnson—Breckendridge [*Breckinridge*] & Lane & Bill [*Bell*] & Everett It is also said that old Sam Houston of Arkansas & Texas is a candidate. But of this we know but little here in the North

Wednesday 7th Cold & Disagreeable I learn that our county has gone republican *Clean* Consequently I must be elected County Commissioner again This is rather more than I had any right to expect as the three towns composing my district taken by themselves gave a majority of 18 votes to the democratic ticket at the last spring election but they now give me 28 majority

Saturday 10th Plowed half the day yesterday & all day to day on the hill. *Lincoln* is *elected* by the accounts

---

[9] An account of these earnings may be found in the Appendix, *post*, p. 227.

Sunday 11th Beautiful fall day After a good deal of pretty rough weather we have now a prospect for some fine weather

Friday 16th weather still favorable to fall work. navigation still uninterupted. finished getting in my corn

Sunday 18th weather blustry & squally by spells Navigation still open

Tuesday 20th Ground frozen pretty hard this morning but still the plow goes. a Steamboat is loading grain today

Wednesday 21st Wind south but dont thaw much I work on the road down toward Bolles' mill. Have two plows going this afternoon

Thursday 22 Wind back in the North again with prospect of winter Snow—windy—wintry. Teams quit plowing & come down about 2 or 3 oclock this afternoon. I have 40 acres fall plowing now done and shall now have to wait a few months for Winter

Friday 23rd Winter in earnest. Mercury below 0 before night The ferry boat is still howling & blustring about but we may consider navigation closed The winter has held off well, though we have not had much good fall weather

Saturday 24th Clear—Cold, winter Went down to Afton for my bobs in the evening did not get them

Sunday 25th Pleasant winter weather A. E. Jackson sold his 80 acres of land on the hill yesterday to G[uy] M. Solsbury [*Salisbury*] for 2,050.$ This I think is a good sale A very lucky cash sale[10]

---

[10] Salisbury was a speculator at Lakeland, according to the 1860 census schedules. This sale is a good example of the rapid increase in the price of land in Minnesota. Probably in 1850 this land, or land of similar

Lakeland Minnesota December 1860 Tuesday 25th Well here is Christmas again. about 2 inches of snow last night which is much needed the roads being almost bare in [places] very pleasant day Alexander & Prudy went to Hastings yesterday to return tonight I was at Hudson yesterday & bought each of the boys a book

quality, could have been acquired at the government price of $1.25 an acre. Ten years later, in 1860, it sold for more than $25 an acre.

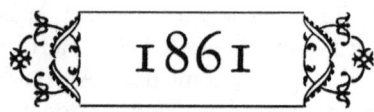

1861 Jany. 1st Tuesday 1st *New years* Fine cold weather Attend the sitting of the Board of Commissioners at Stillwater and return home at night which is to be repeated each day this week. Sleighing pretty good

Sunday 6th Real Minnesota winter Have attended commissioners court every day this year The business was not finished last evening. Board will sit tomorrow I cannot attend *conveniently*

Sunday 13th During past week we have had some very cold weather but it is dry and pleasant. Roads could hardly be any better Snow say from 4 to 6 inches with a little sprinkle every few days just enough to keep the roads nice

February Passes off with but 28 days which happens every time we have a new president to ina[u]gurate

Minnesota March 1861 Friday 1st Warm & Thawing rapidly. Our winter is ruined

Monday 4th this day is to be inducted into the presidency Mr Abraham Lincoln the first Republican ever elected to that office He finds governmental affairs much complicated As some half doz of the slave states have seceeded and are in open rebellion, their leaders declaring they will not submit to republican rule

March 5th Tuesday. Attend the sitting of the board of Com'rs as I also did yesterday. The Presidents inaugural is partly received to day, through by telegraph to St Paul last night & by mail this morning This is quick time

Saturday 9th Take my broom corn over to Mr [Oliver H. P.] Olds' shop to be manufactured[1]

Friday 15 Hawling wood Find Ryan & Clair trespasing on the Sargent place

Saturday March 16th Take my wagon to Afton for repairs

Monday 18th cool Go to Afton for my wagon also to get a wild hive of bees which I am getting of Mr Martin

Saturday 23rd Dark—blustry—wind S. E. Crossd the lake on good sound ice to the broom factory yesterday bring home 12 dz brooms

Monday 25th Go to Stillwater with a load of Brooms Barter them mostly off[2] First wild geese this morning

Tuesday 26th Drive across the ice and out some 15 mile[s] into Wisconsin for a load of oak lumber for Mr Gray.[3] Cool—cloudy and in the evening dark and stormy—driving snow from the northwest Unhi[t]ch on the hill east of lake and lead home Get in about 10 oclock cold, chilly

Saturday 30th Drive out to McHatties to get some

---

[1] Olds's broom factory was in Hudson, Wisconsin. Warner and Foote, *Washington County*, 244.

[2] That Jackson carried broom corn to a factory and then peddled brooms himself shows the primitive organization of trade on the frontier. Thus, instead of selling his broom corn to the factory, Jackson, the primary producer, kept the finished product in his hands to sell to the consumer or to the retail merchant. The frontier had hardly reached the retail handicraft stage of production.

[3] Probably Sheldon Gray, who lived at Lakeland. Census schedules, 1860.

Scotch Seed wheat. Disagreeable day. thawing some but chilly

Sunday 31 Easter Sunday First Larks—right welcome are these little cheerful songsters

Wedn[e]sday 3rd April Pleasant day Help A. Martin thresh

Sunday 7th Cloudy with a little rain in the morning and in the evening the first sunshine we have had since Wednesday The last three days having been rainy decidedly. The ground is just thawing out and we have a very muddy time

Saturday 13th After a backward spring we hitch up & plow an early potatoe patch Learn that fort Sumpter at Charleston S. C. was fired upon yesterday by the rebelious army of the seceeding states. have many fears for the safety of the gallant Anderson who commands a little handful of about 70 men to defend themselves against a force of say 3,000 to 5,000 *Steam boat* up to Catfish this morning—could not get through the ice

Sunday 21st Warm with South wind The news of a battle at Charleston is confirmed Tellegraphic accounts are conflicting. Fort sumpter is surrendered without doubt to the rebels

Monday 22 Papers are filled with "rumors of war" The president calls for 75,000 Volunteers to assist in maintaining the government I was over to Hudson this morning every thing is astir. A meeting at Lakeland to night for raising volunteers, I attend with Preston. Judge McMillen [*McMillan*][4] Mess[rs] Delano[,] Burt

[4] Samuel J. R. McMillan was judge of the first judicial district from 1850 to 1864, associate justice of the state supreme court from 1864 to 1874 and chief justice in 1874–75, and United States senator from Minnesota from 1875 to 1877.

& others from Stillwater are down   Also Rev A. B. Green baptist minister from same place. Rev. Mr. Monger of our place and Rev Mr. Putnam of Afton were also present and earnestly engaged in inlisting men into the service[5]

Thursday 25th   Commence sowing wheat   Club

Saturday 27th   with A. E.[,] Preston & George attend a mass meeting at Stillwater called to consult as to the best method to provide for the wants of the wives Mothers &c of those who have volunteered   As one of the commissioners of this county I consented to give the aid of the county treasury to an am^t not exceeding 5,000$ This is a good act done without authority of law, and I doubt whether the tax payers do not eventually complain of the act

Tuesday [*blank in ms.*]

Wednesday May 1   finish sowing Club & Tea wheat

Thursday 2nd   commence sowing west half of Sal[i]sbury field with Scotch wheat

Friday 3rd   Called to Stillwater as a witness State Vs. Albert Martin

Friday 10th   Finished sowing Wheat yesterday   Too windy to sow oats today so we hawl wood from lakeshore

Saturday 11   Finish sowing oats

Sunday 19th   Cloudy—dark—cold.   weather past week mostly Do. with abundant rain

Wednesday 22nd   Have had 2 days of Spring weather calling this one.   Planted the willow field with corn for Carmoody yesterday   Have a light thunder shower for the first this P.M.   Spring very backward   Plum bushes just begin to look white

[5] With ministers enlisting soldiers, in the North the war was regarded as a crusade against the great power of evil—slavery.

Lakeland June 1861 Monday 3rd warm attend the Commissioners court expecting to stay two or three days, but get through and return with Mr Furber in the evening

July Thursday 4th Preston & Frank go with their uncle & aunt to the cellebration at Hudson Preston raised his flag last evening

Tuesday 9th Drive down to Newport to get a reaping machine take dinner with Mr Seymore Fowler

Wednesday 10th After staying all night and trying reapers till noon today return home without any

Sunday 14th Finish writing a letter to Will, which I had commenced last sunday

Monday 15th Finish cutting 15 acres of Rye for A. E.

Saturday 20th Been haying most of the week. Row over to Hudson this P.M. to look at some reapers

Friday 26th Drive to Stillwater with A. E.[,] George & Mrs. Carmoody pleasant. On Tuesday (23) of this week we had the news of the great battle at Manassas which took place on Sunday (21) and the panic & flight of our forces on Sunday night The reports are now much modified—not near so bad as first given but bad enough yet

Thursday 7th August Drive to the Sweed [sic] neighborhood.[6] get no harvest hands Return by Afton get a load of Posts. The boys cut round the wheat with a cradle preparatory to going in with machine tomorrow

Thursday Aug 8th Go into the harvest with a Brockport self-raking reaper in the Sal[i]sbury field 80 acres[7]

[6] This was probably the Swedish community north of Marine, in what is now New Scandia Township, the first Swedish settlement in Minnesota. It was begun in 1850. Upham, *Geographic Names*, 570.
[7] Self-rake reapers were made on a large scale beginning in 1855 by Palmer and Williams in Brockport, New York. A McCormick agent

Afternoon drive to Stillwater to attend a called meeting of the board of Commissioners to appoint a sheriff instead of G. M. Stickney resigned. Geo. Davis is the lucky man.[8] This day finds me 45 Years old. How our days, months & years do fly

Sunday 11th Into the harvest thick my new reaper Brockport works finely. Have to hold up a few days for grain to ripen

Sunday 18th The harvest is mostly over we have cut including rye 130 acres of grain and have 12 acres to cut tomorrow which winds up the harvest we cut 20 acres Friday (about) I made a full hand binding all day 7 binders to 20 acres, Scotch wheat

Sunday 25th Beautiful day Finished harvesting on Monday 19th Been hawling & Stacking 3 days. about ¼ of stacking done   This is my wifes birth day she being 36

Saturday 31st Finished stacking my wheat last evening just as it commenced to rain this is lucky. A rain at any time during the past week would have been very inconvenient. And at any time when we had a rick open would have been damaging With Dr Johnson & Bro A E drive to Stillwater to attend a convention preliminary to a State convention to be held next Wednesday Delegates [N. C. D.] Draper of Marine [W. H.] Burt & [Louis] Hospes Stillwater[,] A E Jackson Lakeland[9]

reported in 1857 that more Palmer and Williams machines were sold than all other reapers together. Rogin, *Introduction of Farm Machinery*, 96–99.
[8] Davis remained sheriff for ten years. He was later auditor of Washington County. Upham and Dunlap, *Minnesota Biographies*.
[9] The proceedings of the convention are in the *Stillwater Messenger*, September 3, 1861.

Sept 1861 Tuesday 3rd Attend Commissioners court Stay over night at the Sawyer house[10]

Wednesday 4 Evening ride down home with Mess[rs] [John A.] Ford & [John] Holton of Newport

Thursday 5th Return to Stillwater Rema[i]n over night again

Friday 6th Ride down with Mr Middleton to the hill then walk home the commissioners having adjourned

Tuesday 10th With Preston & Frank start about 3 oclock P.M on an excursion north west in quest of cranberries Blackberries and recreation generally Camp at Paro's Brook and sleep pretty well[11]

Wednesday 11th Drive via Stillwater—W[illiam] Rutherfords & on North west Find some cranberries about 10 cllock [sic]. feed—lunch and drive on. country rough & mostly poor. Reach Rice creek a little before sun set[12] Camp. wood & water plenty some fine meadows going to waste for want of men to cut and cattle or other stock to eat them. Weather pleasant

Thursday 12th After a short drive into the Woods and helping to cut a bee tree we drive home

Friday 13th Our Threshing machine makes its appearance

Thursday 19th Break down the threshing machine in the morning and drive to Hastings. get most of my work

[10] The Sawyer House was the leading hotel in Stillwater at the time. It was built by Henry Sawyer in 1857, but it was not until 1860 that it was opened to the public. Warner and Foote, *Washington County*, 526.

[11] Jackson doubtless refers to Spring Creek, which flows through Bayport and empties into the St. Croix. Joseph Perro, a well-known river pilot, had a farm on the creek. Folsom, *Fifty Years in the Northwest*, 359; Upham and Dunlap, *Minnesota Biographies*.

[12] Rice Creek flows through Oneka and Forest Lake Townships in Washington County westward through Anoka County to the Mississippi.

and start home about 10 oclock P.M. Drive (Mule team) over the prairi[e] through a dark rain ballance of the night   Home to breakfast

Newport Wednesday 25th   Drive with Mr Fowler and the Volunteers to Newport   Participate in a good dinner & other exercises   remain over night with my friend G[iles] H Fowler

Newport Sept 26th Thursday   Mr Fowler leaves this morning with the rest of the volunteers for the fort   He leaves an excellent wife and three small children the youngest not 4 weeks old   No wonder our breakfast is eaten in silence   Here is an intelligent and conscientious young husband and father about to sever at least for a long time and very likely for ever the dearest earthly ties [13]   I wish I could go too

Friday 27th   Attend the Co. Convention at Stillwater with Dr Johnson and A. E. Jackson who are delegates. Find the ropes all set for the nomination of [Thomas J.] Yorks for register, [A. C.] Lull for Treasurer[,] [H. L.] Thomas or [Ebenezer] Ayers [*Ayres*] for representative &c &c [14]   I was an aspirant to the nomination for Treasurer

Monday 30th   First frost and it is a stinger

Lakeland Oct 1861 Monday 14th   Meet Mess[rs] McKusick & Furber at the house of Mr Green at Cottage Grove to hear an appeal on a road   Mr Green has an intelligent and interesting family   Evening call at Mr Gages for my wife who had accompanied me that far and drive home by moonlight

[13] Giles Fowler was discharged for disability in March, 1862. *Minnesota in the Civil and Indian Wars*, 1:181.

[14] The proceedings of the convention may be found in the *Stillwater Messenger*, October 1, 1861. Thomas received the nomination for representative over Ayres.

Tuesday 15th   drive to Cottage Grove again, and from there with Mr Strong to Prescott And home again by moonlight

Thursday Nov 7   Drive the wagon to Stillwater Thence with A. E. Jackson to Mr Rutherfords. Find it doubtful whether I can collect my claim against Mr R. owing to his inability to pay. My claim against him is now over 900$ and if lost it will allmost ruin me as I have been depending on this to meet a mortgage against my home place of Seven hundred Dollars

Friday 8th   Ride old Kate up to Holcombs.[15]   Cool

Saturday 9th   Snow Storm (the first) about 1½ inches

Tuesday 19th   very disagreable rain with S. E. wind Navigation still open and the weather has been fine since our Snow storm of Saturday 9th except a little snow Sunday evening

Sunday 24th   Freezing—with some 3 inches of snow on the ground

Monday 25th   Winterish. Take my gun and walk over the hills and through brush & snow to Stillwater to attend an extra sitting of the Commissioners. The lake is frozen over at Stillwater except some spots, and Navigation is closed and Winter is here and has possession. Ride down with Mr Leach after dark Cold & disagreeable

Thursday Dec 26th   Attend an appeal meeting of three commissioners at the house of Mr [Thomas] Persons[16] to settle a road disagreement Owing to a very severe snow storm neither of the other Commissioners attended

---

[15] Probably Edwin C. Holcomb, who is listed in the 1860 census schedules as a carpenter living in Lakeland.

[16] Persons lived at Afton, according to the 1860 census schedules.

1862

1862 Wednesday January 1st   Another New year   The war of 1861 is scarcely begun—where will the end be

Feb 16th Sunday   Good sollid winter   Fort Henry in Tennessee (a rebel establishment) was taken thursday 6th and on thursday last 13th Fort Donaldson was attacked and the fight was raging teribly up to last accounts yesterday with a determination on the part of our forces to *take* it—let it cost what it would   our loss must be heavy

Sunday March 2nd   Snows all day. this added to some 20 inches must give us two feet of snow   Fort Donaldson was surrendered by Gen Buckner Rebel to Gen. Grant (Union) on Sunday 16th with 15,000 prisnors. our loss say 400 killed & 800 wounded   This is costly

Friday 16th   Send a bid on mail rout[e] no 13583 at 622$ for tri weekly as advertised.   570 [for] Do [*tri weekly*] to leave St Paul Tuesdays—Thursdays & Saturdays at 7 A.M. reach Hudson same day at 12 M   Leave Hudson Monday Wednesday & Friday at 1 P.M. reach St Paul same day at 7   on Daily 974$ to leave St. Paul Daily at 7 AM arrive at Hudson Daily at 12 M   Leave Hudson Daily at 1 P.M. arrive at St Paul same day at 7 P.M.

Tuesday 20th   snow going off fast but without much slush   Saw a wild goose for the first   come near getting a shot at it with Mr Robinsons gun

Lakeland April 1862 Friday 4th   Worst of our muddy season is over. Heard some Larks for the first

Sunday 6th   After a stinging freezing cold night it is still cold and chilly though we have a little pale sun shine which thaws the ground a little

Monday 7th   Cold with strong East wind with a little snow   Hawl wood for Carmoody & self

Tuesday 8th   Cold with wind & snow from N. N. E. With wagon and Oliver to drive back I drive to Stillwater facing the storm over very bad roads made up of snow mud & frozen earth to attend court. Being a member of the Grand Jury. This is the first time I was ever called to sit upon a grand Jury. And quite unexpectedly I was chosen by the Court (Judge McMillen presiding) as foreman. This is a distinction of which I feel proud. Nor do I know to whom I am indebted for the honor. As my personal acquaintance with the Judge is but slight, and there are many older men and men of experience in such matters on the Jury

Wednesday 9th   Fine day—some sun shine   Close our labors on the jury before noon and adjourn to ½ past 9 tomorrow morning to give the County attorney Mr. [L. R.] Cornman[1] time to draw up the bills of indictment which are but two in number and both for the crime of Perjury   As our deliberations and findings are secret it might be improper even here to mention the name of the parties at present

Thursday 10th   Pleasant cool partly cloudy. Jury met at 9½ this morning. Mr Cornman having the 2 bills of

---

[1] Cornman, who lived in Stillwater, was also agent for the Phoenix Insurance Company, according to his advertisement in issues of the *Stillwater Messenger* for 1861.

yesterdays finding drawn up we pass upon them sign and report to the court, where upon we are discharged   I ride home with Mr Perin

Friday 11th   Rowed over the lake to Hudson with Mr Perin & Mr Palmer

Saturday 12th   Rain & mud

Sunday 13th   Do. Do.

Sunday 20th   After a backward and disagreeable spring, navigation may now be considered open   No boat except the Allen

Thursday 24th   Plowed a piece of ground and planted some potatoes

Minnesota May 1862   Sunday 4th   Prospect of good weather. Sowed my wheat yesterday

Sunday 11th   warm   We have had a solid week of good weather. Sowed my oats fore part of the week then hauled manure   went to mill &c

Sunday 18th   Cool cloudy & disagreeable   past week mainly good weather   Found our manure pile still frozen so that we had to adjourn & plant broom corn   set out some more strawberries &c. Broom corn say ⅓ plantd ballance ground ready

Sunday 25th   cool—disagreeable—windy—showry. pleasant evening   Planted my corn yesterday

Wednesday 28th   Pleasant. Drive wagon to Stillwater with A. E. & Preston & Mrs Carmoody

Sunday June 1st   Pleasant—Hot—Dry   Drive Oscar, Frank & Willie with their Mother out in the wagon airing

Monday June 2nd   Take my cow Flora to St Paul for sale. Hot & dry   Stop at Watsons[2]

[2] Daniel T. Watson kept a boarding house in St. Paul on Robert Street, between Fourth and Fifth. *St. Paul Directory*, 1863.

Tuesday 3rd   Sell out & come home with capt Tyler. cool

Sept 17 Wednesday   Drive a load of house goods Mrs. Way & Maggie to St Paul[3]   return say 10 oclock at night

Minnesota Sept 1862 Monday 29th   With Martha, Frank & part of a load of Bran drive to St. Paul   Stay over night with Mr Way and return late Tuesday evening the 30th   weather cloudy & a little rainy.   The special business of St Paul just now is shaving Uncle Samuel but during odd spells they put in the time shaving strangers & one another

October Saturday 4   Make a trip to St Paul. load for Mr Pray[4]   Preston & George go along   drive back by Moon light

Friday 10th   first frost this morning. Except some slight touches in the valleys around

1862 Oct. Minnesota Saturday 11th[5]   Drive to St Paul with load of Bran for N[orth] S[tar] Mills   also carry Mrs King & her trunk—on her way to Ft Ripley to Join her husband

Sunday 12th   Pleasant   Drive home from St Paul

Tuesday 14th   Drive another load to St Paul & return home with a load for Clement & Huntoon on Wednesday 15th

1862 Nov Saturday 22   Drive down with Mr [W.] Dougherty to Cottage Grove   Make the acquaintance of

---

[3] Evan J. Way removed with his family from Afton to St. Paul, where he established a produce and commission business. Census schedules, 1860; *St. Paul Directory*, 1863.

[4] Jackson probably refers to Otis A. Pray, who leased the interest of one of the owners of the North Star Mill at Afton during the latter's absence with the Union army. Warner and Foote, *Washington County*, 402.

[5] This entry begins a new volume of the original diary.

Mr Bennett and agree to take 25 sheep to keep on shares. All to be good ewe lambs of last spring I to have all the increase he to have all the wool

Friday 28th   Drive down to Mr Fowlers & stay all night.

Saturday 29th   Meet Mr Dougherty at Mr Bennets & drive home our 25 sheep Each

1862 Dec Saturday 20th   Drive to Stillwater & return. carry up 3 sacks flour for Mr Beach   A. E. Jackson & George & frank go along

Thursday 25th Christmas   pleasant. ground very Icy & sleety   no snow   Alex & Prudy & George dine with us. Winter so far has been very mild. The Ice on the lake is now unsafe to drive upon

1863

Thursday January 1st Newyears again. We have had two rains this winter lately, a thing altogather unusual for Minnesota   Ground still bare and ice on the lake still unsafe   weather mild   This is the great day of America —the great Epochal day that is to mark the end of our American system of African slavery   Upon this day the president Abraham Lincoln has promised to proclaim slavery at an end   This is to be done as a war measure— as a means of weakening the great Southern rebellion. A hap[p]y day for all time to come will this be if the United States government is to be the instrument in the hands and under the guidance of Divine Providence for the liberation of this downtroden african race who have been held in bondage in the Southern States ever since the formation of our confederacy and long before.   African Slavery is in my estimation a relic of barbarism which ought to have been abolished long ago   But the U. S. government had no right under the compact by which the United States were confederated to interfere with it.   It has been looked upon by the good people of the free States as a burning disgrace and only tolerated because we had no right to interfere with it

The election of Mr Lincoln to the presidency in 1860

was considered as an expression of a determination on the part of the people of the free states not to admit any more Slave states. This would secure to the free states the control of the U. S. Senate and break the power of the Slaveholding States to rule the nation Rather than submit to this they resolved to secede from the confederation and as the government would not consent to this, hence the rebellion And as Mr Lincoln and the people of the free states believe that the existance of the war consequent upon this rebellion gives Mr Lincoln as president the right and imposes upon him the duty of thus proclaiming freedom to the slaves of all the insurrectionary States This with other pending measures by which all the slaves of all loyal citizens are to be emancipated and paid for must end this enormously wicked and barborous ins[ti]tution What a shout of gladness will go up from these poor down trodden Darkies this morning wherever it is known that this is the day upon which the proclamation issues which breaks for ever their chains

Minnesota Jany Monday 12 Drive to Stillwater with wagon expecting to get some feed of Mr Rutherford but do not succeed Find that this is the day of the land sale for taxes a good many lands are being sold. I invest $13.16 in lands near Afton for which sum I get an undivided half of 155 acres that was considered worth from 5.00c to 25.00c per acre six years ago

1863 January Wednesday 14 Go to Hudson with some Beef & hides. Pretty cold crossing the ice bridge The winter so far has been very mild The ice is now 10 or 12 inches thick and the indications are that we are now to have some cold weather. No snow yet. My Cutter has not been taken down from its summer quarters

Thursday 15th   very cold with wind in Northwest

1863 Jany Saturday 17th   Weather moderate   W Dougherty takes the sheep to keep a while I having kept them since about the 1st of Dec.

Friday 23rd   Help Dr Johnson to butcher in the midst of a dashing snow storm. The ground is thoroughly frozen and a little snow now will make good sleighing— we have had no sleighing yet. winter has so far been unusually mild

Sunday 25th   Take down the Cutter for the first time this winter   But before we get started to meeting Mr Olds & Lady, Mrs. Jones & Mr O Caldwell & Lady drive up.

Tuesday 27th   Drive to St *Paul* with a load of flour for the North Star Mills. Sledding very good   cold but pleasant winter

Thursday 29th   Drive to St. Paul again   a little snow in the afternoon   Haul 10 bbl flour   easy roads   delightful

1863 January Saturday 31st   Drive to St Paul with load of meal &c   Chilly—we want a little more snow to make the roads tip-top. I sold flour today at 5.00 per bbl. which is higher than it has been for two years or more. Whilst most kinds of goods have been steadily advancing for a year produce has kept low but now wheat flour Pork &c begin to feel the effects of the abundant supply of money or the paper currency that has taken the place of money Heavy brown Sheeting 1 yd wide are held at 40c per yd which is an advance of full three hundred percent in less than two years. Sugar, that we have been buying at 8c are now bringing 15c   Crushed sugar now costs 16⅔ pr [pound?]   These are war times

Sunday Feb 1st   Wind turned to the N. W. last night and blows a gale this morning and continues all day—freezes like bones

1863 Feb Monday 2nd   Wind continues from N. W. and with clear sun shine we have a terrible winter day

Friday 6th   Preston & I drive the team & the young bull Prince of Wales to St Paul.   Stay at Mr Watsons

Saturday 7th   Attend what is called a Ramsey County fair which is a meagre collection of Cattle & horses brought in by their owners & offered for sale at auction.   Offered my bull under a limit of 100.$ no sale   Reach home about 10 Oclock cold and tired   Preston who started from St Paul half an hour ahead of me with the team reached home about 7 or 8 oclock P.M.

Wednesday 11th   With my wife Oscar & Willie go visiting to Mr Perins

Friday 13th   with same list as above go visiting to Oliver Caldwells.   Had a beautiful snow storm on Monday which gives good roads

1863 February Saturday 14   St Valentines   Misty Sleety & rainy.   away goes our nice snow   Evening cold.   Our sloppy snow & running water will be all aglare by morning

Sunday March 1st   frosty & foggy—roads not good   My wife & I were over to Capt Jones[']s yesterday

Monday 2nd   Wrote to Mr Baker at Chicago   also to Shaw & Clark Biddeford Maine—also to S. Madison at Alfred Me

1863 March Tuesday 3rd   cloudy   Mr Doughterty takes the sheep again

Sunday 22nd   A few wild geese made their appearance during the past week.   Last night we had a big thunder shower

Tuesday 24th Cold & winterish Mr Bolles' Mill dam washed out Saturday night

Sunday 29th Beautiful spring day clear but cool with breeze from the North Wild geese begin to be plenty

1863 March Monday 30th Cool Drive to St Paul with some stray Horses which I deliver to Mr E[dward] Webb for his friend & former partner Mr. [F. C.]Maltby.[1] Take tea in the family of our old friend and neighbor Mr. Way. Stay at Mr Watsons and

Tuesday 31st Drive home accompanied by Mrs. Way & Kate First meadow lark

Wednesday April 1st First good warm spring day Over to Hudson with Oliver

1863 April Thursday 2nd Blustry Write to Mr Baker Wrote to Miss Bangs yesterday

Saturday 4th pleasant Saw a robin, the first of the season. Hitch up the team and start the plow this P.M. frost rather near the surface

Sunday 5th pleasant Write to J. L. Stone

Tuesday 7th attend the town election

Thursday 9th Mr & Mrs Perin Mrs Tyler & Sister Mollie & children are down

April 1863 Friday 10th Commence sowing wheat[.] Evening, Thunder with heavy rain

Saturday 11th Rain, Snow & wind from the North. Write to Shaw & Clark Biddeford[,] to R L Wolcott 170 Chatham Square New York City[,] to H J Beston 271 Main St Hartford Ct

[1] Webb and Maltby were associated in the firm of Maltby, Webb, and Company, attorneys and land agents, in 1858 and 1859. Webb was still practicing law in St. Paul in 1863. *St. Paul Directory*, 1858–59, 1863.

1863 April Monday 13th Evening *first Steam boat* up the lake Plenty of Ice in the lake yet

Wednesday 15th Finish sowing my wheat from which I had been driven by the rain on Friday eve. Ground quite wet yet Preston harrows whilst I sow. This begins to look encouraging

Saturday 18 P.M. Drive up to Holcombs and from there to Stillwater having sowed oats during the forenoon. get home about 9 Frank with me. Chilly

1863 April Sunday 19th Cloudy, chilly. Write to E or L Needles, Beloit, Wis in relation to exchanging my place for his. Also to Edward F Hovey No 13 Spruce Street N. Y. Also to C Munro Brown & Co No 74 Bleecker Street N. Y. to the former in relation to the history of the rebellion, to the latter in relation to some invention

Wednesday 22nd Sheep turned to grass weather fine

April Saturday 25th Finish sowing oats up on the hill on Dr Johnsons place. weather fine

May Tuesday 12th go to Stillwater with part of a load of wheat to mill take Dr Johnson along Have an interview with Mr Staples[2] who thinks of buying the Bolls property. Drive home at night through a chilly rain

May 1863 Sunday 17th Morning cool & frosty in places Frank not finding the sheep last night I start out early & ride nearly all day in search for them Find 25—26 & 3 lambs still missing Evening go down to see old "Uncle Bolles" who has dropsey pretty badly and to make the

---

[2] Jackson probably refers to Isaac Staples, who came to Minnesota in 1853 and organized a lumber company at Stillwater in 1854. He also operated a flour mill and a store at Stillwater and owned considerable real estate. Folsom, *Fifty Years in the Northwest*, 413; Warner and Foote, *Washington County*, 600.

matter worse has to be moved out of his old homestead—
reason he got in debt and the creditors & lawyers must
have it It is a burning shame The old man ought to
be left to die upon the place where he has lived and worked
hard for nearly a quarter of a century

Wednesday 27th   finish planting corn

1863 June Monday 1st   Go to Hudson to sell some
Maps &c

Tuesday Wednesday & Thursday 2th 3 4   Sheared
Sheep all the time being impatient to get off on to my new
business viz canvassing for the sale of Victors History of
the Southern rebellion[3]   also the sale of Lloyds Maps &c

[3] Orville J. Victor, *The History, Civil, Political & Military, of the Southern Rebellion* (New York, n.d.). See *ante*, p. 8.

APPENDIX

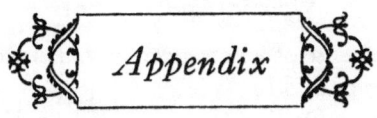

Appendix

[*The following notations are written in the front part of the volume of the Jackson Diary dated August 8, 1852, to April 12, 1854.*]

Prairie Du Chien Wis. Feb 18th 1854.
Distances to St. Paul

Galena to Prairie Du Chien		90
Lansing	35	125
Victory	12	137
Hastings	10	147
Wildcat	12	159
La Cross	13	172
Manteville	20	192
Bonnells Landing	7	199
Winona	6	205
Blue Rock	6	212
Mt Vernon	12	224
Wabeshaw	20	244
Reeds Landing	(5)3	247
Westville	(20)17	264
Wacoota	6	270
Redwing	6	276
Point Douglass	23	209
St. Paul	18	
	226	316

Wabash April 15 1854

Estimated expense of 4 Passengers to Lakeland		150$
Provisions to be laid in		
1 Brl Pork 1 Do Beef	30 ⎫	
2 lb Hams	20 ⎪	
3 Brl Flour	21 ⎪	
fruit	10 ⎬	
1 Brl Sugar	12 ⎪	
Coffee & Tea	10 ⎭	103
2 Horses		200
their expense with hand		40
2 Sets Harness (2 horse)		20
Due on farm		900
" Mr Newell		15
		1428

[*The following notations are written in the front part of the volume of the Jackson Diary dated April 21, 1854, to December 31, 1857.*]

Date of mortgage to Mr Furber Oct 22 1853   Recorded 28th Book B. 8 & 9

Date of Deed to T. A. Wood Dec 8 1851. Recorded Jany 11 *1854*

On E ½ of NW ¼ S 11
also Lot 4 S 2 & Lots 1–2 & 3 S 11
also Lot 2 & 3 S 14
also SE ¼ of SW ¼ of S 2
also N.E. ¼ of SE ¼ of S 4
also N ½ of SE ¼ S 3

Compound   548.89
                 720.00
            $1,268.89

Entered E ½ SW ¼ S 3 June 1/50
          E ½ NW

Pattent Aug 1853

Morgage to Isaac Collis June 1, 1853   720$
  200$ in 3 years int at 12
  520$ in 5 years   "   "
Recorded June 24 1853   Int to June 1858 $432^{00}

Deed from Amos Newell to Jonas Newell Dec 18 1851
  Record[ed] April 1852

Sept 2 1855   Sent by mail to J. R. Moffitt Draft No 1796 from the Mechanics & Manufacturers Bk Providence R. I to City Bk N. Y. for 100$ Date Aug 13   payable to order of D M Leonard assigned to W H Leonard & by him to M Y Jackson & by me to J R Moffitt

[The following notations are written in the back part of the volume of the Jackson Diary dated April 21, 1854, to December 31, 1857.]

May 19th 1854   Meadow   10-45/100 A

May 22nd Sow on South Oats 31 Bus (weight) to about 11 acres
Wednesday 24 Sow on ballance 7 Bus.
Finish harvesting Aug 26

South garden
  plowed Monday May 8

1 acre corn planted May 10 partly dent Ballance flint and sugar

Comes up May 25th (tardy) owing to wet & cold weather

July 23 fit for table use

Aug 24 gather a grist of good ripe flint corn

May 23 1854 Survey of Hill field

South line	62-84/100		
North	60.28	=	61.56
West	86.68		
East	85.10		× 85 89

= 5287 ÷ 160 = 33.04 A

Friday May 26 Commence planting the east part 17 Acres, listed, with yellow dent. finish that part on Tuesday 30

Friday June 2 commence planting South west 6. A. mostly flint. finish Saturday 3rd at noon. plowed & Harrowed

Shoultz and Mathis 4 Bags Extra
Galloway Grocer 16 Bags

Sept 23rd gather an ear of dent corn from that planted June 3rd Sound and ripe enough for seed though much of it is too green for frost yet

Monday 25th Sept Cut the ½ acre of dent corn in the south garden put up in 20 shocks

Wednesday 27th husk an average shock as near as we could tell and weighed the corn and counting 73 lb of ears for a bushel it is yielding 103-41/73 Bus pr acre

APPENDIX

Feb 1 Thresh & measure above half Acre find 33⅓ bus or 66⅔ pr acre after the mice &c took their toll, having stood out in the shock till some time in Jany

Smith bill	9 75		
Oil	2 00		
B Lised [?]	40	11.50	27 88
Iron at Stillw^t	13 64	19 32	19 32
	15.79		39 80
Do Do	5.81		23 91
	21.60	17 16	17 16
Pd Mr Martin	14.18		63 34
	35.78	13 59	13 59
			15.64
		40.00	80.00
			31 35
			20 85
			10 71
			5 41
			33 54
			396 00

Dec 19, 1854 Red Rock

Grain Threshed by Fowler & I

Nov 8	R[ye]	O[ats]	W[heat]	B[arley]
Robinson		213	199	
Green		388	82	
Fisher		589	274	
Norris		565	116	
Hohman		352	110	
Watson		1463	220	125
Hill		381	36	

Gates		335	69	29
Th Furber	150	1188	438	133
John Furber	31	628	177	
McCarty		207	244	
	181	6209	1855	287
			110	
Everett		281	38	
Fowler		97	25	20
	362	6587	2028	307
McKane		877		57
	362	7464	2028	364

Fowler Recd Feb 19 1857

James W Mabin St Paul keeps what is called the Temperance house

Jackson Recd of J S Norris		23.91
" Leach for Robinson		7 00
" Fisher wheat		36 90
" Cash of Mr Fowler		30.00
		.50
Feb 9th		98 31
	of Mr Fowler	57 90
		156 21

[*The following notations are written in the back part of the volume of the Jackson Diary dated January 1, 1858, to October 10, 1862.*]

Muffins 1 pt. Sweet Milk
2 Eggs Small Spoon Butter
Stir to a stiff batter
yeast enough to raise

1859

Jany 6 Log axe   Dr
        8 Bus. corn
        3 sacks Flour   1 90 c
        28½ lb Rope   20 c
        Cash for pulley   90
         "   Rasp   60
        4 Axes & Dressing   3.66
        Mending neck Y. & Sheets [?] 1 70
        133 lb—1 Bbl mess pork
        50 lb Salt

INDEX

Index

AFTON, 8, 11, 57n, 134n, 163n, 176, 193, 198, 201, 208n, 212n; platted, 139, 139n; church services, 139, 141, 142, 149, 150, 152, 153, 162, 163, 165, 167, 171, 172, 174-176, 189; Congregational church, 139n; donation party, 180; mill, 212n, *see also* Bolles, Lemuel
Afton Township, 39n; mounds, 142n
Agricultural implements, 15-19, 38, 194; plows, 11, 15, 74, 81; reapers, 16, 17, 151, 173, 183, 194, 195, 204, 204n, 205; cradles, 16, 204; binders, 17; flail, 17; threshing machines, 17-19, 91-95, 130, 131, 147, 194, 195, 196, 206; prices, 17, 46, 51, 55, 56, 64, 65, 74, 125; harrows, 75, 76; cultivators, 78, 79
Agriculture, beginnings in Minnesota, 10; markets, 19-22, 40, 42, 52, 64, 98, 127, 129, 130, 136, 153, 155, 211, 212, 215-218; fairs, 24, 25, 95; crop conditions, 65, 79, 80, 130, 138-140, 142, 143, 162, 173, 183; Indiana, 95; produce, *see* individual products; societies, *see* individual societies. *See also* Agricultural implements; Binding; Harrowing; Harvesting; Livestock; Planting; Plowing; Prices; Threshing; Winnowing

Aldrich, Cyrus, 175, 175n
Alexander, Martha, 95
Alexander, Simpson, 95
"Alhambra," steamboat, 176
"Allen," steamboat, 211
Allibone, ———, 175
Allibone, John, 173n
Allibone, William, 173n
Allison, William E., 195n
American House, St. Paul, 150, 150n
Anderson, Maj. Robert, 202
Ayres, Ebenezer, 207, 207n

BAILEY, OLIVER, 155n
Baker, M. C., 141, 168, 172, 179, 217, 218
Baptist church, Minneapolis, 113n; River Falls, Wis., 129; Hudson, Wis., 167; Lakeland, 169, 169n
Barley, price, 44; threshed, 144
Barns, construction, 14
Beach, ———, 213
Beans, 52, 54, 60; markets, 12, 51n, 55; prices, 51, 52, 55, 59, 64
Beckner, ———, 99
Beef, preserving, 61, 73; price, 224
Bees, 61, 64, 66, 201, 206
Bell, John, presidential candidate, 197
Belland, Henry, 38, 38n
Bennett, ———, 213
Bennett, Capt. ———, 111, 112
Bennett, Mrs. ———, 112

{ 233 }

Bennett, Dora, 112
Binding, 16, 17; binders, see Agricultural implements
Bissell, Elijah A., 39, 39n, 41, 44, 55, 62, 66, 74, 77, 79, 142n
Bissell's Mounds, 142, 142n
Blake, Edward, 45, 45n, 46
Blocher, ———, 94
Blueberries, 20
Boardman, Martha A., see Brown, Mrs. William R.
Bolles, Lemuel, 129, 134, 176, 219; mill, 11, 132, 141, 198, 218
Bonsell, Miss ———, 126
Bonsell, Charles, 188, 188n
Bonsell (Bonsall), Samuel P., 115, 116, 136, 145, 146, 150, 154; election clerk, 153; estate, 163
Bonsell, Mrs. Samuel P. (Mary Perrin), 115, 146, 157, 165, 172; marriage, 179. See also Caldwell, Mrs. Oliver
Boutwell, Rev. William T., 172, 172n
Bradley Hotel, Galena, 123
Brawne, Jonathan, 71, 71n, 72, 73n, 74, 75, 77, 78, 81
Breckinridge, John C., 197
Brissett, Amable, 53, 53n
Brissett, Edmund, 38, 38n, 42, 45, 49-51, 59, 70, 75
Brockport, N. Y., reapers, 204n
Broomcorn, 20, 201, 211
Brophy, Michael, farm, 112, 112n
Brown, E. Harrison, 39, 39n, 40-43, 45-64, 66-72, 74-77, 80, 81
Brown, John, of Osawatomie, 186, 187
Brown, John W., 41, 41n, 52-54
Brown, Mrs. John W. (Mary Mooers), 51, 51n
Brown, Joseph, Brown's brother, 61
Brown, Joseph R., 41n, 67n
Brown, William R., biographical sketch, 2-5; justice of the peace, 4, 5, 48, 58, 71, 79; land claim, 4, 5n; carpenter, 4, 47, 60, 63, 67, 73, 75, 82; diary described, 32; counselor in lawsuit, 39, 40, 41, 43, 79; religious beliefs, 47n; deputy register of deeds, 51, 52, 58, 62, 64, 65, 70; in postal service, 61, 73
Brown, Mrs. William R. (Martha A. Boardman), 4, 37, 37n, 38, 43, 50, 51, 56, 57, 60, 65, 66, 67, 72, 73, 75, 80
Brownsville, 106, 107, 107n, 110
Brunson, Rev. Alfred, 42n
Buchanan, James, administration criticized, 174
Buckingham, John, 117, 117n
Buckingham, Philo, 86, 88, 89
Buckwheat, 174
Buford House, Delphi, Ind., 121
Bunker Hill Day, celebration, 183
Bunnell, Willard, 107n
Bunnell's Landing, see Homer
Burnet House, Hastings, 195, 195n
Burnett House, Logansport, Ind., 120
Burt, W. H., 202, 205
Bush, John, 53, 53n, 54
Butter, prices, 63, 65, 155. See also Dairy products

CAIRNES, ———, 117
Caldwell, Rev. ———, 171
Caldwell, Hezekiah, 128, 128n
Caldwell, Martha A., see Jackson, Mrs. Mitchell Y.
Caldwell, Oliver, 119, 119n, 131, 133, 137, 141, 176, 179, 183, 194, 210, 216-218
Caldwell, Mrs. Oliver, 216, 218. See also Bonsell, Mrs. Samuel P.
Caldwell, Prudence, see Jackson, Mrs. Alexander E.
Caldwell, William, 125, 125n, 131, 133, 137, 138, 141, 146-148, 152-154, 161, 175, 180, 193, 204
Caldwell, Mrs. William, Sr. (Elizabeth Alexander), 125, 125n, 141, 148, 153, 161, 183

INDEX   235

Caledonia, 107n
Calumet River, 100
Cannon Falls, cattle raised, 19
Carli, Dr. Christopher, 59, 59n, 68n
Carli, Mrs. Christopher, 67n, 68n
Carli, Paul, 67, 67n
Carli, Mrs. Paul (Lydia Ann), *see* Carli, Mrs. Christopher
Carmoody, John, 182, 203, 210
Carmoody, Mrs. John, 204, 211
Carpenter, ———, 98
Catfish Bar, 144, 144n, 160, 202
Catfish Mound, 145
Cavileer, Charles T., 3n, 37, 38n, 40-43, 45, 46, 50, 52, 53, 55-57, 60, 62, 64-66, 68, 71, 78, 79, 81; partnership with Brown, 3, 47, 47n; saddler, 3, 4, 52; leaves Red Rock, 4; claim, 4, 5n, 50
"Cecilia," steamboat, 39, 74, 77, 81
Chapman, ———, 97n, 103
Chatfield, 153, 156
Chicago, 62; market, 98; described, 101; hotel, 122
Chicago and Galena Union Railroad, 103n
Christian church, Wabash, Ind., 6, 89, 90
Christmas Day, 31, 132, 166
Cincinnati, Newcastle, and Michigan Railroad, 90, 91n
City Hotel, Lafayette, Ind., 118, 122
Civil War, enlistment, 202, 203, 203n, 207; effect on prices, 216
Clair, ———, 201
Clement, Carlos, 184, 184n, 212
Collis, Isaac, 225
Columbus, Ia., 106
Congregational church, Afton, 139n; Hudson, Wis., 168
Constitutional convention, election of delegates, 161, 161n, 162
Cooper, James Fenimore, *Stories of the Sea*, 27
Corn, 11, 41, 46, 55, 71, 163; broom, 20, 201, 211; prices, 68, 76, 134, 136-138, 143; planted, 79, 125, 126, 137-139, 149, 171, 172, 181, 182, 203, 211, 220, 226; growing time, 129; damaged, 139, 139n, 142; plowed, 140; harvested, 143, 183, 226; threshed, 156
Corn meal, price, 154
Cornman, L. R., 210, 210n
Cottage Grove, 51n, 71n, 72n, 117, 207, 212; church services, 163
Cottage Grove Township, 11, 37n, 72n
"Cottage Spring," Jackson's home, 116, 124, 129, 131, 137, 148
Cox, ———, 94
Cox, D. M., 145, 172
Cranberries, 20, 52
Cressy, Rev. Edwin W., 113, 113n
Crosby, Henry W., 57, 57n, 69
Cummings, Lindsey, 68, 71, 72
Cummings, Robert, 39, 39n, 44, 55, 68, 68n, 71, 72
Currency, scarcity, 23, 24, 167, 216
Currier, ———, 97n, 99, 100

Daggett, Elias, 169, 169n
Dairy products, at fairs, 25. *See also* Butter
Davis, George, 205, 205n
Davis, James S., 37, 51, 55, 59, 62, 68, 73, 74, 76, 78, 80, 81
Davis, Mrs. Mary Haskell (Mrs. William Oliver), 48, 48n, 72
Dayton, ———, 143
Delano, ———, 202
Delphi, Ind., 88, 121, 130, 134
Democratic party, 164, 165, 185, 185n
Denmark Township, 39
Dentan, Francois, 77, 77n
Dentan, Samuel, 54n
Description and travel, Indiana, 98-101; Illinois, 101-104; Wisconsin, 104-106, 178; Minnesota, 106-118; Mississippi River, 106-118; Washington County, 115, 206; St. Croix Valley, 178

Detroit, Eel River, and Illinois Railroad, 91n
Doctors, 30
Doe, Hilton, 38n, 80
Dougherty, W., 212, 213, 216, 217
Douglas, ———, 156
Douglas, Stephen A., candidate for president, 197
Dousman, Hercules L., mail contractor, 61, 61n
Downing, David, 177n
Downing, James, 177n, 180, 196
Draper, N. C. D., 205
Drew, Edward B., 107
Drew, James M., 8n
Dugas, William, 65, 65n
Du Luth, Daniel G., sieur, in St. Croix Valley, 10

ECONOMIC CONDITIONS, 21-24, 79, 79n, 157n, 166, 166n, 174. *See also* Currency; Prices
Edwards, ———, 130, 131
Eel River, 91, 91n, 99
Eggs, prices, 155, 167
Elections, presidential, *1852*, 87, *1860*, 197; Lakeland, 153, 175, 176, 180, 218; delegates to constitutional convention, 161, 162; Washington County, 161, 162, 164, 185, 192; Minnesota, 164; Five Million Loan, 170
Elgin, Ill., 102
"Equator," steamboat, 173; wrecked, 182, 182n
Everett, Edward, vice-presidential candidate, 197
"Excelsior," steamboat, 137

"FALCON," steamboat, 82
Falstrom (Faulstrom), Jacob, 39, 39n, 40, 41, 43-46, 79, 79n
Falstrom, John, 79, 79n
Faribault, David, 64, 64n, 65, 65n
Faribault, Jean Baptiste, 64n, 113, 114, 114n
Farmers' clubs, 25; Lakeland, 154; activities, 154n
Fayette County, Ind., 5, 115

Fences, 15, 37, 67
Ferguson, John H., 62
Ferrall, Daniels, and Co., 190
Finch, ———, 112
Findley, Samuel J., 64, 64n
First U. S. Infantry, at Fort Snelling, 82n
Fishing, *see* Social life and recreation
Five Million Loan, 171n; meetings to protest, 169, 170; election, 170
Flora, Alexander, 91, 92, 93
Flora, Mrs. Alexander, 91, 92
Flour, 42, 47, 52, 53; exported from Minnesota, 21, 22; imported, 22; prices, 57, 138, 154
Ford, Dr. James, 89
Ford, John A., 3n, 41, 52, 53, 55, 59, 62, 63, 65, 81, 206; store, 37, 37n, 53n, 58; blacksmith, 37n, 46, 57, 67, 71, 75
Ford, W. I., 128
Fort Donelson, 209
Fort Henry, 209
Fort Snelling, 4, 10, 42n, 47, 82, 113; distributing point for mail, 41, 46, 49, 61, 62n; supplies obtained from, 41, 42, 52, 59, 64, 65, 81; market, 42, 52, 64, 130, 153; infantry regiment, 52n, 82n; surgeon, 74n
Fort Sumter, 202
Fort Wayne, Ind., 86, 91n
Foster, Joel, 108, 108n
Fowler, ———, 129, 132, 194-196, 213
Fowler, Giles H., 129n, 207, 207n
Fowler, Seymore, 129n, 204
Fowler, William, 129n
"Fred," steamboat, 176
Freeborn County, cattle, 19
Freeport, Ill., 102, 103
Freight, charges, 21, 22, 41
Fremont, John C., presidential candidate, 153
Fruit trees, 137, 161, 203
Furber, ———, 72, 79, 117, 224

INDEX 237

Furber, Joseph W., 51, 51n, 117n; county commissioner, 193, 196, 204, 207
Furber, Theodore, 72, 72n, 117n

GAGE, B. F., 188, 188n, 189, 207
Galena, Ill., 97, 123, 123n
Galena and Chicago Union Railroad, 123, 123n
Garden Prairie, Ill., 102
Gardens, 72, 81, 82. *See also* Vegetables
Gavin, Daniel, 54n
Getchell, Charles S., 139, 139n, 196
Gibson, Rev. A., Baptist minister, 129, 129n, 131, 134, 135
Gilbert, ———, 97n, 102
Gleim, E. H., steamboat captain, 123n, 124n
Good Templars, 25
Gorman, Gov. Willis A., 110
Gosse (Goss), Joseph, 157, 157n
Graham, William A., vice-presidential candidate, 87
Graham House, Rock Island, Ill., 118
Granger, Lt. Robert S., 52, 52n
Grant, Ulysses S., captures Fort Donelson, 209
Grant Township, 185n
Gray, Sheldon, 201, 201n
Gray Cloud Island, 38n, 42n, 45n, 54, 54n; trading post, 47n
"Greek Slave," steamboat, 117, 117n
Greely, Miss ———, 55, 55n
Greely, Elam, 55, 56n, 57, 74, 114n
Greely, Himan W., 115n
Greely, John, 115
Green, ———, 207
Green, Asa B., steamboat captain, 182, 182n; Baptist minister, 203
Green Bay and St. Paul Railroad, 114, 114n
Grigrich (Grigerige, Gregridge), Joseph, 40, 40n

Gristmills, 63; Bolles', 11, 132, 141, 198, 218; Phalen Creek, 65n; Rutherford's, 185, 185n; Stillwater, 219, 219n

HALE, JOHN P., presidential candidate, 87
Half Way House, 150, 150n
Hamlin, Hannibal, vice-president, 197
Hammond, ———, 107
Harris, Albert, 56n, 59
Harris, Mrs. Albert, 56
Harrowing, 76, 125, 137, 181; harrows, *see* Agricultural implements
Harvesting, 129, 141, 142, 151, 184, 195; methods, 16; vegetables, 37; hay, 140, 151, 162, 163, 183, 204; rye, 140, 162, 173, 194, 204, 205; corn, 143, 183, 226; wheat, 194; oats, 225
Haskell, Clara, 48
Haskell, F. A., 185
Haskell, Joseph, 11, 41-45, 48, 52, 53, 55-57, 60, 62-64, 66, 67, 69, 72, 74-78, 81, 139n, 151
Haskell, Mary, *see* Davis, Mrs. Mary Haskell
Haskell, Ralzaman, 139n
Haskell, Sophia, *see* Norris, Mrs. James S.
Hastings, 196, 206; Burnet House, 195, 195n; foundry, 195n; bank, 195n
Hay, 38, 43, 46, 48, 50, 55, 56, 59, 71, 142; harvesting method, 16; damaged, 42, 62, 71; harvested, 140, 151, 162, 163, 183, 204
Helm, J. Holton, 143
Helm, R. D., 145
Hennepin County Agricultural Society, 24
"Heuer," steamboat, 80
Hill, ———, 196
Hill, Lewis, 70, 70n, 73, 79
Hitt, J. W., 70
Hobart, Ind., 100

Hoffstrom, Hettie, 184, 185
Holcomb, Edwin C., 208, 208n, 219
Holcombe, William, 58, 58n, 76
Holton, David, 80, 80n
Holton, John, 42, 42n, 43, 46, 53, 62, 63, 69, 71, 73, 74, 76, 80n, 206
Holton, Mrs. John, 60
Homer (Bunnell's Landing), 107, 107n
Hone, David, deputy sheriff, 45, 45n, 55, 81
Hoover, George, 137
Hopkins, Daniel, 37, 37n, 41; store, 43, 52, 53n, 68, 76, 80
Hospes, Louis, 193, 205
Hotchkiss, ———, 107
Housekeeping, 28
Houses, construction, 13-15, 66; sod, 13; frame, 13, 15; log, 13, 14, 112; furnishings, 13; conveniences, 28-30
Houston, Samuel, 197
Houston County, 107, 107n
Hovey, Edward F., 219
Howe, ———, 55
Hoyt, Dr. Otis, 191, 191n, 192
Hudson, Wis., 114, 125, 130, 134n, 161, 196, 199, 202, 220; churches, 134, 163n, 167, 168n; market, 136, 155, 215; Masonic lodge, 167; broom factory, 201, 201n; July 4 celebration, 204; mail service, 209
Hunting, *see* Social life and recreation
Huntoon, Lucius A., 167, 167n, 184n, 212
Hurlbut, Lemuel, 63n

IAMS, JOHN, 107, 107n, 175
Illinois, 21; described, 101-104
Illumination, 28
Imlay, D., 86
Immigration, Minnesota, 2, 9, 12, 21
Indiana, railroads, 7; fair, 95; described, 98-101; sugar making, 147
Indiana House, Wabash, Ind., 119
Inver Grove, antiloan meeting, 170
Irvine, John R., 49, 49n
Isabel River, 117, 117n

JACKSON, ALEXANDER E., 6-8, 86n, 90, 96, 97, 110, 119, 127, 134, 141, 143, 150, 164, 168, 169, 171, 172, 174, 183, 184, 193, 198, 199, 203-205, 207, 208, 211, 213
Jackson, Mrs. Alexander E. (Prudence Caldwell), 7, 86, 86n, 90, 119, 125, 134, 141, 168, 169, 171, 180, 183, 185, 199, 204, 212, 213
Jackson, D. Imlay, 85, 85n, 121, 128, 130, 134, 140, 145, 156, 159, 163, 172
Jackson, Daniel, 5, 6, 8, 88, 88n, 120, 128
Jackson, Ellen Jane (Mrs. D. Imlay Jackson), 85, 85n, 121
Jackson, Frank, 89, 89n, 119, 122, 141, 152, 153, 163, 171, 174, 189, 204, 206, 211-213, 219
Jackson, George, 119, 126, 203, 204, 212, 213
Jackson, Henry, 55, 66; justice of the peace, 39, 39n, 40, 41, 44; storekeeper, 65; postmaster, 79, 79n
Jackson, Mitchell Y., 29, 31; biographical sketch, 5-9; assessor, 8, 138-140, 149-151, 162, 163, 172-174, 175n; register of deeds, 8; county commissioner, 8, 192, 192n, 197, 200-205, 207, 208; book salesman, 8, 220; Lakeland house, 13, 14; financial condition, 23, 157, 166; political activities, 25, 87, 153, 162, 164, 175, 195, 197; library, 26; Mason, 26, 124; diary described, 32; sells warehouse, 90; withdraws from Christian church,

INDEX   239

90; sells threshing machines,
91-95; journeys between Indiana and Minnesota, 97-124; preempts land at Lakeland, 116;
buys Lakeland farm, 116; school
trustee, 136; election judge, 153;
in lyceum debate, 168; church
trustee, 169; on grand jury, 210
Jackson, Mrs. Mitchell Y. (Martha
A. Caldwell), 7, 25, 86, 110,
116, 119, 119n, 126, 134, 141,
142, 145, 152, 153, 156, 163,
165, 167, 168, 171, 174-176,
180, 189, 194, 205, 217
Jackson, Myron B., 9n
Jackson, Oscar, 88, 88n, 119, 125,
129, 141-143, 145, 174, 182,
211, 217; illness, 176, 189-193
Jackson, Preston T., 5n, 9n, 13n,
19, 25, 86, 119, 125, 141, 142,
171, 189, 193, 196, 202-204,
206, 211, 212, 217, 219
Jackson, Raymond A., 33, 123,
124n
Jackson, Sarah Ellen, 121
Jackson, William, 183, 194, 211,
217
Johnson, Mrs. Clarence H., 33
Johnson, Dr. Edward, 176, 176n,
189-192, 205, 207, 216, 219
Johnson, Herschel V., vice-presidential candidate, 197
Johnson, W. H., 139n
Jones, Sterling, 134, 134n, 146,
216, 217
Jones, Mrs. Sterling, 167
"Julia Dean," steamboat, 118.

KANOT, ———, 178, 179
Kansas, 153; subject of lyceum debates, 26, 168; constitution rejected, 174; John Brown in, 186
Kaposia, Sioux village, 4, 58n;
Methodist mission, 4, 5n, 39n,
42n, 79n
Kavanaugh, Rev. Benjamin T.,
Methodist missionary, 3, 42, 46,
46n, 56, 60, 66, 70

Kavanaugh, William B., Methodist
missionary, 3, 42, 46, 46n, 56,
60, 66, 70
King, Mrs. ———, 212
King, David, 79, 79n
King, William R. D., vice-presidential candidate, 87
Kingsley, A. D., 144, 144n, 152,
169
Kinnickinnick, Wis., 145
Kinnickinnick River, 108
Knox Co., O., 85

LA CROSSE, WIS., 106, 107
"Lady Franklin," steamboat, 123,
124n
Lafayette, Ind., 118, 122, 156
Lake Harriet, 113n
Lake Johanna, 112n
Lake Pepin, 108, 117
Lake St. Croix, 6, 67n, 69, 70, 72,
114, 144n; ferry, 198. *See also*
St. Croix River
Lake Superior, 134
Lakeland, 8, 25, 32, 39n, 124,
153n, 155, 161, 184n, 188n,
201n, 208n; sirup production,
20; library association, 26, 180;
described, 114; sawmill, 114n;
platted, 114n; school, 129, 135,
136, 141, 154, 168-170, 184;
church services, 129, 131, 141,
145, 149, 153, 162, 163, 165,
167-169, 171, 172, 174, 176,
180, 188, 189; post office, 131,
144n; lyceums, 146, 168; elections, 153, 164, 175, 176, 180,
218; Jackson's Addition, 158,
158n; Baptist church, 169, 169n;
antiloan meeting, 169, 170; donation party, 180; Republican
meeting, 184; Civil War enlistment, 202
Lamare-Picquot, 74n
Lamont, Daniel, 54n
Lamont, Jane (Mrs. Moses S.
Titus), 54, 54n
Lancaster, Wis., 105n

Land, speculation, 4, 22, 23, 101; prices, 23, 101, 102, 105, 112, 156, 157, 198, 198n, 199n, 215
Lane, Joseph, vice-presidential candidate, 197
Langhery, James, 128
Lansing, Ia., 106
Laporte, Ind., 99
Lard, price, 155
La Roche, Leonard H., 65, 65n
Lavicinia (Lavisinia), ———, 37, 38, 46
Leach, George W., 136, 156, 169, 208
Le Claire, Antoine, 63, 63n
Le Claire, Michel, 63, 63n
Le Claire, Ia., 118
Lehmicke, Rudolph, 185
Leith, ———, 46
Libraries, 26; Lakeland, 26, 180
Lincoln, Abraham, supported by Minnesota Republicans, 195; elected president, 197; inaugurated, 200, 201; emancipation proclamation, 214, 215
Livestock, oxen, 11, 69, 73, 77, 78; breeds, 19, 25, 63, 63n, 64, 73, 74; pigs, 19, 38, 43, 49-51, 67, 78, 131, 143, 154, 155; poultry, 20, 25, 37, 43, 63, 67, 73, 143, 155; prices, 20, 37, 38, 143, 154, 155, 217; at fairs, 25; sheep, 25, 29, 213, 216, 217, 219, 220; cattle, 37, 39, 42, 45, 52, 56, 64, 70, 72-74, 127, 129, 196, 211, 217; castrated, 38, 176; butchered, 43, 45, 51, 70, 131, 154, 188, 216; horses, 57, 58, 63, 75, 77, 156; bred, 72, 80; mules, 207
Lloyd, J. T., maps, 220
Lockport, Ind., 120
Logansport, Ind., 88, 91n, 120
Logansport and Northern Indiana Railroad, 91n
Lowell, Jacob, 184, 184n
Lull, A. C., 207
Lumber industry, 79, 181; Washington County, 10, 12; camps, 20, 51n, 178; Marine, 44n; St. Croix Falls, 51n; Stillwater, 74n, 219; Wisconsin, 179
Lyceums, Mt. Carmel, Ill., 2; questions debated, 26, 146, 168; Lakeland, 146, 168
"Lynx," steamboat, 70, 77, 82

McCoy, FRANCIS, 53, 53n
McHattie, ———, 45, 67, 72, 201
McHattie, Alexander, 45n, 68, 76
McHattie, John, 45n, 48, 50, 50n, 51, 52, 56, 57, 57n, 60, 69
McHattie, Mrs. John (Jane Middleton), 50n, 57, 57n
McIlrath, Charles, 195, 196n
McKackum, ———, 137
McKean, Elias, 129n, 184, 184n
Mackey, Andrew, 57n
Mackey, Mrs. Andrew, 57
McKnight, ———, 51
McKusick, John, 51, 51n, 55, 74, 207; county commissioner, 193, 196
McLeod, Alexander R., 62, 62n, 64, 65, 65n, 79
McMillan, Judge Samuel J. R., 202, 202n, 210
Madison, S., 217
Madison and St. Paul Railroad, 114, 114n
Maiden Rock, 108, 117
Mail service, Point Douglas, 39n; St. Croix Falls, 39n; Red Rock, 41, 46, 49, 55, 61, 63, 65, 67, 70, 71, 73, 80; Minnesota, 61n; Hudson, Wis., 209; St. Paul, 209
Maltby, F. C., 218, 218n
Manassas, battle, 204
Mann, John S., 112, 113
Marengo, Ill., 102
Marine (Marine Mills), 44, 56, 170n, 178, 193, 204n, 205; sawmill, 44n; region described, 175
Marine Lumber Co., 44n, 45n, 56, 56n, 63

INDEX 241

Marion, Ind., 86
Marsh and Co., 92
Marshall, Rev. C. H., Congregational minister, 168, 168n, 171, 173, 174, 180; donation party for, 180
Martin, Albert, 134, 134n, 135, 137, 140, 188, 201, 202, 203
Mason, J. C., 139n
Mason City, Ia., 9
Masonic Order, 154; Wabash, Ind., 26; St. Paul, 114, 114n, 130, 150, 150n, 167
Massilon, O., threshing machines, 93n
Mege, Alexander, 49, 49n
Meloy, John C., 195, 195n
Mendota, 65n, 74, 74n, 75n; Sibley's residence, 52, 114; hotel, 113, 113n; region described, 113; Faribault house, 113n
Mendota House, Mendota, 113, 113n
Merchants' Hotel, Chicago, 122
Methodist church, Hudson, 134
Mexican War, 80, 81
Michigan City, Ind., 100, 118, 122, 122n
Michigan Southern Railroad, 123
Middleton, ———, 46, 206
Middleton, James, 45, 45n
Middleton, Jane, *see* McHattie, Mrs. John
Middleton, Samuel, 12
Middleton, William, 12, 45n, 68
Middleton family, 45n, 52
Miller, ———, 158
Miller, John, 42, 42n
Milwaukee, market, 21, 98; wheat prices, 22; agriculture in region, 98
Minneapolis, 112; fairs, 24; hotel, 74n; Baptist church, 113n
Minnehaha Falls, 3, 113
Minnesota, settlement, 2, 9, 12; farms in *1850*, 12; exports and imports, 21; described, 106-117; rainfall, 110

Minnesota City, 107
Minnesota Farmer and Gardener, 22
Minnesota Historical Society, cornerstone ceremony, 150, 150n
Minnesota House, Stillwater, 114, 114n
Minnesota Territorial Agricultural Society, 24
Mississippi River, levels, 80, 81; rapids, 118
Moffitt, J. R., 131, 147, 194, 196, 197, 225
Monfort, A. C., 41, 41n
Monteville, 107
Mooers, Hazen, 47, 47n, 49, 50, 51, 51n, 55, 70, 75
Mooers, John, 51, 51n, 64
Mooers, Mrs. John, 51
Morgan, Mrs. ———, Jackson's sister, 120
Morgan, I. Finley, 129, 129n, 135, 143, 153
Morgan, John, 150n
Morgan, Milton, 119, 119n, 129, 137, 143, 156
Morgan, Mrs. Milton, 143
Morgan, W. W., 169, 169n
Morrill, A. R., 195, 195n
Mount, ———, 99
Mount Carmel, Ill., 2, 3
Mount Vernon, 107
Mount Vernon, O., 5
Mumford, Capt., *see* Monfort, A. C.
Munger (Monger), Rev. Enos, Baptist minister, 169, 169n, 171, 172, 174, 179, 180, 188, 189, 203
Myers, N. D., 168

NEEDLES, ———, 219
Nevada, Ill., 103, 103n
New Albany, Ind., 122n
New Albany and Salem Railroad, 122, 122n
New Orleans, 21
New York Weekly Tribune, 27

Newark, Ind., 93, 94, 98
Newcastle, Ind., 91n
Newell, ———, 224
Newell, Amos, 116, 130, 225
Newell, Dr. George C., 175, 175n
Newell, Harriet A., 129, 129n, 162
Newell, Jonas, 116, 149, 150, 225
Newport, 4, 5, 129n, 204, 206
Nobles, Rev. Lemuel, 162, 162n
Norris, James S., 11, 41, 43-46, 48, 55, 58, 60, 61, 66, 68, 69, 71-76, 79, 81, 227
Norris, Mrs. James S. (Sophia Haskell), 48
North Star Mills, Afton, 212, 212n, 216
Northup, Anson, 74, 74n
Northwestern Farmer and Horticultural Journal, 26, 169; subscribers' club, 154

OAK GROVE, 25
Oats, 65, 71, 75, 77; markets, 21, 130; threshed, 61-63, 69; winnowed, 62-64; weight, 64; prices, 64, 69, 137, 138; planted, 79, 80, 125, 126, 136-138, 148, 211, 219, 225; harvested, 129, 140, 151, 225; yield, 152
O'Kane, John, 89
Olds, ———, 216
Olds, Oliver H. P., 201, 201n
Oliver, John, 127, 127n, 172
Oliver, Mrs. William, *see* Davis, Mrs. Mary Haskell
Orstott, Mrs. ———, 98
Osterhaut, ———, 97n, 101
Otis, Benjamin T., 78, 78n
Otisville, Ia., 37
"Otter," steamboat, 41
Owatonna, 176n

PALMER, ———, 211
Palmer and Williams, 204
Parker, Asa S., 193
Parker, James, 63, 63n, 77
Paro's Brook, *see* Spring Creek
Patch Grove, Wis., 105

"Patriot," boat, 89
Paulding, Commodore Hiram, 168, 168n
Pavilion Center, N. Y., 92
Pearce, ———, 58
Perin (Perrin), Moses, 115, 116, 126, 146, 154, 161, 211, 217, 218; proprietor of Lakeland, 114; sawmill, 114n; school trustee, 136; election judge, 153
Perin, Mrs. Moses, 146, 161, 218
Perrin, Aaron, 115
Perrin, Mary, *see* Bonsell, Mrs. Samuel P.; Caldwell, Mrs. Oliver
Perro, Joseph, 206n
Persons, Thomas, 208
Petree, Capt. ———, 120
Pettijohn, Eli, 54n
Pettijohn, Mrs. Eli, *see* Prescott, Lucy
Pettit, John U., 146, 146n
Phalen Creek, 62n, 65n
Phalen Falls, 64
Phelan, Edward, 62, 62n, 65n, 79
Phoenix Insurance Co., 210n
Pierce, Edward, 70
Pierce, Franklin, presidential candidate, 87
Pig's Eye, 77n
Pilot Knob, 113, 113n
Piqua, O., 130, 194
Pitts, Hiram A., 93n
Pitts, John A., 93n
Pittsburg, Ind., 121
Planting, methods, 16; vegetables, 74-76, 80, 81, 181, 191; oats, 79, 80, 125, 126, 136-138, 148, 211, 219, 225; corn, 79, 125, 126, 137-139, 149, 171, 172, 181, 182, 203, 211, 220, 226; wheat, 148, 149, 161, 181, 192, 193, 203, 211, 218, 219; potatoes, 192, 211
Platteville, Wis., 104
Plowing, 78, 80, 136, 137, 148, 149, 160, 169, 181, 186, 191, 198, 211, 218; cost, 11, 15;

INDEX 243

methods, 15; vegetables, 76; potatoes, 80, 202; corn, 140; plows, *see* Agricultural implements
Plummer, Capt. Samuel M., 82, 82n
Plymouth, Ind., 98
Point Douglas, 45n, 108; mail service, 39n
Politics, farmers' activities, 25. *See also* Democratic party; Elections; Republican party
Pomeroy, Judge ———, 97n, 99
Pond, ———, 53, 53n, 54
Pond, Gideon, apples exhibited at fair, 25; Presbyterian missionary, 53n
Pond, Samuel W., Presbyterian missionary, 53n
Pork packing, 20
Port Byron, Ill., 118
Porter County, Ind., 99
Potatoes, 11, 12, 76, 193; markets, 21, 77, 129; winter storage, 60, 73; steamed for pigs, 67, 67n; varieties, 75; prices, 77, 138; plowed, 80, 202; planted, 192, 211
Prairie du Chien, Wis., 11, 61n, 62n; described, 105; telegraph, 174
Pray, Otis A., 212, 212n
Presbyterian church, Wabash, Ind., 89; Hudson, Wis., 163
Prescott, Lucy (Mrs. Eli Pettijohn), 54, 54n
Prescott, Philander, 54n, 59, 59n, 74, 81
Prescott, Wis., 38n, 53n, 108, 117
Prices, living expenses, 7; farm labor, 11, 15, 61; farm implements, 17, 46, 51, 55, 56, 64, 65, 74, 125; livestock, 20, 37, 38, 143, 154, 155, 217; pork, 20, 65, 216, 224; freight, 21, 22, 41, 125; wheat, 21, 22, 95, 138, 216; in *1857*, 22; land, 23, 101, 102, 105, 112, 156, 157, 198,

198n, 215; household necessities, 29, 52, 55, 56, 64, 65, 80, 125, 216; clothing, 37, 41, 52, 53, 55-57, 64, 65, 67; vegetables, 40, 46, 68, 154, 182; barley, 44; beans, 51, 52, 55, 59, 64; flour, 57, 95, 138, 154, 216, 224; butter, 63, 65, 155; oats, 64, 69, 137, 138; potatoes, 77, 138; labor, 82, 95; travel expenses, 119n, 120, 224; coffee, 125, 224; lard, 155; sugar, 167, 216, 224; beef, 224; tea, 224
Purinton, James, 43, 43n, 44-46, 51, 58, 62
Putnam, Rev. Simon, Congregational minister, 139, 139n, 141, 149, 150, 163, 167, 171, 175, 203; donation party for, 180
Putnam House, Stillwater, 196, 196n

RAILROADS, Indiana, 7, 91. *See also* Five Million Loan; individual railroads
Ramsey, Alexander, candidate for governor, 165, 165n
Ramsey County, fair of *1863*, 25, 217
Ray, Henry, 127
Ray, Mrs. Henry, 119
Ray, J. H., 119, 121, 123, 127, 148
Ray, Mrs. J. H., 119, 122
Reads Landing, 108
Recreation, *see* Social life and recreation
Red Rock, 5n, 42n, 53n, 77n, 129; mission, 3, 4, 5n; store, 37
Red Wing, 38n, 108; Sioux village, 54, 54n; mission, 54n; hotel, 106, 107n; platted, 107n
Red Wing House, Red Wing, 107
"Regulator," steamboat, 140
Reiner, Dr. J. H., 170, 170n
Renfro, William C., 55, 55n
Rensselaer, Ind., 145, 156, 159
Republican party, 8, 153, 164, 176, 180, 185, 185n, 192, 197; Wash-

ington County conventions, 163, 175, 184, 185n, 205, 207, 207n; Lakeland, 184; state conventions, 195, 205, 205n
Rice, C. H., 178, 178n
Rice Creek, 206, 206n
Richards, ———, 94
Richmond, Ind., 91n
River Falls, Wis., Baptist church, 129n
Robert, Louis, 40, 40n, 65, 75, 76, 81
Robertson, ———, 168
Robertson, Andrew, 47, 47n, 56, 69
Robertson (Robinson), Daniel A., 110, 110n
Robinette, Joseph, 65, 65n
Robinson, see Robertson, Daniel A.
Robinson, ———, 209
Robinson, Thomas, 110n
Rock Island, Ill., 118
Rockwood, B. L., 39, 39n, 41, 55, 60, 69, 71, 79, 81
Rollingstone colony, 8, 8n, 107n
Rouser, Evans, Daniels, and Co., 186
"Royal Arch," steamboat, 123, 123n, 124, 124n
Russell, ———, 61
Russell and Co., Massilon, O., 93n
Rutherford, ———, 208, 215
Rutherford, James, 185, 185n
Rutherford, William, 185n, 206
Ryan, ———, 201
Rye, harvested, 140, 162, 173, 194, 204, 205; threshed, 144

ST. ANTHONY, 112, 113; hotel, 74n, 110n; described, 111
St. Anthony Falls, 3; development, 42; described, 111
St. Croix Falls, Wis., 71n, 72n; lumber industry, 11, 43n, 51n, 56n; mail service, 39n
St. Croix River, 32, 127; navigation closes, 143, 154, 165, 176, 208; navigation opens, 148, 160, 169, 192, 202, 211, 219. See also Lake St. Croix
St. Croix Valley, settlement, 9, 10; Du Luth in, 10; timber, 10; lumbering, 15; mail service, 39n
St. Louis, 3; market, 21
St. Paul, 38n, 53n, 97, 97n, 106, 108, 113, 118, 150, 157, 158, 165, 196; market, 19-21, 40, 64, 127, 129, 211, 212, 216-218; pork packing, 20; shipping point, 22; justice court, 39, 39n, 40, 41, 43, 44; stores, 49n, 69n; hotels, 74n, 110n, 113, 150, 150n, 159; post office, 79, 79n; described, 109-111; rainfall, 110; navigation closes, 143; navigation opens, 181; boarding houses, 184, 211n; Republican convention, 195; telegraph service, 201; mail service, 209; commission business, 212n; lawyers, 218n
St. Peter's, see Mendota
Salisbury (Solsbury), Guy M., 198, 198n, 203, 204
Sanderson, Reuben H., 153, 153n, 155, 163
Sargent, ———, 138, 201
Sargent, Mrs. ———, 141
Sawmills, St. Croix Falls, 43n; Stillwater, 51n; Phalen Creek, 65n; Lakeland, 114n; Pierce County, Wis., 117
Sawyer, Henry, 206n
Sawyer House, Stillwater, 206, 206n
Schoolcraft, Henry R., expedition, 172
Schools, 31; Lakeland, 129n, 136, 141, 154, 168
Scott, Winfield, presidential candidate, 87
Shakopee, 9
Shullsburg, Wis., 104, 104n
Sibley, Henry H., 52, 52n, 64, 65, 74, 75n; land claim, 114; governor, 165n

INDEX

Sibley House, 42n
Simpson, James W., 64, 64n, 65
Sixth Minnesota Volunteer Regiment, 4
Slavery, discussed, 186, 187
Smallpox, Kinnickinnick, Wis., 145
Smith House, Plymouth, Ind., 97n
Snelling House, St. Paul, 113
Soapmaking, 30, 37, 38, 80
Social life and recreation, 26, 27, 47, 48, 56, 57, 179, 180; berry picking, 20, 26, 27, 206; hunting, 27; fishing, 27, 40, 57, 69, 126, 161; children's, 30, 31; picnic, 172. *See also* Lyceums
Spofford, Jacob E., 178n
Spring Creek, 206, 206n
Standart, G. H., 121
Staples, Isaac, 219, 219n
Stearnes, Charles E., 184n
Stearnes, George H., 184n
Steele, Franklin, 42, 42n, 49, 52, 64, 65, 75-77, 81
Stewart, H. L., 61
Stillwater, 55, 56, 59, 76, 115, 151, 162, 175; population, *1850*, 12; produce shipped, 20; market, 20, 51, 55, 60, 130, 132, 143, 153, 154, 182, 201, 213; wheat prices, 21, 22; currency, 24; newspaper, 27; lumber industry, 51n, 56n, 74n, 219n; store, 51n; social life, 57; hotels, 74n, 114, 114n, 196, 196n, 206, 206n; described, 114; prison, 114; land office, 114, 116; Masonic lodge, 130; assessors' meetings, 139, 150; commissioners' meetings, 145, 163, 193, 197, 200, 201, 204, 205, 208; Republican conventions, 163, 175, 184, 185n, 205, 205n, 207, 207n; business conditions, 166, 167; region described, 178; Bunker Hill celebration, 182, 183; court session, 203, 210; meeting for soldiers' families,
203; land sale, 215, gristmills, 219n
Stillwater Lumber Co., 51n, 56n
Stillwater Messenger, 19, 169, 195
Stone, J. L., 218
Stouffer, ———, 139
Stoves, 14
Strawberries, 211
Strong, ———, 150, 157, 208
Sugar, making, 147; price, 167
Swedish element, 204, 204n
Sweetser, W., 128

Tanner's Lake, 196
Taylor's Falls, 78n, 178
Tefft, B. F., *Speeches of Daniel Webster*, 27
Telegraph, St. Paul, 110n; Atlantic cable, 174
Thanksgiving Day, 132, 132n
Thayer, Rev. Charles, 163, 163n, 167, 168, 172
Thomas, Hewitt L., 139, 139n, 163, 169, 176, 207, 207n
Thompson, Kitty Ann Jackson, 118n
Thompson, Noah S., 118, 118n, 122, 156, 157
Thompson, Mrs. Noah S., 118
Threshing, 129, 144, 152, 155, 164, 196, 202; methods, 17-19, 61, 61n, 63, 69; cost, 61; oats, 61-63, 69; Indiana, 91-95; barley, 144; rye, 144; corn, 156; machines, *see* Agricultural implements
Timber, St. Croix Valley, 10; Mississippi River islands, 109
Titus, Mrs. Moses S., *see* Lamont, Jane
Toledo, O., 85, 86, 88, 89, 120
Train, *see Traineau de glace*
Traineau de glace, 47, 47n, 52, 53, 55, 59
Transportation, *see* Freight; Railroads
Trees, species along Mississippi, 109

Turner, Dr. George F., 74, 74n
Twin Cities, surrounding country described, 111
Tyler, Freeman C., 114, 115, 117, 125, 132, 163, 212; sawmill, 114n; election judge, 153
Tyler, Mrs. Freeman C., 115, 219
Tyner, Daniel H., 137, 137n

UNDERWOOD, ———, 97n, 104
Urbana, O., 2

VAIL, WALTER R., 51, 51n, 55, 57, 62
Valparaiso, Ind., 99
Vanorks, Maj. ———, 170
Van Vorhes, Andrew J., 184, 195, 196n
Vasa, 78n
Vegetables, 12, 39, 67, 78, 80, 125, 163, 175, 183, 193, 194; winter storage, 13, 37, 48, 48n, 49, 60, 66, 70-73, 78; markets, 20, 40, 153; at fairs, 25; harvested, 37; prices, 40, 46, 68, 154, 182; planted, 74-76, 81, 181, 191; plowed, 76. *See also* Beans; Potatoes
Venoia, ———, 58
Vermont House, Mason City, Ia., 9
Victor, Orville J., *History of the Southern Rebellion*, 220, 220n

WABASH, IND., 127; Jackson's residence, 6, 8, 85-97; Presbyterian church, 89; Christian church, 89, 90; hotel, 119
Wabash Canal, 7, 87, 89
Wabash County, Ind., 6, 95
Wabash County Agricultural Society, 6
Wabash Railroad, 91, 91n
Wabasha, 107, 117
Wabasha County, 51n, 53n
Wacouta, 117
Walker, Orange, 44, 44n, 184
Walker Miss S. J., 90
Walker, W. P., 89

Walker, Gen. William, 168, 168n
"War Eagle," steamboat, 118
Warren, Ill., 103, 118, 123
Washington County, 8; settlement, 9, 12; topography, 10; lumber industry, 10, 12, 13, 15; early farmers, 11; population, 12; number of farms, *1850*, 12; market gardening, 12, 20; pioneer houses, 13; fences, 15; elections, 161, 162, 164, 185, 192, 197; property valuation reduced, 174; Republican conventions, 175, 184, 185n, 207, 207n; commissioners' meetings, 196, 197, 200, 201, 204, 205, 207, 208; sheriff, 205; described, 206
Watson, Daniel T., 184, 184n, 195, 211, 211n, 217, 218
Way, Evan J., 212, 212n, 218
Way, Mrs. Evan J., 212, 218
Way, Kate, 218
Way, Margaret, 212
Webb, Edward, 218, 218n
Wells, 15
Wentworth, David, 80, 81
Western Farm and Village Association, 8
Wheat, 11, 79; markets, 21; prices, 21, 22, 95, 98, 138, 216; screened, 76; threshed, 91, 92, 94, 144; harrowed, 137; planted, 148, 149, 161, 181, 192, 193, 203, 211, 218, 219; harvested, 151, 194; yield, 152; varieties, 202, 203, 205; bound, 205
Whitcher, E. B., 196n
White, Harley D., 53, 53n, 54
Whiteside, M., 134
Whorton, Benjamin, 90
Wild Cat Creek, 106, 106n
Wild life, Minnesota, 3, 27; partridges, 66; ducks, 66, 169; gophers, 74, 77; prairie chickens, 158, 180; geese, 158, 169, 180, 191, 201, 217, 218; song birds, 169; pigeons, 172
Wilson, ———, 155

INDEX

Winnowing, oats, 62-64
Winona, 107, 143; rainfall, 110
Winona County, sheriff, 107n
Winslow, Miss ———, 160
Winslow, James M., 110, 110n, 111, 158, 159, 160
Winslow, Mrs. James M., 160
Winslow House, St. Paul, 159
Wisconsin, described, 104-106; lumbering, 179
Wolf Creek, Wis., 178

Women, household activities, 28-30
Wood, ———, 172
Wood, T. A., 116, 224
Wood Lake, Wis., 179
Woodbury Township, 45n
Worth, Edward, 39, 39n, 40, 41, 44, 46, 79

York, Thomas J., 184, 207
Young, ———, 177

www.ingramcontent.com/pod-product-compliance
Lightning Source LLC
Chambersburg PA
CBHW031624160426
43196CB00006B/266